Ribble: valley and river

RIBBLE

valley and river

A local and natural history

by Malcolm Greenhalgh

For Julia & Stuart
with my
best wishes
[signature]

Happy
Christmas

Also available from Carnegie:

Wildlife of Lancashire, Manchester & North Merseyside, ISBN 978-1-85936-118-4
Colin Pooley (ed.), *Rivers and the British Landscape*, ISBN 978-1-85936-120-7
Derek Beattie, *A History of Blackburn*, ISBN 978-1-85936-113-9
Peter Aughton, *Liverpool: A People's History* (new edn, 2008), ISBN 978-1-85936-161-0
Marjorie Searson, *Longton in the Nineteenth Century*, ISBN 978-1-85936-124-5
Peter Shakeshaft, *St Anne's on the Sea*, ISBN 978-1-85936-159-7
Mike Clarke, *The Leeds and Liverpool Canal*, ISBN 978-1-85936-013-2
David Brazendale, *Lancashire's Historic Halls*, ISBN 978-1-85936-106-1
David Hey, *A History of Yorkshire: 'County of the Broad Acres'*, ISBN 978-1-85936-122-1

Forthcoming:
Alan Crosby, *A History of Lancashire* (2010), ISBN 978-1-85936-152-8
Stephen Bull, *The Civil Wars in Lancashire, 1640–1660* (2009), ISBN 978-1-85936-105-4
David Hunt, *A History of Preston* (new edn, 2009), ISBN 978-1-85936-171-9

full details and secure online ordering at **www.carnegiepublishing.com**

Ribble: valley and river: A local and natural history

First published in 2009 by
Carnegie Publishing Ltd
Chatsworth Road,
Lancaster LA1 4SL
www.carnegiepublishing.com

British Library Cataloguing-in-Publication data
A catalogue record for this book is available from the British Library

ISBN 978-1-85936-181-8 (*limited edition hardback*)
        978-1-85936-135-1 (*softback*)

Designed, typeset and originated by Carnegie Book Production, Lancaster
Printed and bound in Malta by Gutenberg Press

HALFTITLE
A detail of Speed's map of Lancashire, early seventeenth-century, with the river Ribble and the famed Lancashire mosses prominent features of the landscape.

FRONTISPIECE
The Ribble at Cow Bridge in summer, a watercolour by Denys Ovenden.

Contents

Acknowledgements

I would first like to thank Carnegie Publishing, especially Anna and Alistair, for publishing what for me is the most important book I have ever written. I would also like to single out Dr Alan Crosby, who has kindly let me use his knowledge of the history of Lancashire.

My thanks goes also to: Bowland Game-Fishing Association; the Lancashire Wildlife Trust; The Wildfowl and Wetlands Trust; Alan Ashcroft of the local history section of Leigh Library; and the staff of the regional history section of Manchester Reference Library; the late Alan Brindle; Dr Dmitri Logunov of the Manchester Museum; Ray Ball; Stuart Crofts; John Hartley, Glenys Latham; Mike McKavett; Dr P. H. Smith MBE; Denys Ovenden; Brian Rafferty; Harry Shorrock (the greatest Lancashire naturalist of the twentieth century); Jason Smalley; Ken G Spencer; Miss D. Worsley-Taylor. I am also indebted to two friends of long ago who started me on my work on the Ribble: the late Alan Storey and Eric Twelves.

Finally, I would like to thank you, who bought this book. All royalties have gone to the Ribble Valley Conservation Trust or the Hodder Consultative Trust. You have made a contribution to my river.

All of the photographs were taken by the author, except for: Stuart Crofts pp. 43, 99 (top), 142 (top) 195; Mike McKavett pp. 42, 54 (top), 99 (bottom), 110, 119, 142 (bottom), 162 (bottom), 196, 198, 262 (bottom), 263 (top), 278, 279; Brian Rafferty pp. 54 (bottom), 199 (bottom), 263 (bottom), 275; Jason Smalley pp. 14, 15, 115, 218; P. H. Smith pp. 30, 35, 118 (top), 138 (top), 199 (top), 207, 211, 264, 267, 270, 271; and Michel Roggo p. 103. My thanks to them all.

The Ribble catchment includes not only the Ribble itself, but the rivers Hodder, Calder, Darwen and Douglas. Together these drain much of central and northern Lancashire as well as part of west Yorkshire.

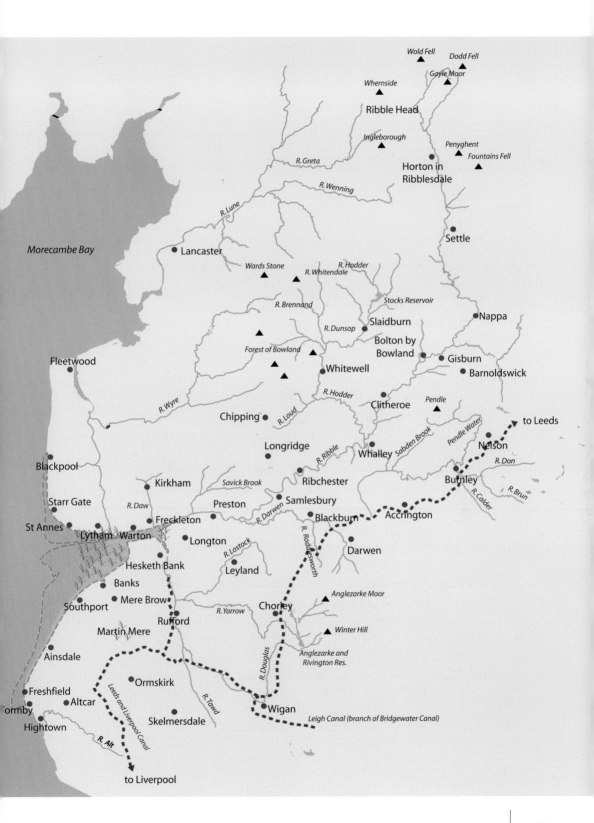

Morecambe Bay

Wold Fell ▲
Dodd Fell ▲
Gayle Moor ▲
Whernside ▲

Ribble Head

R. Greta

Ingleborough ▲

Penyghent ▲
Fountains Fell ▲

Horton in
Ribblesdale

R. Wenning

R. Lune

Lancaster ●

Settle ●

Wards Stone ▲
R. Whitendale ▲
R. Hodder

R. Brennand

Stocks Reservoir

Slaidburn
R. Dunsop
Nappa ●

Bolton by
Bowland

Forest of Bowland ▲
▲

Gisburn ●
Barnoldswick ●

Fleetwood ●

▲
▲

Whitewell ●

R. Hodder

Pendle ▲

Clitheroe

R. Wyre

Chipping ●

R. Loud

Longridge ●

R. Ribble

Whalley ●

Sabden Brook

Pendle Water

Nelson ●

to Leeds

Blackpool ●

Kirkham ●

Savick Brook

Ribchester ●

Burnley ●

R. Don

R. Calder

R. Brun

Starr Gate ●

R. Daw

Preston ●

Samlesbury ●

St Annes ●

Freckleton ●

R. Darwen

Blackburn ●

Accrington ●

Lytham
Warton

Longton ●

R. Lostock

Darwen ●

Hesketh Bank ●

Leyland ●

R. Roddesworth

Banks ●

Mere Brow ●

Anglezarke Moor ▲

Southport ●

Rufford ●

Chorley ●

R. Yarrow

Martin Mere

Winter Hill ▲

Ainsdale ●

Ormskirk ●

Anglezarke and
Rivington Res.

R. Douglas

Freshfield ●

Altcar ●

Skelmersdale ●

R. Tawd

Wigan ●

Leigh Canal (branch of Bridgewater Canal)

Formby ●

Hightown ●

R. Alt

Leeds and Liverpool Canal

to Liverpool

Introduction

Of the many rivers which flow along the valleys of 'merrie England',
there are few that in the richness of antiquarian and historical
associations, the loveliness of the district it waters, or the numbers
of objects of beauty and interest along its course, exceed our own
RIBBLE.'

William Dobson, *Rambles by the Ribble* (3rd edn, 1877)

The River Ribble and its tributaries have been an important part of my life for
well over forty years. I was twelve years old when I first walked its estuary
saltmarshes with my binoculars in winter to watch the huge flocks of waders
and wildfowl. Later I spent several years researching the estuary wildlife,
earning my Ph.D. and the Zoological Society of London's Prince Philip Prize
for Zoology, and writing many scientific articles and my first book, *Wildfowl
of the Ribble Estuary* (1975).

Just as the Ribble has a remarkable wildlife estuary, so its source and its
tributaries are equally important. The Ribble itself rises in what is probably
the finest limestone scenery in the British Isles, its source dominated by
the three great peaks of the Yorkshire Dales: Ingleborough, Penyghent and
Whernside. For almost five years I was fortunate enough to help run a field
centre and lead biology and geography courses in the dales and fells around
the Ribble headwaters.

For the last twenty-two years I have been a freelance researcher and writer,
and the Ribble Valley downstream of Settle and the River Hodder – Ribble's
most beautiful tributary – which flows from the north, having drained the
Forest of Bowland, have been my open-air laboratory. In the last decade
this laboratory has been extended to include the tributaries which flow from
industrial Lancashire into the Ribble: the Calder, a once polluted sewer,

Grove Head: source of the Ribble.

which flows through Burnley; the Darwen, which rises on wild moors before meandering around the back of Blackburn Rovers football ground; and the Douglas, which flows from the aptly named Winter Hill before losing most of its water in reservoirs and collecting pollutants in Wigan town centre.

The Ribble system is unique among British rivers in that it forms the boundary line between what is still largely an idyllic rural scene to the north and the grime and urban sprawl of old industrialised Lancashire to the south. What we see today – the rivers and streams, countryside around them, and the wildlife that live here – is thus largely a consequence of history and

prehistory. Man and nature together have moulded the primeval countryside which was forged by the last Ice Age. Here, history and natural history are inextricably linked.

There is no doubt that the Hodder valley is one of the most beautiful in England. That is not only my opinion. It is rumoured that the Queen has intimated that she would retire here if she could! The Craven hills where the Ribble rises form one of the finest pieces of limestone scenery in Britain, while the valley down to the tide is a scene of green tranquillity, with lovely woodlands and lush pastures. Even the urban tributaries rise on fine areas of moorland and, having escaped town, pass once more through splendid countryside. Much of the coast around the estuary has been developed, but we have the most magnificent saltmarshes in Europe, while the sand dunes that still exist between Southport and Liverpool are quite splendid. An integral part of our coast is the extensive flat mosslands that were once a marshy wet wilderness. Yet millions of people live within easy reach and every dry day of the year thousands of feet set out to tramp the country. People want to live here, and every year a little more countryside is converted into estates of executive homes. People want clean water for drinking, watering their lawns and washing their cars. Every year a little more water is abstracted from the Ribble and its tributaries. For the past fifty years the British government, now backed by the European Union, has urged farmers to increase their productivity and has subsidised the draining of wet fields, the turning of wildflower meadows into grass monocultures and the grubbing up of hedgerows. There is a conflict: we want the wilderness, but we want the wilderness trained. That conflict is sure to grow, for people and votes will always come before wilderness and wildlife.

This then is a record of what was at the start of the third millennium, and of how it came to be here. It is a personal view and based largely on personal observations made as I walked and waded here. I can only urge future generations to be heedful of the words of Gerard Manley Hopkins:

What would the world be, once bereft
Of wet and of wildness? Let them be left,
O let them be left, wildness and wet;
Long live the weeds and the wilderness yet.

Malcolm Greenhalgh
Lowton
December 2007

CHAPTER ONE

The source of the Ribble

'For I had weighed the mountains in a balance,
And the skies in a scale.'

G. K. Chesterton, *Femina Contra Mundum*

An anonymous sixteenth-century manuscript states that 'The Ribble is a river verie rich of Salmon and Lampreie dooeth in manner inviron Preston in Andernesse and it riseth neere to Ribblesdale above Gisburne.'[1] In the same century (in the late 1530s) John Leland, Henry VIII's antiquary, wrote that, 'Ribil riseth in Ribilsdale above Salley Abbey and so to Sawley. A III. Miles above Sawley it reseyvith Calder that cummith by Whalley and after another water called Oder.'[2] In fact both of these descriptions were wrong, or at least many kilometres out. The Ribble rises a very long way above Gisburn, and the Hodder joins the Ribble above, not after, the confluence of the Ribble and the Calder. Leland probably never saw the river close to its source of its confluence with the Hodder, though he certainly did cross it at Preston.

In his *Britannia* (1582) William Camden reported that, 'this river cometh with a quick and hasty stream out of the hills of Yorkshire, taking his course first south-bound by three exceeding high mountains, Ingleborrow Hill at the spring head'. Michael Drayton (1612) took another of the 'three exceeding high mountains' as his source of the Ribble in his poem *Polyolbion*:

> From Penyghent's proudfoot as from my source I stride,
> That mountain, my proud sire, in height of all his pride
> Takes pleasure in my course as in his first born flood.[3]

Of course, geographical knowledge was always somewhat uncertain in the sixteenth and seventeenth centuries, and although these various writers were incorrect in describing the source of the Ribble they were similarly vague or imprecise with many other rivers and natural features. Indeed, the exact source of the river was very uncertain to all concerned until recent times, not only because it is hard to pinpoint such a location anyway (which is the true headstream?), but also because it is only in the past 150 years or so that people have really been very interested in such aspects of landscape and topography. In reality, the Ribble does not rise on Ingleborough, or Penyghent, or on Whernside, the third of the Three Peaks of the Yorkshire Dales National Park, although tiny rills from the first two do contribute to the growing stream. Instead, a spring rises at 544 metres above sea level on the northern side of Gayle Moor, in a place that is labelled Grove Head on the Ordnance Survey map. For the sake of absolute precision, the point at which that trickle emerges from the wet, peaty moorland is at grid reference SD812835. The trickle heads north, then turns to the south-west and is given the name Long Gill. That is the source of the River Ribble.

There is, however, another beck that could lay a claim to be source of the Ribble; it is certainly one of the highest headwaters. A couple of kilometres to the north-west of Long Gill is Wold Fell. Several small streams, some of which run dry in long summer droughts, drain this extensive moor. Those draining away to the west carry water to the River Lune and so to the Irish Sea, and those draining to the east carry water to the River Ure and eventually the North Sea. But two becks which rise at 490 metres on Cow Pasture, the southern slope of Wold Fell, flow south and meet at Newby Head Farm (433 metres) and then join with Long Gill at High Bridge, close to the Ingleton–Hawes road. According to Frederick Riley, writing in 1914, one of these two becks 'rising out of Wold Fell must be accorded place of honour as being the true source of the Ribble'.[4]

Below Newby Head the growing stream is now called Gayle Beck. It flows on in a southerly direction, through the farmsteads of Gearstones and about a kilometre from the Ribblehead railway viaduct until, near the hamlet of Selside, it is joined by Cam Beck. At that confluence the stream is re-named the Ribble. This is perhaps apt, for though the streams that give rise to the Ribble are above Selside, here we find the area known as Ribblehead with its famous viaduct and inn. Three kilometres below Selside, and already an important trout stream, the infant Ribble reaches the highest village in the valley, Horton-in-Ribblesdale.

The climate around Ribble source and estuary

The source of the Ribble is an inhospitable place or, rather, the weather can be inhospitable. Professor Gordon Manley summarised the climate of this part of England quite vividly in *Climate and the British Scene* (1952): 'The unique exhilarating horribleness of such weather is the more appreciated when one knows that two hours distant one finds ham and eggs.'[5]

A comparison of plain meteorological statistics between the two geographical extremes on the Ribble – Ribblehead close to the source and Southport by the mouth of the estuary – illustrates the harshness of the Pennine climate. At Southport the mean January temperature is 5.5°C and at Ribblehead 1.2°C; the mean July temperature at Southport is 15.6°C and at Ribblehead 12.2°C. On the human frame the contrast is one of relative comfort and discomfort, but for wildlife the effect is profound. For instance, around Southport grasses have at least a 300-day growing season, whereas at Ribblehead the growing season is barely 200 days. This also, of course, means a very short growing season for crops, and in the past this militated against arable agriculture except for bare subsistence, and also reduced the opportunities for the establishment of improved high-quality pasture.

At Southport, 76 centimetres of rain falls every year, on an average of 185 days. At Ribblehead, beneath the cloud-gathering peaks of Ingleborough and Whernside, an annual average of 200 centimetres of rain falls on 240 days. Even in drought years, such as 1955, 1976, 1976 and 1993, Ribblehead is drenched by about 170 centimetres, more than twice Southport's annual average. On one famous day, 2 December 1954, 13 centimetres of rain landed

The Ribble headwater, Long Gill, with mist clearing from Ingleborough following heavy rain.

Iam Sike, Shivery Gill and Far Mares Gill join with the head of Long Gill to create the infant Ribble as they flow down Gayle Moor.

on the Ribble's source in a period of 24 hours. Snowfall shows a similar pattern. Southport averages around 12 days per year with snow or sleet recorded falling and fewer than five days with lying snow. At Ribblehead falling snow or sleet is recorded on about 35 days *per annum* and lying snow, in north- or east-facing hollows, on 50 or more days. These are impersonal statistics, and my diaries record some personal sufferings. In 1969 I was out on the moors on 77 days scattered through the year: it precipitated on me on 42 of those days; I experienced snowfall in every month from November to April, and lying snow from November to mid-May. In 1979 I spent 167 days in the dale and on the moors: it rained and snowed on 91 of those days and I noted lying snow in every month except July, August and September. In 1989 in 91 days out in the hills I experienced snow or sleet falling on four and it rained on 22 (that was a particularly mild, dry year). More recently there has been less snow but lots of rain: in 1999 I spent 40 days in the upper dale and saw no sleet or snow falling; but it rained on 21 days.

The effect of low temperature and high precipitation in the headwater moorlands is made worse by the chilling effect of the wind. At Southport the average strength of wind throughout the year is Force 2–3, at Ribblehead, Force 4. However, the incidence and strength of gales linked to the passage of Atlantic depressions is very similar between coast and high fell. Inland, in the lowlands and on the lower slopes, woodlands, hedgerows and buildings hinder wind-flow and thus reduce the strength of gales. On 15 January 1954, for example, an 85 mph (135 kph) gale stopped three steam trains that were trying to thunder their way over Ribblehead viaduct.

Most lowland people are sensible enough not to venture on the high moors when the forecast warns of teeming rain or thick blizzard. Yet even on balmy days in late spring, when people are sunbathing at Blackpool and Southport, comfort on the moors may mean an extra sweater and thermal mittens. Lowland folk know nothing of 'hoggs' squarls' (cool, wet, windy April days), 'gosling storms' (gales with sleety rain in May) and 'cow-quakes' (hard frost or snow in May) – or rather, they may not know the names, but for well over a hundred years innumerable walkers and hikers from the lowlands have been very well aware of the weather itself.

No wonder, then, that, away from the steepest slopes and limestone scree, the land around the source of the Ribble is mainly waterlogged bog. Here you will find bog-mosses (*Sphagnum*) and cotton-grass (*Eriophorum angustifolium*) growing on the open mires and more rushes (*Juncus*) than grasses on many undrained upland pastures.

Newby Head, the highest farm in the valley, was once an inn.

History and prehistory of the Ribble source

In its 90-kilometre journey to the sea the Ribble falls 544 metres, but in its first 11 kilometres to the confluence of Cam Beck with Long Gill, close to Selside, it falls 276 metres, or roughly half its total descent. The first part, across Gayle Moor, is through steep moorland to Newby Head on the col between the heads of Uredale (Wensleydale) and Ribblesdale. Here is Newby Head Farm, the highest dwelling in the valley. Up to 1919 the farm was an inn of some antiquity, for the high moorland road that passes Newby Head was originally a drove-road used by Scottish cattle-dealers taking their stock south to English markets. The drovers would herd their stock on Newby Head Pasture while availing themselves of refreshment at the inn.[6]

Only two Pennine inns were (and still are) higher than Newby Head, Tan Hill Inn, at 536 metres, on Arkengarthdale Moor and the Cat and Fiddle, at 515 metres, between Buxton and Macclesfield.

Gearstones, five kilometres downstream, is also strategically positioned close to the junction of the Hawes–Ingleton road with a side branch of Cam High Road, a green drove-track of Roman origin that is now part of Dales and Pennine Ways. This is the high-level route which crossed the Dales from Lancaster, up the Lune valley to Burrow in Lonsdale and then on to Ingleton, Cam End and the superb high ridge between Wensleydale and Raydale, before descending to the fort at Bainbridge and probably on to Catterick. It is a notably fine piece of alignment and its strategic route was designed for military purposes. The road was built in about AD 75 as the Romans divided the high Pennines into manageable chunks in order to prevent unrest and possible rebellion among the Brigantes, the Iron Age or British tribe which occupied most of Yorkshire and Lancashire and whose history is discussed in more detail below (page 13). The Romans built a series of forts at strategic locations and linked them by roads such as the route over Cam End.

Today Gearstones is a scattering of old, lichen-encrusted farm buildings, but in the eighteenth century it was the site of a twice-yearly fair, when Scottish drovers brought herds of cattle there and English dealers came to barter for them. Gearstones was then also an inn and, during the fairs, an immense quantity of ale was supped there. Carts, wagons and packhorse trains broke their journey at Gearstones as they travelled the turnpike roads and green-tracks between Ribblesdale and Lunesdale in the south and Wensleydale, upper Wharfedale, and Mallerstang and the Eden valley in the north. Although these may now seem largely empty lands, there has always been the need to cross the high fells and move from dale to dale. In 1751, for example, a new turnpike trust was authorised to link Lancaster and Richmond, partly with lowland valley roads and partly by improving

and upgrading the line of the old Roman road over Cam End. Part of this
spectacular high-altitude route was later replaced by the present route down
Widdale to Hawes.

We are fortunate to have a very detailed and vivid account of the inn at
Gearstones dating from its heyday as a resting place (though maybe not a
very agreeable one) for those using these lonely routes. In 1792 the inveterate
traveller and diarist John Byng, journeying from Askrigg to Ingleton, recorded
his distinctly unfavourable impressions of the inn:

> Crossing a ford, Mr Blakey led me to a public house – call'd Grierstones,
> the seat of misery, in a desert; and tho' (unluckily for us) fill'd with
> company, yet the Scotch fair held upon the heath … added to the horror
> of the curious scenery; the ground in front crowded by Scotch cattle
> and the drovers; and the house cramm'd by the buyers and sellers, most

of whom were in plaids, fillibegs, &c. ... at length we procured some boil'd slices of stale pork, and some fry'd eggs, with some wretched beer and brandy: – to which my hunger was not equal; and from which my delicacy revolted ... The only custom of this hotel, or rather hovel, is derived from the grouse shooters, or from two Scotch Fairs: – when at the conclusion of the days squabble, the two Nations agree in mutual drunkeness, the Scotch are allways wrap'd up in their plaids – as a defence against heat, cold or wet ... all the Yorkshire around [is] black and frightful.[7]

The profitability of Gearstones Inn was enhanced in 1869 when a temporary town was built for around 3,000 navvies a little over a kilometre away on the flat moorland of Batty Green. The Midland Railway Company was building its celebrated Settle to Carlisle line, pushing it northwards through the heart of some of the most difficult terrain in England by means of an unequalled sequence of magnificent engineering works – viaducts, tunnels, deep cuttings and high embankments. The most difficult section had to be constructed between Ribblehead and Mallerstang, at the head of the Eden Valley. The first task was the marking out of the route the line should take, and one of the engineers doing the job was snowed in at Gearstones for 12 days early in 1870. The labour involved the construction of the famous Ribblehead viaduct, among the greatest monuments of Victorian civil engineering, 398 metres in length with 22 arches and attaining a maximum height over the surrounding moorland of 49.5 metres. About 26,000 cubic metres of dressed stone and 170 cubic metres of mortar were used, and the work was frequently hindered and made all the more dangerous when scaffolding was blown aside by severe gales. To the north of the viaduct a 2,360 metre-long tunnel had to be dug beneath Blea Moor. There was no modern machinery: the navvies used explosives, picks, shovels and, with no electricity, around £50-worth of candles every month. When they were not working, feeding or sleeping, Gearstones Inn was the centre of social life for the hundreds of navvies who had been brought to these wild and inhospitable moors. But the opening of the line in 1875 meant the end of Gearstones as an inn. The navvies departed. There was no longer a need for drovers to herd cattle south, nor for markets and fairs to be held there. Trains could carry much more quickly than drovers or packhorse trains. In 1911 the inn closed and Gearstones became a hill farm.[8]

Downstream of Gearstones, Gayle Beck has cut its way through Carboniferous limestone bedrock to produce the narrow gorge of Thornsgill. The river now flows through some of the world's classic limestone country, with limestone crag, scree and pavement, shakeholes and potholes and, in

Thornsgill, two caves – Thornsgill Cave and Katnot Cave. The bed of the infant river has been etched and forged by water and boulders swirled around by the water to produce low waterfalls, plunge pools and pots. Crossing the river here is a narrow packhorse bridge, reputedly (but not really) of Roman origin. Before Henry VIII swept away England's monasteries, Ribblehead belonged to the monks of Furness Abbey and their highest grange, Thorns House, lies in ruins here. A grange was a large commercially run farm exploiting agricultural resources on the monastic estate, staffed by lay brethren [*conversi*] and using hired labour drawn from the surrounding area. Thornsgill is left behind as Gayle Beck flows past Ingman Lodge and Colt Park, both also once granges of Furness Abbey but both rebuilt, Ingman Lodge in 1687 by someone with the initials CW, according to a carving over the front door.

When the Normans invaded England, Selside – a Norse Viking settlement and meaning 'a farm by the sallows' – was the highest settlement in Ribblesdale to be recorded in Domesday Book. It was confiscated by the Crown, became part of Furness Abbey holdings, and then, after the Dissolution, remained as a hamlet of small farmsteads. To the west the land rises quickly to the summit of Simon Fell (650 metres), the eastern buttress of flat-topped Ingleborough (724 metres), and to the west Penyghent (694 metes), which broods over Ribblesdale like a recumbent lion.

This area of limestone country has long been inhabited. Late Palaeolithic people colonised upper Ribblesdale as the Ice Age came to a close around 12,000 years ago but, like the Mesolithic people who followed, they would have been nomadic hunters and fishers and had very little impact on the countryside. They were followed by Neolithic people who settled in the dale, cleared patches of forest and, besides being hunter-gatherers, were simple agriculturists. Dating from about 2500 BC is Giant's Grave, a Neolithic chambered burial mound five kilometres east of the Ribble at the foot of Penyghent (SD 857733). Measuring 16 by 15 metres, this was a complex structure when built, though many of the larger stones were robbed out long ago, and it perhaps implies that there was a well-organised and fairly substantial community in the area. During the Bronze Age (from about 1700 BC) and the Iron Age (from about 500 BC) the density of settlement and the level of exploitation of the resources of the valley increased.[9] The landscape was changed significantly in consequence. Until quite recently there was a general belief, among historians and archaeologists as well as in the popular view, that the Romans came to a wild and untamed landscape, where huge tracts of primeval forest were inhabited by blue-painted Celtic warriors who lived in huts in small clearings. Archaeological investigation, and the work of landscape historians, palaeobotanists and environmentalists (researching ancient ecologies) have disproved this. The Iron Age or Celtic inhabitants of Ribblesdale, as elsewhere in the country, were settled farmers, living in substantial stone-built houses or huts, in communities with yards, outbuildings and enclosures for animals as well as intricate patterns of fields edged with stone walls and boundary banks extending across the slopes of the valley sides. Traces of these field systems occur on several better-drained slopes (the easiest to see are viewed on the limestone pasture below Malham Cove at the head of Airedale), and the archaeological record is ever more detailed as fieldwork, aerial photography and systematic assessment reveal new settlement sites.

In the Iron Age period, and into the early decades of the Roman era, the Pennines of Yorkshire and Lancashire were the heartland of a large tribe known as the Brigantes. Compared with tribes in southern and midland England relatively little is known about the Brigantes, but the available evidence – and contemporary accounts – suggest that the kingdom of Brigantia was a loose confederation of sub-groups of smaller tribal communities, few of which are known by name. There is circumstantial evidence to indicate, though, that one such tribe may have lived in the Dent/Ingleborough area, and another in Craven. The former group were responsible for building the spectacularly sited walled hillfort which occupies the relatively flat summit plateau of Ingleborough. Inside the wall were many circular huts and the foundations of these are still visible. Brigantia was ruled by a royal family whose power-base lay east of the Pennines, in the area roughly between Ripon and Darlington, centred on Catterick and Stanwick near Richmond.

In the first decades of the Roman occupation of the south and the midlands, from AD 54 onwards, Brigantia – a tough nut for even the Romans to crack – was left in relative independence, its rulers accepting the overlordship of Rome but maintaining local autonomy. This comparatively favourable circumstance came to a dramatic end in AD 69, as a result of an acrimonious marital split. The queen of Brigantia, Cartimandua, like her much better known contemporary, Boudicca, was a formidable personality but, unlike Boudicca, was pro-Roman. Her husband, Venutius, was anti-Roman. In AD 69 a faction led by Venutius rose against his wife and her Roman allies, and the Romans intervened militarily to protect their own interests. Brigantia was invaded, and by AD 72 the Romans had taken the territory, reaching and garrisoning Carlisle. They immediately took steps to prevent a recurrence of such a threat, building the roads through the Pennines which have already been noted, and siting forts at the heads and mouths of dales and in strategic passes.

Auroch print (*left*) and human footprints (*right*). People moved in small numbers into the Ribble catchment soon after the end of the late Ice Age. They left few traces. The most vivid are footprints, preserved in peat and clay on the beach in the Freshfield/Formby area. When these people walked here, the sea was away to the west. Amongst the animals they hunted here was the auroch, or wild cattle. Judging from the size of their footprints, it is clear that they were much larger than our modern cattle. The footprints have been dated to 3,500–4,000 years ago, though some believe they might be even earlier.

Prehistoric forest clearance

The outer coat of a pollen grain is extremely tough and can survive intact for thousands of years even when buried in wet peat. From the structure of this resistant outer coat, the pollen grains of different plant species can be identified under a microscope. By examining the pollen found at various depths in peat bogs, and by using radiocarbon dating methods, it is possible to see how vegetation cover has changed since the last Ice Age.

Throughout northern England this research has shown that until the Neolithic period (perhaps five or six thousand years ago) the countryside was clothed in a deciduous forest which included large amounts of wych elm (*Ulmus glabra*) as well as the dominant oaks *Quercus petraea* and *Q. robor*. Weed seeds of species such as stinging nettle (*Urtica dioica*) and common chickweed (*Stellaria media*) were then rare in the pollen record. However, the arrival of Neolithic people coincided with a virtual disappearance of elm pollen and an increase of weed seeds in the record. For many years it was assumed that the Neolithic people were directly responsible for this, and from the 1960s to the 1980s scientists agreed that they had cleared the forest quickly and selectively felled elm trees so that their livestock could eat their highly palatable leaves. By cultivating large areas of ground, it was argued, Neolithic people encouraged the increase of weeds.[10]

However, it seems that the elm decline was nothing to do with Neolithic people clearing forests. Rather, some form of Dutch elm disease caused the elm decline; and the creation of glades in the forest by the sudden death of the elms might, in part at least, have led to the increase of weeds.[11] Neolithic people certainly did make clearings in the forests of upper Ribblesdale, but compared with those in other parts of Britain the extent of these was probably small.

When we examine the distribution of artefacts in northern England we see that the high concentrations occur along the east coast and valleys of rivers flowing to the North Sea, the lower Eden Valley and parts of Cumbria. The Ribble and its surrounding countryside are relatively impoverished of artefacts, which might suggest that the population was quite small, maybe numbering no more than a very few hundreds. In Ribblesdale it is likely that the forest was cleared only gradually, and in a piecemeal fashion, over a period of at least two thousand years, from the Neolithic into the Roman era and beyond.

After the Romans abandoned northern England towards the end of the fourth century AD, the British inhabitants remained, continuing the lifestyles of small-scale upland farming which they had carried on largely uninterrupted throughout the Roman period. Subsequently the region experienced successive waves of settlement and colonisation. By the beginning of the fifth century there had already been incursions of Picts from Scotland, and Anglo Saxon peoples were starting to settle on the east coast. The Angles gradually moved westwards, reaching Ribblesdale sometime in the middle of the seventh century and they were followed by the Danes, also from the east, at the end of the eighth century. Angles and Danes settled mostly in the lowlands and many settlements in the Yorkshire Dales have names which derive from Old English and Old Danish (see page 233). From about the middle of the ninth century Norse Vikings, who had spread from south-west Norway, via Shetland and Orkney to Ireland and the Isle of Man, came across the Irish Sea to the coast of Cheshire, Lancashire and Cumbria. They penetrated the Ribble valley from the west and founded farmsteads on the higher, vacant land. One Norse settlement excavated at Ribblehead dates from the late ninth century and consisted of a long stone farmhouse and stock pens built from limestone slabs. Many farms and villages throughout the Ribble catchment have Old Norse names. No ancient site in upper Ribblesdale offers the visitor more than traces of field boundaries, stone hut-circles and burial mounds, but the natural features more than compensate.

A short walk above Selside is Alum Pot, the name of which is a corruption of Heln Pot or 'Hell's Mouth'. It is a 63-metre deep chasm surrounded by a plantation of larch (*Larix decidua*) and a drystone wall to prevent sheep straying too close and falling to their deaths. A small stream, which rises on Borrins Moor, tumbles down the southern lip of the Pot. Even in hot summers, Alum Pot is damp and cool and full of life. The limestone strata underlying the slopes of Ingleborough and Simon Fell are like a Swiss cheese, full of holes that interconnect to produce some of the finest potholing opportunities in Britain. The entrance to one such 'hole', Long Churn Cave, is barely 100 metres north-west of Alum Pot, and the Long Churn system eventually enters Alum Pot 15 metres below the surface. The Rev. John Hutton of Kendal first investigated this cave in 1781, but he was unable to reach Alum Pot: 'We went 157 yards along [Long Churn Cave], till we came to a steep

Thorns Gill Bridge is a typical packhorse bridge of upper Ribblesdale.

Newhouses Tarn
is the only natural
lake in the Ribble
valley.

rock, fully 12 feet perpendicular, where we stopped; a wise consideration! We might have descended, perhaps, without danger, but the question was how we might get up again, which, without ropes or a ladder, would have been totally impracticable.'[12]

In 1847 John Birkbeck and William Metcalfe led three others down that first 3.6 metre pitch of rock and waterfall and in 1870 Boyd Dawkins, with a party of twelve others, was the first to descend to the bottom of Alum Pot. They were lowered in a large bucket using a winch and rope. A full exploration of the extensive Long Churn/Alum Pot system is one of the great pot-holing experiences of the Dales, with subterranean waterfalls, chambers with long stalactites and fragile calcite straws extending down from the roof, deep pools that must be swum or waded, and walls etched by trickling water and decorated with calcite sculptures. At the entrance to Alum Pot from the cave system a gleam of light penetrates the pitch darkness from above, and the only sounds are the tinkling of the waterfall into the black abyss and the singing of birds in the sun-drenched trees, 15 metres overhead.

This cave and pothole system continues on as a remarkable piece of drainage, for it extends beneath the Ribble without flowing into the river. From the bottom of Alum Pot the water flows for over one kilometre through

Horton-in-
Ribblesdale church,
with Penyghent in
the background.

underground passages to Foothaw's Hole, some 300 metres from the right bank of the river. After very heavy rain, excess water flows from Foothaw's Hole and down Foothaw's Beck to the Ribble, but when flows are normal, no water escapes from Foothaw's Hole. Instead it continues on through subterranean passages that carry it below the Ribble to an outflow at Turn Dub and from there it flows to the Ribble. Close to Turn Dub, in a hollow in the dale pasture, is New Houses Tarn. Natural lakes are rare in the Pennines and this tarn was formed as recently as the early nineteenth century, when an underground water-filled passage in the limestone bedrock became blocked. Instead of flowing into the Ribble, the water was forced to the surface and formed the tarn, one of the finest natural trout lakes in England.

Cam Beck, which with Gayle Beck forms the Ribble close to Ribblehead, rises on the south side of Cam Fell. Along the summit of this great ridge the Romans built Cam High Road. As the beck flows from the undulating peaty moor it suddenly enters the steep-sided craggy Ling Gill after passing beneath Ling Gill Bridge, a sixteenth-century packhorse bridge that was rebuilt in 1765 and renovated in 1932. Up Cam Beck from the bridge is open moorland, but downstream the beck descends rapidly into the gill where bird-cherry (*Prunus padus*), rowan (*P. aucuparia*) and thorn-scrub survive beyond the reach of nibbling herds of sheep. Ling Gill Bridge is on the green-track that heads north from the village of Horton-in-Ribblesdale to Wensleydale.[13] This section is now is part of the Pennine Way. Another green track from Horton

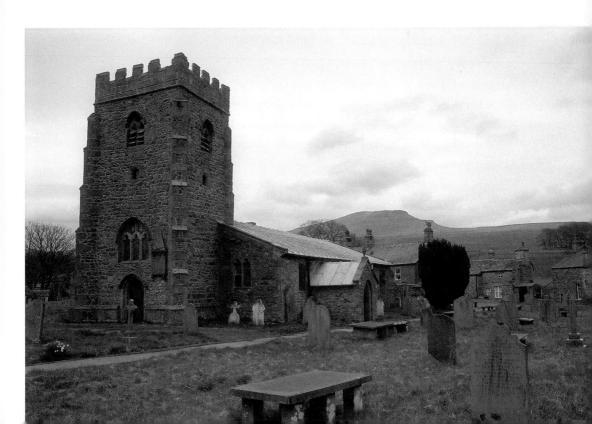

heads north-west to cross Cam Beck at Nether Lodge, close to the bottom of Ling Gill. This second track, now part of the Ribble Way, eventually reaches Gearstones and proceeds on to Lunesdale and Mallerstang. Just before it crosses Cam Beck the track passes over the smaller Brow Gill Beck by the natural, water-carved limestone arch known as God's Bridge. High Birkwith Farm, which lies at the head of the lane north of Horton where the two green tracks separate, was built in the fifteenth century as a grange of Jervaulx Abbey, but after the Dissolution it became a farm and inn for drovers. It ceased trading as an inn late in the nineteenth century.

Horton-in-Ribblesdale is an old village and, save for a few terraces and modern houses built for railway and quarry workers, it is still a small farming community. The church, dedicated to St Oswald, is Norman, built in the early years of the twelfth century with later additions (including the tower) during the reign of Henry VIII. Whereas the names of hamlets higher in the dale have Norse origins, the word Horton comes from the Old English *Hortune* – the settlement in the mire. Yet, although the village has a recorded history which stretches back over a millennium, and a long unrecorded existence

Stainforth Foss: a waterfall into a plunge pool.

before that, what we see in the valley around the village has been mostly created in the last three centuries.

Horton is a honey-pot for day-trippers to upper Ribblesdale. On warm summer days the car park will be full by breakfast time as walkers set out to climb one of the Three Peaks – Ingleborough, Penyghent and Whernside – or even attempt all three in the day. The Ribble Way and the Pennine Way pass through the village, those following these long distance routes stopping, by tradition, at the Penyghent Café for a mug of tea. Speleologists burrow underground in caves and potholes, while members of Manchester Angling Association cast their delicate wet flies to trout in the river. Many visitors, however, come here just to wander about on the lower slopes of Penyghent and visit two great potholes. Hull Pot is a vast chasm with an opening 54 metres by 13.5 metres and with a depth of 17.4 metres: it is an open hole in the ground with daylight reaching the bottom. In contrast the entrance to Hunt (or Thund) Pot is only 4.5 by 1.8 metres, but it falls away to blackness, having a depth of 30 metres.

Between Horton and Settle the valley is very narrow and the main road, the minor road known as Stainforth Lane, the railway and the river all run parallel within a half kilometre strip of land. The name of the village of Stainforth is of Anglo-Saxon origin, but the words Foss or Force in the names of the nearby waterfalls on the Ribble (Stainforth Foss) and high up Stainforth Beck (Catrigg Force) are from the Old Norse. A short distance downstream the village of Langcliffe takes its name from the Old English meaning Long Cliff, describing the straight, very steep slope that extends down the east side of the valley between Stainforth and Settle. To the east of this 'long cliff' the landscape of well-drained limestone pastures and crags extends to Malham Moor and then over to Wharfedale. On the western side of the valley the land rises to the extensive crags of Moughton, which have long been a source of quarried limestone. Over 5,000 years ago the valley floor here was swamp and, above the present Helwith Bridge, there was a narrow shallow lake. The prehistoric inhabitants of the valley fished the lake, hunted in the swamps, and lived on the drier limestone.

In May 1838 an apprentice plumber called Michael Horner visited the entrance to a narrow cave then called Foxhole, set in crags a couple of kilometres east of Langcliffe. He managed to squeeze through and inside picked up what was subsequently identified as a bronze fibula from the Bronze Age. He took his find to Joseph Jackson of Settle who entered the cave on the day of the coronation of Queen Victoria, 28 June 1838, and renamed it in her honour. He found some bronze implements and a few Roman coins. In the 1860s and 1870s a thorough archaeological excavation was made of the cave deposits, and subsequently other caves in the area (Moughton Fell,

Jubilee, Horseshoe, Kinsey, Yew Tree, Attermire) were investigated. These
have revealed fascinating information about the animals and people who lived
here over many thousands of years.[14]

The oldest cave deposits have been dated at about 135,000–114,000 years
ago, long before the last Ice Age. Then, hippopotamuses (*Hippopotamus
amphibius*), straight-tusked elephants (*Palaeoloxodon antiquus*) and narrow-
nosed rhinoceroses (*Stephanorhinus hemitoechus*) roamed the area which is
now upper Ribblesdale, though it is impossible to imagine that landscape
when we look at the valley today.

Deposits dating from the last Ice Age, in the period of about 70,000–12,000
years ago, included the remains of bison (*Bison priscus*), spotted hyena
(*Crocuta crocuta*), cave-bear (*Ursus deningeri*), woolly rhinoceros (*Coelodonta
antiquitatis*) and woolly mammoth (*Mammuthus primigenius*). It seems likely
that they were here as the Ice Age drew to a close and in its immediate
aftermath, for when the area was in the full grip of glaciation there was thick

ice flowing down Ribblesdale and the climate and environment would not have supported animal life or any significant vegetation.

The cave deposits revealed that as the icecaps and glaciers retreated northwards, other species such as lynx (*Lynx lynx*), red fox (*Vulpes vulpes*), wolf (*Canis lupus*), badger (*Meles meles*), brown bear (*Ursus arctos*), red deer (*Cervus elephas*), reindeer (*Rangifer tarandus*) and probably elk (*Alces alces*) began to colonise the district. The remains of one elk found in lake deposits at Poulton le Fylde near Blackpool, dated at 12,400 years ago, had a spear or arrowhead embedded in the thorax and another in the foot, indicating that Palaeolithic hunters had followed the wild animals northwards. Tools made from reindeer antler and harpoons found in Victoria Cave near Settle are also of Palaeolithic origin.

The discovery of several artefacts, including a polished basalt axe imported from County Antrim, Northern Ireland, confirm that people had settled in upper Ribblesdale by the Neolithic period, around 5,000 years ago. Aurochs, a species of wild cattle (*Bos primigenius*), wild horses (*Equus ferus*), mountain hares (*Lepus timidus*) and wild boars (*Sus scrofa*) were then grazing the grasslands of the Dales. It is likely that the Ribble valley had its richest ever mammalian fauna at this time, when the human population was comparatively small. As the population grew, sporadically but inexorably, over the next two thousand years and into the Roman period, some of the largest and most impressive mammal species became extinct, not (as had been the case with the narrow-nosed rhino or woolly mammoth) purely because of the effects of climatic changes, but because *Homo sapiens* hunted them to extinction. Elk, lynx, wild horse, mountain hare and reindeer disappeared in the late Neolithic to Iron Age. The brown bear and aurochs had vanished by the end of the Roman period, around AD 400. Wolves survived to at least 1305, when there was a report of them killing eight cattle in the Ribble valley. Wild boar were highly prized beasts of the chase and in 1295 they were sufficiently abundant in and around Ribblesdale for 80 to be captured alive and taken from Pendle to Pontefract Castle. It is said that James I hunted wild boar at Hoghton Tower near Preston in 1617, but that is unlikely, at least in the wild, for there is no good record of the species in north-west England after 1500.

More recently, the roe deer (*Capreolus capreolus*) became extinct in the region by the end of the eighteenth century, its return and current abundance being a twentieth-century phenomenon. Red deer became extinct about the beginning of the nineteenth century. The wild cat (*Felis silvestris*) was probably finally exterminated in the late seventeenth century, the pine marten (*Martes martes*) in about 1880, and the last Ribble valley polecat (*Mustela putorius*) was recorded from Horton-in-Ribblesdale in 1892 (though it survived in the adjacent Lune valley until about 1912).

Evolution of the dale vegetation[15]

Those of us who enjoy Ribblesdale – and all other Pennine dales – are impressed with the beauty of the place. High impressive fells brood over the valley. There are undulating peat blanket-bogs covered with cotton grass and the bog moss *Sphagnum*, and heather (*Calluna vulgaris*) moor on drier, acid, peaty slopes. Where there is no peat, the ground is well drained and the limestone is close to the surface, there are sweet grassy pastures; but where there is no peat but the ground often waterlogged, there are tracts of wet acidic pasture where clumps of rushes predominate. Some of the steepest slopes are dominated by limestone scar, crag and scree. At the bottom of the dale, on either side of the river, are open fields bounded by almost geometrically precise drystone walls. On Cam Fell and the north side of Blea Moor are planted blocks of conifers that in the last thirty years have grown into pine forest. Otherwise there are few woodlands: patches of trees around Alum Pot, scrubby woodland in Ling Gill, shelter belts close to farmsteads. These features we admire and love to explore on foot, but it is clear that this is not a natural countryside.

When the last Ice Age ended the bare rock and clay left behind by the retreating glaciers and snowfields was initially colonised by an arctic-alpine flora including alpine meadow-rue (*Thalictrum alpinum*), mountain avens (*Dryas octopetala*), purple saxifrage (*Saxifraga oppositifolia*), hoary whitlow-grass (*Draba incana*), crowberry (*Empetrum nigrum*), cloudberry (*Rubus chamaemorus*) and heather. Judging from the fossil record, several species now long extinct in upper Ribblesdale also occurred, including dwarf arctic birch (*Betula nana*), arctic willow (*Salix herbacea*) and Norwegian mugwort (*Artemisia norvegica*).

However, with the amelioration of the Pennine climate the forest quickly spread across the land, initially of birch (*Betula pendula* and *Betula pubescens*), but culminating in a mixed mainly broad-leaved forest of oak, alder (*Alnus glutinosa*), wych elm and hazel (*Corylus avellana*). Very little open ground existed during this forest period about 7,000 years ago. Only the tops of the highest fells were above the tree-line, so that the plateaux of Ingleborough, Penyghent and Whernside were the chief refuges of non-forest plants. It is also likely that some plants of open country survived on narrow ledges on the steepest crags, where trees could not take root and survive.

About 7,000 years ago, however, the climate began to change from a fairly dry one that encouraged tree growth to a very warm and wet one. This meant that the gentler slopes and summits, with their less effective natural drainage, tended to become seriously waterlogged. Bog moss and cotton grass thrived in these wet conditions and they spread rapidly. The waterlogged ground was deficient in oxygen, so that the older dead moss and cotton grass decomposed very slowly and this, in turn, produced blanket-bog peat. The oxygen deficiency in the ground also suffocated the roots of the forest trees which grew on or at the edges of the waterlogged areas. They died, fell, and became overwhelmed by the growing thickness of peat. Thereafter, forest persisted only on the steeper, better-drained slopes.

Beginning about 5,000 years ago the climate became drier and the growth of the great blanket bogs came to an end. It is likely that these areas of blanket-bog were then gradually colonised by birch scrub and heather moor with bilberry (*Vaccinium myrtilus*) on drier peat, and that oak, alder and ash (*Fraxinus excelsior*) once more began to extend their range. But then, about 2,500 years ago, the climate again became wetter and cooler. This resulted in blanket-bog spreading rapidly once more across the poorly drained areas of moor. The tree line, which had at one time been just below the summits of the highest fells and close to the 600 metre contour, was lowered to about 540 metres. However, forest could reach that altitude only on the steeper, better-drained slopes, and close to the tree-line there would have been tree-scrub rather than dense woodland with tall majestic oaks. So, looking north-east from the tree-less summit of Simon Fell (650 metres), forest on the lower

A trace of the ancient forest is revealed as wood, from a tree overwhelmed by the developing blanket bog about 2,500 years ago, is exposed in eroding peat.

slopes below across South House and Borrins Moor would have given way to scrub almost to the summit of Park Fell (563 metres). Looking east, to where there are now lush pastures by the Ribble around Horton, there would have been swampy forest probably dominated by alder and willows (*Salix* species). Beyond the river, beginning around Foul Gutter Ridge, Black Bank (black: peat) and Thorns Moss the forest would peter out and blanket-bog must then have extended to the distant Blea Moor, Gayle Moor and Cam Fell, with the occasional rotting birch or oak stump sticking up from the flat blanket of peat that was covered by a mosaic of bog moss, cotton-grass and heather moor.

Furness Abbey, a Cistercian foundation originally based at Tulketh, Preston, had big flocks of sheep grazing over a large proportion of upper Ribblesdale.

If *Homo sapiens* had never visited upper Ribblesdale, that is what it would be like today. But of course they have, and it isn't. For humans have felled trees to provide fuel, building materials and to provide clearings where they could grow crops of oats and barley and to graze their goats, sheep and cattle. Neolithic, Bronze Age, Iron Age, Roman, Dane, Anglo Saxon and Norse all settled here, and all etched away a little more of the native forest. However, landscape change continued, and indeed accelerated, with the gradual growth of population and the extension and diversification of economic activity during the medieval period and into the modern age. Among the most important contributions to the process of landscape development were those which came about as a result of the Norman Conquest and the emergence – and then disappearance – of the monasteries as major landowners.

In 1068, two years after the Conquest, a major rebellion against the new regime took place in Yorkshire. William I would not tolerate such a threat to his crown. He marched north, retook York and then, to reduce the chances of further rebellion in northern England, adopted a scorched earth policy. A contemporary chronicler recorded that William 'continued to comb forests and remote mountain places, stopping at nothing to hunt out the enemy hidden there … He cut down many in his vengeance, destroyed the lairs of others, harried the land and burned homes to ashes [and ordered that] the whole region north of the Humber might be stripped of all means of sustenance'.[16] A high percentage of the upland farmsteads and hamlets throughout northern England – including the Ribble valley – were burned to the ground and their inhabitants either evicted or put to the sword.

When the Domesday Survey recorded the assets of the Pennines less than a generation later, in 1086, the term 'vasta est' (it is waste) was very widely used. Historians continue to debate whether this means that these areas were those which had been destroyed by William's army during the 'Harrying of the North' in 1069, or whether the term had other meanings. The evidence is ambiguous, but there is no doubt that the Domesday Survey indicates that this part of England was thinly populated. Central Lancashire (then legally a part of Yorkshire – it gained its independence in 1182) and the adjacent part of

Yorkshire through which the upper Ribble flows had a population of only four people per square mile (12.5 per sq km), and upper Ribblesdale only 0.4 per square mile (0.15 per sq km), compared with an average density of 32 people per square mile (12.5 per sq km) in England as a whole. In 1068 there were at least 64 inhabited settlements (farmsteads, hamlets, villages) in Ribblesdale, but by 1086 only 16 at the most were listed as paying taxes. There were very few recorded settlements above the 250 metre contour and in general the land appears to have been regarded as almost worthless. At Domesday the average value of English land was 32 shillings per square mile, but for the land within the Ribble catchment the equivalent value was only about 4 shillings.[17] The reliability of figures such as these is always subject to some doubt, but the overall impression is clear. Whether the low population densities and the poverty of the area were the result of the events of 1068–69 is, however, more uncertain. Suffice it to say that this part of Yorkshire may well have suffered greatly from William's vengeance, but that it had never been a densely populated or wealthy area. The figures derived from the Domesday Book may just reflect the position which had prevailed for centuries.

Once the political and military situation had stabilised, after 1070, William I gave extensive lands and estates to loyal supporters who had helped him in his conquest of England. The creation of great territorial estates held by powerful lords (or barons) was part of the king's strategy for ensuring that the regime remained firmly in control of the outer areas of the kingdom, and at the same time they acted as a front-line defence against possible incursions from Scots, the Welsh and others. Within fifty years, the Normans had introduced the continental forms of monasticism to England, and new monasteries were being established in considerable numbers across the country. They were frequently sponsored by major landowners, who endowed the new foundations with extensive estates to provide for their future income. Founding a religious house in this way was at once an act of piety, a step towards ultimate salvation, an insurance policy and a mark of status in this world. In the Yorkshire Dales and adjacent districts by 1300, a series of great monastic houses held large tracts of upland territory which had been given to them by the major landowners in the previous two hundred years. Some of these monasteries, such as Bolton Priory (usually, though incorrectly, known as Bolton Abbey) in Wharfedale, were situated in the Dales, but others, such as Fountains and Furness, were rather more distant.

In Ribblesdale several monasteries had estates. We have already encountered some of the granges, or large-scale commercial farms, by which these estates were managed. Jervaulx Abbey at the foot of Wensleydale, founded in 1156 by Akarius FitzBardolph, held moorland and fellside lands in upper Ribblesdale. In 1124, Stephen, Count of Mortain (who became king in 1135) granted lands to the monks of his new monastery at Tulketh in Preston. Three years later they moved to Furness Abbey, which by 1300 controlled a very extensive upland estate at the head of Ribblesdale. Further down the valley, William de Percy made comparable donations in 1147 for the founding of Sawley (or Salley) Abbey (see page 58), and in 1296 Henry de Lacy provided a major endowment of lands for the establishment of Whalley Abbey (page 172).

The Cistercian order became particularly celebrated for the management of sheep. Prior to their arrival the small amounts of wool produced in the region was largely for local consumption, but during the twelfth and thirteenth centuries large tracts of the lower dales and the limestone uplands were turned over to intensive wool production by Cistercian foundations such as Furness and Fountains. By the end of the thirteenth century about 110 tonnes of wool was being exported *per annum* from monastic farms and granges in the central Pennines through York market alone, most of it going for export to Flanders and Italy.[18] The profit from wool was in considerable measure responsible for the splendour of the magnificent abbeys for which the Cistercians are now so famous. Even after the Dissolution of the Monasteries from 1536 by Henry VIII, the production of wool continued to increase, for the monastic lands were sold, either as individual farms to yeoman farmers or as estates to wealthy gentry who then hired shepherds to tend their flocks. Most farms then supported up to three flocks, each consisting of about 200 breeding ewes. In the early seventeenth century an estimated 18,000 sheep grazed the limestone turf that extended from Ribblesdale to Malham.[19] Such was the profit from the wool that many families could afford to rebuild their farmsteads within two or three generations of making the original land purchase. Many farmhouses, not only in Ribblesdale, but also in the Hodder and Calder valleys, date from this period (1610–80). The effect of high densities of sheep on the moorlands is not only to prevent the regeneration of woodland. Intensive grazing can also destroy heather/bilberry grouse moorland, as happened in the twentieth century on the Rivington/Anglezarke Moors (p. 181), and it may also determine the species of grass growing on grassy moors (see page 35). For some eight hundred years, therefore, intensive grazing was a major factor influencing the landscape and the ecology of substantial areas of the Ribble valley and the surrounding hills.

How true Judith Turner's conclusion: 'For [man] has altered our primaeval woodlands from when he first began using the products of the forests in sufficient quantity to modify their nature until the present day, when we ourselves must bear the responsibility for so much of the highly artificial nature of our so-called natural environment.'[20]

One of the most conspicuous features of the countryside within the Ribble catchment is the drystone wall. These walls are important habitats for wildlife,

Small tortoiseshell butterfly. Its caterpillars feed on nettles, and the urine from sheep sheltering in the lee of dry stone walls encourages the nettles.

for they provide nest sites for birds such as wheatears (*Oenanthe oenanthe*), pied wagtails (*Motacilla alba*) and wrens (*Troglodytes troglodytes*); pathways and cover for small mammals such as wood mice (*Apodemus sylvaticus*) and weasels (*Mustela nivalis*); and a firm substrate for a variety of lichens, mosses, some epilithic ferns and flowering plants such as biting stonecrop (*Sedum acre*). Sheep often take shelter in the lee of drystone walls, and the high concentrations of nitrogen and phosphorus in their urine encourages the growth of stinging nettles, and with them the insect life associated with nettles (for instance, the small tortoiseshell butterfly *Aglais urticae*), even at comparatively high altitudes. Arthur Raistrick described how walling in the dales and on the moors occurred during two distinct periods, the sixteenth and the late eighteenth and early nineteenth centuries, and produced three recognisably different forms of land enclosure.[21]

Before the sixteenth century most of upper Ribblesdale was unenclosed – that is, it comprised open country without fences, hedges or walls. Even in the valley bottom, the permanent '*ing*' and '*ley*' meadow place-names of the Angles and Danes, the water meadows by the river, village pastures and the fields where villagers cultivated their vegetable and cereal crops were often not walled, although the arable land might be fenced in with a bank and thick impenetrable hedge of blackthorn (*Prunus spinosa*) or hawthorn (*Crategus monogyna*) to keep crops and grazing animals apart. Beyond this hedge the land was common rough pasture. Similarly in upland farmsteads, the Norse tradition had a system of communal grazing on common land, with small tofts (walled enclosures) close to the houses for growing oats. During the monastic period, when the sheep population of the Pennines was expanding rapidly, disputes occurred with increasing frequency when stock wandered to graze on the land belonging to adjacent villages or abbeys. To try to prevent this, distinctive boundary markers might be laid out to demarcate: often a ditch or a ridge marked with stones or boundary crosses was used. Some of these crosses – or more usually, their bases – still exist. During the later sixteenth century a combination of increasing population pressure which encouraged the extension of arable land and better pasture, and the reorganisation landholdings following the Dissolution, encouraged further enclosure of the lower slopes and the common meadows in many communities. The process was piecemeal and undertaken by agreement between the lord of the manor (who owned the commons) and his tenants, or was imposed by manorial lords as part of their management strategies for their estates. The field patterns produced by this process tend to be irregular, with many smaller fields carved one by one out of the waste.

Until the early eighteenth century, despite this, very extensive areas of open moor and unenclosed hillsides, and meadows and pastures remained in

Many bridges, such as this one across the Ribble at Stainforth, were built or rebuilt during the enclosure of the valley farmland.

Riverside mills, manufacturing paper or wool products, were a constant threat of pollution. Happily they are not today.

the dale. These tracts were still mostly common land, where each tenant of the manor had the right to graze a fixed number of cows or sheep. From the middle of the eighteenth century, however, a series of Enclosure Acts greatly reduced the area of open land of this type and effectively saw the end of this right. Landowners promoted private legislation so that they could extinguish the manorial common rights over these open uplands, and then divide the land into regularly shaped fields. The Enclosure Acts included clauses which defined the character and dimensions of the new boundaries: thus, new stone walls might have to be 'in all places made 34 inches broad at the Bottom and 6 feet high, under a Stone not exceeding 4 Inches in thickness ... there shall be laid in a Workmanlike Manner 21 good Throughs in every rood of Wall, and the first 12 to be laid on at a height of 2 Feet from the Ground, an the Wall at that height to be 2 Feet broad'.

The long-term effect of enclosure was not only to transform the landscape, but also to reorganise and reshape patterns and practices of agriculture.

It was perhaps one contributory factor in the 'drift from the land' which began to accelerate in the early nineteenth century, as – with more efficient agricultural techniques – there was less work for labourers and their families. So the countryside was divided up, as the Enclosure Acts had stipulated, to produce many of the key features in the landscape as we see it today. In the valley bottoms into straight-walled, rectangular or square fields of about 3.5 hectares and on the moors into long walled strips of equal width, covering 15 or more hectares. Man had made his conspicuous mark even on the high fellsides and remote moors.

Natural history of upper Ribblesdale

Upper Ribblesdale lies to the north of the Mid-Craven fault, a break in the rock strata that uplifted the Carboniferous limestone to the north. The fault line runs along Giggleswick Scar and then carries on eastwards, north of Settle, to produce the classic limestone scenery of Attermire and Great Scars and, at the head of neighbouring Airedale, Malham Cove. In the Craven district limestone is the dominant geological influence upon the scenery. Carboniferous limestone is also called Mountain limestone here, for it makes up the bulk of the great fells of Whernside, Ingleborough, Penyghent, Blea Moor and Cam Fell. The flat-topped summit caps of these fells, which are especially distinct in the first three named, are formed from a sequence of shales, limestone and gritstone that gives a stepped or banded appearance. This sequence is known as the Yoredale Series, and on top of it is a layer of Millstone Grit. Upper Ribblesdale is, therefore, classic limestone country, with some very special forms of wildlife.

Vegetation of upper Ribblesdale

The vegetation of the moorlands around the Ribble headwaters is a mosaic of different types, each of which requires certain conditions of soil acidity and is influenced by whether or not the soil is limey, soil depth, drainage, the presence of a layer of peat, and the intensity of grazing by sheep.

Where the soil is limey and well drained, rich limestone grassland is dominated by the sheep's fescue (*Festuca ovina*) with lesser quantities of blue moor grass (*Sesleria albicans*), quaking grass (*Briza media*), sweet vernal grass (*Anthoxanthum odoratum*), crested hair-grass (*Koeleria macrantha*), crested dogstail (*Cynosurus cristatus*) and Yorkshire fog (*Holcus lanatus*). On well-drained steeper slopes, where the soil is more acidic, wavy hair-grass (*Deschampsia flexuosa*) may be dominant. Where the ground is a little wetter, common bent (*Agrostis capillaris*) may be co-dominant with sheep's fescue. Several species of small sedges may be found amongst these grasses, including glaucous sedge (*Carex flacca*), birdsfoot sedge (*C. ornithopoda*), pill sedge (*C. pilulifera*) and spring sedge (*C. caryophyllea*). Where the soil is completely

Lesser celandines are woodland glade flowers, but they commonly grow in damp fields that were once wooded.

waterlogged in winter, tussocks of purple moor-grass (*Molinia caerulea*) are dominant, and where the waterlogged soil is particularly limey will be found also the large yellow sedge (*C. flava*).

All the grasses mentioned in the last paragraph provide top-quality or reasonable grazing and sheep will seek them out. Where grazing is particularly intensive these species may be completely or almost completely removed by sheep and their place taken by the tougher, less palatable mat grass (*Nardus stricta*). Large areas of moorland pasture in upper Ribblesdale are over-grazed mat grass moor with, in areas of wetter acidic soils, moor rush (*Juncus squarrosus*). Many over-grazed damp pastures have extensive stands of soft rush (*Juncus effusus*) that, in winter, give the pasture a brown appearance in contrast with the green of well-drained or improved pastures.

In late spring and early summer large expanses of flat, blanket-bog moorland are white with the fruiting heads of common cotton-grass. By contrast, where the acidic peat is better drained, as at the edges of peat hags or on steeper slopes, heather and, in even drier areas, bilberry may clothe the moor.

Wherever the soil is well drained and greater than about 30 centimetres deep, stands of bracken (*Pteridium aquilinum*) may occur up to the tree-line of 540 metres. The first frosts of autumn kill that year's growth, and it is only late in spring that the new fronds can safely emerge from the ground. Rather as in deciduous woods, several species of spring wildflower can be found in bracken stands, species that complete their flowering before the bracken has grown and cut out the light. Lesser celandine (*Ranunculus ficaria*), bluebell (*Scilla non-scripta*) and primrose (*Primula vulgaris*) are especially common in this niche.

Sphagnum bogs are usually small in upper Ribblesdale, and are found in wet hollows or where water seeps from sloping ground to produce a 'flush'. These mossy bogs have some quite fascinating plants associated with them, including the pink-flowered cross-leaved heath (*Erica tetralix*), bog rosemary (*Andromeda polifolia*) and cranberry (*Vaccinium oxycoccus*) that trail across the lime-green *Sphagnum* and the sulphur-yellow spikes of bog asphodel (*Narthecium ossifragum*) that stick vertically upwards. The insectivorous sundew (*Drosera rotundifolia*) occurs in the *Sphagnum*, whilst another insectivorous species, butterwort (*Pinguicula vulgaris*) tends to occur at the edges of bogs, often on bare wet mud.

Mossy saxifrage is common in the damp limestone grasslands of upper Ribblesdale.

Many other plant species can be found in the limestone grassland and acid bogs. Some are quite conspicuous, such as the gorse. The large straggling bushes of the common gorse (*Ulex europaeus*) flower on the lower slopes continuously from October, through the winter, with the bulk of blooms opening in April and May. By contrast, the smaller rounded bushes of the western gorse (*Ulex gallii*) are in flower only in the period July to September.

Other species of flowering plants are less conspicuous but extremely beautiful. Among the limey fescue grassland may be found spotted orchid (*Dactylorhiza fuchsii*), greater butterfly orchid (*Platanthera chlorantha*), fly orchid *(Ophrys insectifera*), fragrant orchid (*Gymnadenia conopsea*), early purple orchid (*Orchis mascula*) and common twayblade (*Listera ovata*). In at least one site, green-flowered helleborine (*Epipactis phyllanthes*) flowers on a calcareous slope sheltered by hawthorn bushes. White helleborine (*Cephalanthera damasonium*) used to occur under scattered trees at one site, but I have not found it since 1971.

Among the grasses of well-drained acidic slopes, tormentil (*Potentilla erecta*), heath bedstraw *(Galium saxatile)*, sheep's sorrel (*Rumex acetosella*) and milkwort (*Polygala vulgaris*) are common, while on moister ground can be found the moschatel (*Adoxa moschatellina*) and field gentian (*Gentianella campestris*).

One feature of the slopes leading to the summits of Ingleborough and Penyghent, and on some lower slopes, is exposed limestone in the form of cliff, scar, scree and pavement. These are often well drained, though water often seeps from above through pockets of calcareous soil, and they are out of reach of the nibbling sheep. They provide niches for some very special plants.

Saxifrages are well represented, with the purple saxifrage being especially spectacular in spring on the higher crags. Where the rock is kept damp by a trickle of water the yellow mountain saxifrage (*S. aizoides*) is common; Hunt Pot is a notable site. Where the soil is deeper, the mossy saxifrage (*S. hypnoides*) can be very common. Rue-leaved saxifrage (*S. tridactyilites*) is especially abundant on screes. The starry saxifrage (*S. stellaris*) is one to look out for as it used to occur in damper rocky areas on both Ingleborough and Penyghent, but it seems to have disappeared in recent years.

Arctic sandwort (*Arenaria norvegica*) and the Yorkshire sandwort (*A. gothica*) occur on limestone screes close to rock faces and occasionally in the grykes (the deep cracks between the clints) of limestone pavement. Upper Ribblesdale is the only location in Britain of this latter species, which also occurs in the limestone mountains of the French Jura. The deep blue flower heads of spiked speedwell (*Veronica spicata*) can also be found on limestone together with the poisonous baneberry, also called herb Christopher (*Actaea spicata*). Other species often associated with limestone outcrops include hoary whitlow grass (*Draba incana*), alpine cinquefoil (*Potentilla crantzii*), mountain pansy (*Viola lutea*), alpine lady's mantle (*Alchemilla alpina*), alpine pennycress (*Thlaspi caerulescens*) and the two grasses, alpine meadow-grass (*Poa alpina*) and yellow oat-grass (*Trisetum flavescens*). Wild thyme (*Thymus praecox*) is common in the limestone country of upper Ribblesdale and with it was found, in 1811 and 1854 but not since, the parasitic thyme boomrape (*Orobanche alba*). Where the rock or scree is very wet, alpine bistort (*Polygonum viviparum*) often occurs.

An outline of the Ribblesdale limestone rock garden would be incomplete without mention of the abundant ferns, six characteristic species being the maidenhair spleenwort (*Asplenium trichomanes*), wall-rue (*A. ruta-mararia*), green spleenwort (*A. viride*), rigid buckler fern (*Dryopteris submontana*), limestone polypody (*Gymnocarpium robertianum*), hard shield fern (*Polystrichum aculeatum*) and the brittle bladder fern (*Cystopteris fragilis*).

The limestone gorges of upper Ribblesdale, together with fenced-off pothole entrances and other corners inaccessible to the nibbling sheep, have a scrubby woodland vegetation. Ash, rowan, bird cherry, blackthorn and hawthorn often occur with, in some sites, yew (*Taxus baccata*) and wych elm. Growing beneath these may be grasses, including false-brome (*Brachypodium sylvaticum*),

tufted hair-grass (*Deschampsia caespitosa*) and cock's-foot (*Dactylis glomerata*). Dog's mercury (*Mercurialis perennis*), wild garlic (*Allium ursinum*), herb Robert (*Geranium robertianum*), sanicle (*Sanicula europaea*) and woodruff (*Galium odoratum*) often flower in the shade. A similar flora may also be found beneath alders and the non-native sycamore (*Acer pseudoplatanus*) along the banks of the river where they are fenced off from grazing sheep and cattle.

Most pastures and meadows in the valley bottom from Newhouses south to Settle have been ploughed and re-seeded with more productive species of grass such as perennial rye (*Lolium perenne*), or at have least been drained, sprayed with herbicide and treated with large doses of NPK fertiliser. Thus the traditional flora of the wet pastures and water meadows that were enclosed around 200 years ago has been lost to grass monoculture with a few resistant weeds. There are, however, a few places where it is still possible to find a richer flora, including a wide variety of grasses such as cock's-foot, crested dogstail, meadow foxtail (*Alopecurus pratensis*), sweet vernal grass, Timothy (*Phleum pratense*) and Yorkshire fog. White clover (*Trifolium repens*), red clover (*T. pratense*), yellow

LEFT
The twayblade (*Listera ovata*) is one of the commonest orchids in upper Ribblesdale. This one is in the lee of a dry stone wall by the lane leading to New Houses.

rattle (*Rhinanthus minor*), eyebright (*Euphrasia rostkoviana*) and meadow buttercup (*Ranunculus acris*) add colour. Some fields even have a showing of species such as lesser celandine and bluebell that grew here when the field was woodland, hundreds of years ago.

Animal life in upper Ribblesdale

The red fox has earths high on the fells surrounding the Ribble headwaters, one vixen descending over 350 metres to the valley floor to raid chicken runs. Several other mammals occur to, or almost to, the summits of the highest fells. Common shrews (*Sorex araneus*) and pygmy shrews (*S. minutus*) can be found at high level wherever there is cover in the form of drystone walls, scree or cairns. I have caught common shrews to 620 metres on Simon Fell, 490 metres on Penyghent and 420 metres on cotton-grass moor on Cam Fell. Moles (*Talpa europaea*) occur wherever there are earthworms in the soil for them to eat, so they occur to around 500 metres in better-drained limestone grassland. Field voles (*Microtus agrestis*) are widespread, occurring wherever there is rough grassland or heather-bilberry moor. Bank voles (*Clethrionomys glareolus*) are far more of a valley species, although I have found them living in scree to 310 metres. As their name suggests, wood mice are primarily woodland rodents, though they do occur in hawthorn scrub and amongst bracken to around 400 metres. Otters (*Lutra lutra*), badgers and roe deer can be seen in upper Ribblesdale, though they are much commoner further down the valley (page 109) and in the Hodder valley (page 121).

RIGHT
A brood of newly hatched dunlin chicks from a nest at Ribblehead. Within half an hour of hatching their parents had led them over 100 metres away to feed in an area of *Sphagnum* bog and shallow pools.

The bleak expanses of open moorland from which the headwaters of the Ribble rise have important breeding bird populations. On the wet tops, golden plover (*Pluvialis apricaria*) are most conspicuous because of their plaintive far-carrying whistle, but wherever there are bog pools dunlin (*Calidris alpina*) will be found nesting with the plovers. Dunlins can easily be detected by the purring trill of the male as he announces his territory, but once nesting is under way he tends to be silent and the pairs less conspicuous. In one three km² plot on the high moors in 1974 there were 16 pairs of golden plovers and three pairs of dunlin. The same study area also held a pair of teal (*Anas crecca*) that raised their ducklings on an overgrown boggy pool, several pairs of red grouse (*Lagopus lagopus*), at least six pairs of snipe (*Gallinago gallinago*), a pair of redshanks (*Tringa totanus*), three pairs of curlew (*Numenius arquata*) and a pair of short-eared owls (*Asio flammeus*). A pair of merlins (*Falco columbarius*), that had a nest just off the study plot, hunted the 120 pairs of meadow pipits (*Anthus pratensis*) that were the most abundant birds here. Meadow pipits are the favourite host species of female cuckoos (*Cuculus canorus*) on the moors, and in April and May the dale resounds to the onomatopoeic calls of the males.

Some forty years ago, early in 1966 there was a meeting between Walter Flesher (one-armed gamekeeper and BBC radio naturalist), John Wilson (RSPB warden), and me to plan the guarding of the last pair of nesting peregrines (*Falco peregrinus*) in the Yorkshire Dales. We talked of having a 24-hour guard that spring but, alas, our plans came to nought because the nest-site was abandoned. The dales peregrines had been exterminated by the same combination of egg-collecting, theft of chicks for falconry and poisoning by organochlorine insecticides which had decimated the bird of prey populations elsewhere in Britain. A ban on the use of these noxious chemicals, together with a reduction in nest robbery, has resulted in a slow recovery and, happily, today the peregrine hunts once more over the moorlands of upper Ribblesdale. So too do the buzzard (*Buteo buteo*) and raven (*Corvus corax*), species that have extended their range in the Pennines since the 1980s.

One species that has probably become extinct in the whole Ribble catchment in recent years is the black grouse (*Tetrao tetrix*). It is a species that requires a quite complex mosaic of habitats: scrub, trees, heather moor, lightly grazed grass-sedge-rush moor. The tidying up of moorland edges and increased sheep densities leading to over-grazing have been its downfall both here and in many British areas. From being a quite common species in the 1950s, it has not been recorded for well over a decade.

Whinchat (*Saxicola rubetra*), stonechat (*S. torquata*), wheatear and ring ouzel (*Turdus torquatus*) are moorland species that are rarely seen on the open moor. Ring ouzels can be found nesting in steep-sided ravines or 'cloughs' within easy reach of worm-rich pastures. Wheatears nest commonly in scree, in drystone walls and, where these are lacking, in any suitable cavity (one pair nested successfully by Ling Gill in a hole formed when a boulder fell from the bank into the stream). Whinchats and stonechats both nest in bushes such as hawthorn and gorse, bracken and bramble (whin is the local dialect term for gorse). Stonechats are residents and very susceptible to hard winter weather so that populations disappear after a hard winter and slowly recover over several years. After a run of mild winters in the late 1990s and 2000s, several populations of stonechats had developed. By contrast the whinchat is a summer visitor, and its population has declined in recent years because of drought conditions in its African winter quarters.

In winter, the high moors are almost birdless, save for the occasional carrion crow (*Corvus corone*) flapping overhead, seeking some rotting sheep carcass. A walk over the moors may, however, reveal two very special winter visitors. Snow buntings (*Plectrophenax nivalis*) are visitors from the high arctic and most commonly associated with the coast. However, quite large parties may be encountered (my own record count is of 124 on Blea Moor in February 1975) as they drift like snowflakes across the moor feeding on sedge and rush fruits. Lapland buntings (*Calcarius lapponicus*) are much rarer, but possibly overlooked: I encountered them seven times, with 19 the largest party between 1969 and 1976.

Below the wild open moor the high level improved pastures have a different breeding bird community. Lapwings (*Vanellus vanellus*) replace golden plovers. In rushy fields, snipe and curlew occur in higher densities (in a 1.2 square kilometre study plot there were seven pairs of snipe and five pairs of curlew in 1999). Skylarks (*Alauda arvensis*) are fairly scarce on the open moor, but plentiful in the high pastures (the 1999 study plot had 27 pairs). Pied wagtails nest in drystone walls and jackdaws (*Corvus monedula*) and starlings (*Sturnus vulgaris*) in barns on the high pastures.

Lapwing, curlew, redshank (*Tringa totanus*), snipe, skylark and yellow wagtail (*Motacilla flava*) are the main ground-nesting birds of the riverside meadows and pastures of the valley bottom. However, during the last quarter of the twentieth century the populations of these species declined with one, the yellow wagtail, now extinct in upper Ribblesdale (in 1971 I counted eight pairs between Horton and Langcliffe, but there was none in 1999). The reason for this decline is almost certainly more intensive management of the meadows and, especially, the early cutting of grass for silage that destroys nests and unfledged young. Before the early 1970s, when the grass crop was taken as hay, the cut usually took place in July, when eggs had hatched and young fledged.

Common sandpipers (*Actitis hypoleucos*) nest amongst riverside vegetation and dippers (*Cinclus cinclus*) and grey wagtails (*Motacilla cinerea*) in cavities by Gayle and Cam Becks and the infant Ribble downstream to beyond Settle. They can also be found nesting by the tiniest of streams: in 1967 one pair of dippers nested on a ledge about three metres down Hunt Pot. By contrast, sand martins (*Riparia riparia*) excavate burrows in vertical earth banks by the river and, because there are few of these in upper Ribblesdale, sand martins are scarce here compared with Big Ribble.

The permanent and semi-permanent pools on the open moor, often associated with *Sphagnum* bogs and flushes, have a rich aquatic animal

community. In late March, some pools are a mass of frog (*Rana temporaria*) spawn, though prolonged freezing at these high levels often results in a low hatch-rate. High-level pools throughout the Ribble catchment sometimes have populations of palmate newts (*Triturus helveticus*), whereas pools at lower levels have common newts (*T. vulgaris*). Flying around these pools in summer and early autumn may be large red damselflies (*Pyrrhosoma nymphula*), common darters (*Sympetrum striolatum*), black darters (*S. danae*) and the four-spotted chaser (*Libellula quadrimaculata*), for the larvae of these four dragonflies are the main predatory invertebrates of these pools. The pools also have huge

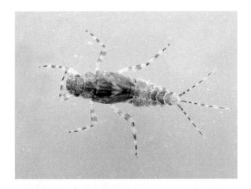

TOP LEFT
One of the
commonest of
the many species
of mayflies in
Ribblesdale is the
blue-winged olive
(*Serratella ignita*).
Its sturdy nymphs
have banded legs
and tail filaments.

TOP RIGHT
The adult emerges
from the river
mainly in June–
October and has
grey wings and
three tails.

CENTRE LEFT
The upland
dun (*Ameletus
inopinatus*) is a
mayfly of mountain
streams and its
nymph can be
found in Cam Beck
and the headwaters
above Ribblehead.

CENTRE RIGHT
Stoneflies demand
the cleanest of
water. One of the
largest, *Dinocras
cephalotes*, has
a nymph up
to 3 cm long
and is common
throughout the
Ribble above
Settle (also in the
Hodder).

RIGHT
The males of
large stoneflies are
flightless, so this is
a female. They can
be seen April/May.

populations of non-biting midges (Chironomidae) and, where there is a flow of water through *Sphagnum*, the biting black-fly (*Simulium*). Lesser water-boatmen are often abundant in moorland pools and include the species *Sigaria lateralis*, *S. venusta*, *S. nigrolineata* and *Callicorixa wollastoni*. Two species of pond-skater, *Gerris costai* and *G. gibbifer*, as well as the small whirligig-beetle *Gyrinus minutus*, can be found on the surface of the peaty pools. Four non-aquatic insects are closely associated with *Sphagnum*-moss: a long-horn beetle

Saperda populnea, a mirid bug *Capsus wagneri*, the large marsh grasshopper (*Stethophyma grossum*) and, especially where there is cross-leaved heath with the *Sphagnum*, the bog bush-cricket (*Metrioptera brachyptera*).

Cotton-grass moor is inhospitable for 'soil' invertebrates because the peat is low or lacking in oxygen. One species of crane-fly *Tipula subnodicornis* manages to cope and it often occurs in huge numbers, its larvae providing food for the wader populations of the moor. The larvae of a small metallic copper coloured beetle *Plateumaris discolor* survive by feeding on the cotton-grass roots and tapping the internal oxygen channels of the roots. The larvae of Haworth's minor moth (*Celaena haworthii*) feed on the shoots and fruits of cotton-grass and the white-marked light brown adults can be seen flying by day over the moor.

Moths are particularly numerous on grassy moorland around the Ribble headwaters. The brown larvae of the antler-moth (*Cerapteryx gramineus*) feeds on mat-grass and rushes, the tiny caterpillars of the whitish micro-moth *Coleophora caespitiella* on the fruits of rushes, and the larvae of *Procus strigilis*, *Petilampa minima* and *Arenostola pygmina* on sheep's fescue. The hairy caterpillars of the ruby tiger moth (*Phragmatobia fuliginosa*) can be found feeding on several grass species on damp upland grasslands. Mottled grasshoppers (*Myrmeleotettrix maculatus*) occur through the summer in lightly grazed dry fescue-bent grassland.

Butterflies are not common on the high grassy moors. The Scotch argus (*Erebia aethiops*) was recorded from Whernside in the nineteenth century, but not since then; it has colonies in Cumbria. The larvae of the large heath (*Coenonympha tullia*) feed on purple moor-grass, cotton-grass and some sedges. The small green hairstreak (*Callophrys rubi*) is common on bilberry moor from late April.

Above Settle, the river Ribble is primarily a brown trout (*Salmo trutta*) stream, although some salmon (*S. salar*) reach here from the sea to spawn and their parr grow in the river for up to three years before they head downstream to the sea. The river here also has eels (*Anguilla anguilla*), miller's thumbs (*Cottus gobio*), minnows (*Phoxinus phoxinus*) and stone loach (*Noemacheilus barbatula*). Grayling (*Thymallus thymallus*) and chub (*Leuciscus cephalus*) can be found close to Settle.

The upper Ribble has a great assembly of river invertebrates, though what was a thriving population of the native crayfish (*Austropotamobius pallipes*) in the 1980s between Settle and Horton seems to have greatly declined or even disappeared (I could not find one in June 2005). The reason for this may be that American signal crayfish (*Pacifastacus lenuisculus*) has been released into the river (it is spreading from Long Preston) and with it a fungus which kills the native species. Of the other river invertebrates stoneflies and upwinged

With such a rich invertebrate life, the Ribble upstream of Settle supports a high density of breeding dippers, which feed by going underwater in search if their insect prey.

flies (mayflies) are of great interest, for their diversity in terms of the number of species and abundance are indicative of water quality. My surveys have revealed no fewer than 20 species of stoneflies and 22 species of upwinged flies living in the river and its feeders.[22]

There are also healthy populations of caddis-flies, including the caseless, predatory green larvae of *Rhyacophila dorsalis* with a similar species *R. obliterata* in the higher feeders, and the net-spinning *Hydropsyche instabilis*. Such diverse populations indicate that the water flowing down to Settle is of top quality.

Upper Ribblesdale is an important part of the Yorkshire Dales National Park, and one of the most beautiful corners of our overcrowded island. Its prehistory and history are long, and illustrate well how the evolution of the countryside has been affected by the evolution of the human society there. The management of agriculture and tourism within this part of the valley should be sympathetic to cause of maintaining this beauty and its wildlife.

Folly Hall, built in 1679 by Richard Preston, is one of Settle's oldest buildings and now houses the Museum for Craven Life.

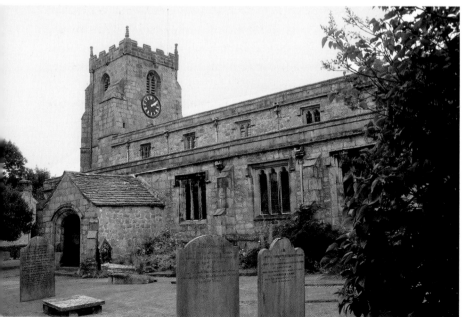

St Alkelda's Church at Giggleswick is the mother church of the townships of Giggleswick, Rathmell, Settle, Langcliffe and Stainforth. A board inside the church lists all its vicars from 1230, though there was a church here long before that, perhaps to pre-Norman times.

CHAPTER TWO

Little Ribble, Big Ribble

... a country streaked with tangled clouds and sunshine, with square-topped Ingleborough in the far north, with the deep curved vale of Ribble here and there shooting a flash of silver flood amongst the trees, with joyful old Pendle, a knowing old dog of a mountain curled up beyond the gap of the Calder.

William T. Palmer, *Wanderings in Ribblesdale*, 1951.

Settle marks the downstream limit of what I call the Ribble headwaters. Thus far small streams, rising in springs welling up from the underground catacombs of caves and potholes or from peat bogs high on the fells, have bubbled their way rapidly down to form and then to swell the infant Ribble. At Settle the valley opens out. The high fells of Craven – Ingleborough, Penyghent, Whernside and Cam Fell – are left behind. Now the Ribble is no longer a moorland stream; nor is it yet the big river that it becomes below its confluences with Hodder and Calder. So the Ribble between Settle and Preston can be divided into two quite discrete sections: Little Ribble and Big Ribble.

Little Ribble

Settle is on a major Pennine crossroads. Ancient Roman roads and drovers' tracks, now widened and converted into metalled roads, head due north through the town to Wensleydale and meander south to the urban conurbations of industrial Lancashire. Running south-east to north-west is the great cross-country route linking the woollen towns of the West Riding of Yorkshire with the Irish Sea and Lake District holiday resorts. On a summer weekend or bank holiday the A65 carries a continuous stream of traffic. This route follows the

Castleberg Crag
overlooks the town
of Settle.

Craven Fault that lifted the land to the north and formed a limestone cliff
– Giggleswick Scar – to the west of the town. South of Settle, too, is the
major railway junction where the line to Lancaster diverges from the famous
Settle and Carlisle line, the latter heading off to Ribblehead, Mallerstang and
the Eden Valley.

Settle appears in the Domesday Survey as 'Setel', and by the reign of Henry
III (1216–72) it had been granted a charter to hold a market. However, little
of the present town predates the seventeenth century. Settle is overlooked by
the crag of Castleberg, described by Thomas Pennant in 1773 as 'a monstrous
limestone rock that threatens destruction'.[1] Standing on this outcrop, the
town and its market place are almost at one's feet; beyond is Giggleswick,
and stretching into the distance are the fells of Bowland, Little Ribble and
the blue-grey of Pendle.

The now neglected 'ebbing-and-flowing' well.

Giggleswick, the village of the Anglian chieftain Ghikel, has its roots in the Dark Ages. It too is mentioned in Domesday and had a parish church long before Settle, so that people from the town walked there for Sunday worship. The present Giggleswick church dates from the fourteenth century, and is built on the site of two earlier ones. The village also has a notable public school, founded in 1507.

Just outside the village, beneath Giggleswick Scar, is the curious ebbing-and-flowing well. By tradition this is a well of mystical properties. It has an inflow through an oval opening in the back of the stone trough that makes up the well and two small outflows at the sides. Water magically rises and then, when level with the grating covering the well, the inflow ceases and the level falls. Of course, there is nothing magical at all, for the phenomenon is simply the result of a siphon action. During droughts there is no flow or ebb, and in times of heavy rain the well remains full. The well was once very famous. Michael Drayton wrote, in 1616, that:

> At Giggleswick where I a fountain can you show
> That eight times in a day is said to ebb and flow.[2]

And Dr Gibson, who edited Camden's *Britannia*, described it as 'the most noted spring in England for ebbing and flowing'.[3] However today the well has been taken from the tourist trail because it lies next to what was the main A65 (since the Settle bypass was built, the B6480 that carries traffic north from the town), there are no car parking facilities and to examine the well one must walk from Giggleswick along the road. The internal combustion engine rules, even here!

Long Preston
Deeps, where
the river flows
sluggishly through
the bed of a
post-glacial lake.
Yellow water lilies
cover much of the
surface in summer.

At Cow Bridge
the river ceases to
meander through
the Deeps, flowing
seawards through a
series of pools and
riffles.

Long Preston Ings

From Settle and Giggleswick the Ribble flows south for two kilometres to the new Settle bypass and then, suddenly, the character of the river changes completely. Instead of an alternating series of deeper pools and shallow rocky riffles, with the land rising steeply on either side, the river deepens, its flow becomes sluggish, and it meanders with wide sweeping loops through a flat marshy floodplain that in places is over one kilometre wide. As the crow flies it is just over five kilometres from Settle bridge to the southern end of this flat expanse, where Wigglesworth Beck flows into the Ribble upstream of Cow Bridge near Long Preston village; but with its meanderings the river flows twice that distance.

This unique area is known as Long Preston Ings or Deeps, and its origins lie in the geomorphological processes that took place at the end of the last Ice Age. Before then the Ribble upstream of Cow Bridge flowed eastwards

TOP LEFT
Bog-bean and marsh marigold are amongst many species of water, waterside and marsh plants found along the Deeps.

TOP RIGHT
The monkey-flower (*Mimulus guttatus*) is common throughout the Ribble system, growing on exposed sand or gravel at the waterside. However it is not a native, having been introduced to Britain from North America.

BOTTOM LEFT
Ragged robin was common in wet meadows throughout the Ribble catchment up to the 1950s and 1960s. Drainage, the use of herbicides and re-seeding with grass monocultures have resulted in it being very scarce today.

BOTTOM RIGHT
Globe flowers have always been scarce in the valley, but they can be found in undrained, marshy areas over limestone.

to join the River Aire between where Gargrave and Skipton stand today. However, as the last Ice Age drew to a close, huge mounds of boulder clay, deposited by the ice-sheets and glaciers, blocked the route from Cow Bridge to the Aire. These boulder clay mounds, rounded and oval in appearance and called drumlins, dominate the landscape on either side of the A65 between Hellifield and Gargrave. Without them the Ribble to this point would flow to the Humber and North Sea, and not to the Irish Sea. Upstream from this boulder clay dam (above Cow Bridge) the river water backed up to form a wide shallow lake which subsequently silted to produce the Ings, and the river cut an outflow that headed south-west to the Irish Sea instead of east. The Ings are therefore the broad flat floor of a temporary post-glacial lake.

Looking more like a coastal fenland river rather than an upland one at 130 metres above sea level, the bed of the Ribble as it flows through the flat, marshy, dried-up lake bed is mainly silt. The aquatic flora is typical of a lowland river, with yellow water-lily (*Nuphar lutea*), pond water crowfoot (*Ranunculus peltatus*), broad-leaved pondweed (*Potamogeton natans*) and perfoliate pondweed (*P. perfoliatus*). In the damp margins are amphibious bistort (*Polygonum amphibium*), creeping yellowcress (*Rorippa sylvestris*), green figwort (*Scrophularia umbrosa*), slender speedwell (*Veronica filiformis*), giant bellflower (*Campanula latifolia*), sand leek (*Allium scorodoprasum*), spiked water-milfoil (*Myriophyllum spicatum*) and water horsetail (*Equisetum fluviatile*).

The curlew is one of the characteristic breeding birds around Little Ribble, but much rarer in the fields around Big Ribble.

The water meadows around the Ribble at Long Preston Deeps flood in winter, but in summer are grazed or a cut of silage taken. Some fields have been 'improved', but others remain wet with extensive stands of rushes and with water forget-me-not (*Myosotis scorpioides*), marsh marigold (*Caltha palustiis*) and ragged robin (*Lychnis flos-cuculi*). There are some semi-permanent pools and, close to the river, calcareous springs with a fascinating flora that includes marsh cinquefoil (*Potentilla palustris*), birdseye primrose (*Primula farinosa*), bogbean (*Menyanthes trifoliata*), marsh lousewort (*Pedicularis palustris*), butterwort and fen bedstraw (*Galium uliginosum*). Amongst the rushes are the blunt-flowered rush (*Juncus subnodulosus*), the few-flowered spike-rush (*Eleocharis quinqueflora*) and slender spike-rush (*E. uniglumis*), and black bog-rush (*Schoenus nigricans*). Among many sedges are fen cotton-grass (*Eriophorum latifolium*), tawny sedge (*Carex hostiana*), long-stalked sedge (*C. lepidocarpa*) and brown sedge (*C. disticha*). A few sites in the area have marsh valerian (*Valeriana dioica*), globe flower (*Trollius europaeus*), spotted orchid and early marsh orchid (*D. incarnata*), and one site has narrow-leaved marsh orchid (*D. traunsteineri*), a rare species in north-west England.

Ornithologically the water meadows have breeding and wintering communities that are common enough on lowland wetlands but unusual in the middle reaches of Pennine valleys. Mute swan (*Cygnus olor*) and shelduck (*Tadorna tadorna*) breed along with larger numbers of moorhen (*Gallinula chloropus*), lapwing, redshank, snipe, sedge warbler (*Acrocephalus schoenobaenus*) and reed bunting (*Emberiza schoeniclus*). Yellow wagtails were common here until their population crashed in the 1970s and early 1980s; as the 1984 Settle Bird Report put it, 'Breeding population still decreasing as more and more meadows are used for silage.'[4] By 2000 they were gone. Out of the breeding season up to 500 golden plovers, 4,000 lapwings, 200 snipe and 1,500 curlews gather to probe the damp ground for worms and insect larvae. Winter wildfowl include flocks of up to 500 wigeon (*Anas penelope*), 400 teal and 250 Canada geese (*Branta canadensis*).

Large red damselfly, common blue damselfly (*Enallagma cynthigerum*), blue-tailed damselfly (*Ischnura elegans*), common hawker (*Aeshna juncea*), brown hawker (*A. grandis*) and common darter can be seen here. In 2000 two new dragonflies were recorded for the Deeps: a male banded demoiselle (*Calopteryx splendens*) and two male black darters.[5] By 2007 the once rare banded demoiselle had become a common dragonfly along the entire Ribble from Preston to Settle.

Up to the end of the nineteenth century, wet boggy water meadows were common in the dales. Subsequently drainage, the use of herbicides and re-seeding with more productive grasses have destroyed most. Long Preston Ings is therefore a major and precious remnant of a once widespread habitat.

Reed buntings nest in the wetlands around Long Preston Deeps.

The banded demoiselle did not occur anywhere in the Ribble catchment fifty years ago. This lovely damselfly now occurs commonly through the Douglas system and along the Ribble from Preston to Long Preston.

Cow Bridge to the Hodder and Calder confluences

The names of many of the villages on Little Ribble downstream of Long Preston are derived from Old English (or Anglo-Saxon) forms, Long Preston was *Prestune*; Paythorne means 'Pai's thornbush'; Gisburn was *Ghiseburn* ('the gushing stream'); Bolton was *Botheltun* ('village or farmstead with its buildings'); Sawley was *Sallai* or *Salley* ('the willow clearing'); Grindleton was *Grendeltun* ('farmstead by the gravelly stream'); and Wigglesworth was once *Winchelesuuorde* ('Wincel's enclosure'). There are also names derived from the Old Norse, such as Hellifield, which was *Helgefeld* ('Helgi's open land'). Clitheroe was *Cliderhou*, probably from a mixed Old English and Norse root meaning 'hill of the loose stones' (*clitter* is still a dialect word for scree or stone debris).[6]

The peel at Hellifield was built during the mid-fifteenth century by Lawrence Hammerton under licence from Henry VI. On the other side of the river, the original Wigglesworth Hall was the home of Sir Stephen Hammerton who was executed at Tyburn in 1537 on the orders of Henry VIII, following his involvement in the Pilgrimage of Grace. The bridge at Paythorne is medieval, and the farms above this tiny hamlet were founded, after the clearance of secondary woodland and scrub, in the fifteenth and sixteenth centuries. One is now called England's Head, a name which is a misconstruction of Ing-land's Head: the upper limit of the meadows. Upstream of England's Head is Nappa, a name first recorded in 1251 and meaning the enclosure on a bowl-shaped hilltop. The remains of the enclosure are a kilometre to the east of Nappa ford,

Swineden Enclosure was a medieval pig compound. Today it is a large area of boggy rushes.

by the footpath linking Swinden Moor Head and Swinden Hall. Swinden: the valley of swine. The Iron Age mound of Castle Haugh and a tumulus between Paythorne and Gisburn reveal that settlement in this area can be traced back to the Iron Age, and perhaps earlier. Both Paythorne Bridge and Nappa ford were – and still ought to be – sites of interest on the third Sunday of November, for this is Salmon Sunday, when people used to gather there to watch salmon spawning in the shallow gravel-strewn riffles.

Gisburn is the family seat of the Lords Ribblesdale, although up to the Dissolution it was a holding of nearby Sawley Abbey. The first Lord Ribblesdale still influences the valley here for, early in the eighteenth century, he planted 1,200,000 oaks and large numbers of other trees.[7] Many of these still flourish, giving this stretch of the Ribble a notably wooded appearance and with some very fine stands of grand mature trees.

Bolton-by-Bowland is one of the most beautiful and secluded villages in Little Ribblesdale. Bolton Hall dates from the mid-fourteenth century and came to fame in 1465 when Henry VI took shelter here when on the run after the Battle of Hexham (see page 63). King Henry's Well is named from this less than comfortable visit. It was Henry's pleasure to give small presents to those who gave him shelter: here he presented his host, Sir Ralph Pudsey, with a pair of gloves, a pair of boots and a spoon. Later, during the reign of Elizabeth I, another Pudsey was accused of illegally mining silver in his estate's lead-mines and smelting the silver to cast forged silver shillings. To

Bolton-by-Bowland rivals Downham (see page 158) as 'most beautiful village' in the valley.

Tosside Beck joins the Ribble at Bolton-by-Bowland. Note how, in the distance, the stream has been fenced off to grazing cattle, whereas in the foreground it has not. One project of the Ribble Catchment Conservation Trust is to use fencing to maintain healthy bank side vegetation and to prevent erosion of the banks by livestock. Thus wildlife in the valley – both aquatic and waterside – benefits, and the farmer loses no land!

avoid arrest he fled on horseback, and is said to have driven his horse to leap Rainsber Scar, the cliff that forms the Ribble gorge at Bolton, and headed to London where he successfully pleaded his innocence. The point where he made the leap is called Pudsey's Leap. Upstream of Rainsber Scar, Little Ribble flows through a steep-sided gorge with a tight loop called Denham Wheel. 'Wheel' comes from the Angle for a whirlpool, and there is one other on Big Ribble, Sale Wheel just downstream of Calderfoot.

Sawley is a modernised form of the older name Salley. William of Normandy gave lands here to William de Perci who had helped in the conquest of England. In 1147 his grandson, William Baron Percy granted

lands to the Cistercian order, to found a new monastic house. Twelve monks
and lay brothers came here from Fountains Abbey, receiving further financial
support from the founder's daughter, Maud de Percy, Countess of Warwick.
Sawley faced major problems from the outset: its site was low-lying and
prone to dampness; the harvests were said to be poor; and the climate, so the
monks claimed, was inhospitable. After 1296 it faced severe competition, and
incessant rivalry from the newly founded Whalley Abbey a few kilometres
down the road, and in the early fourteenth century the abbey's lands suffered
from the vicious attention of Scots who invaded northern England under
Robert Bruce. Perhaps for these reasons, the abbey buildings were never
completed. It was laid out in the late twelfth century according to the standard
monastic plan, with a full-sized cloister, but the church was never finished
and the nave remained only half the intended length. In the late fifteenth
century there were more funds available, and the chancel was reconstructed
with new aisles, but the strange truncated church stayed. Today this oddity,
unique among Cistercian houses, is still easily visible. In the spring of 1536
the abbey surrendered during the first phase of Henry VIII's Dissolution of
the Monasteries, but in the autumn of that year it was one of the northern
houses which was restored during the popular rising known as the Pilgrimage

Clitheroe Castle was built on a Carboniferous limestone reef-knoll.

of Grace. In March 1537 its last abbot, William Trafford, was executed and the abbey dissolved for the second time. Although what now remains is carefully preserved, the ruins are relatively scanty compared with other Cistercian houses such as Furness and Fountains. The high-quality dressed stonework was robbed out and used in other buildings in and around Sawley. The village and abbey of Sawley are at the downstream end of a narrow gorge, where the valley widens into a broad flat floodplain. Once these wet meadows were

covered with willow-carr, as the name of the village (clearing in the sallows, or willows) recalls.

Clitheroe is the largest town on the banks of Little Ribble. Its Old English and Norse name derives from the town's most conspicuous feature, the great limestone rock on which the castle is built. As with many other frontier regions of England, William I presented the lands of Clitheroe to a loyal subject, Gilbert de Lacy, who became Lord of the Honour of Clitheroe. The town is dominated by the ruins of its castle, which from its limestone reef-knoll commands a magnificent view over the surrounding lowlands and fells. For two centuries there has been argument about the date of its construction, some – such as Thomas Whitaker – arguing that it was built immediately after the Norman Conquest. It is now accepted that some form of defensive structure existed here by 1102, but that the present castle building probably dates from the late twelfth century.[8]

The castle was comparatively simple in plan. It had a small keep, about 13 metres high and 6 × 6 metres in area with walls three metres thick; there is a small chapel dedicated to St Michael and some stables, a court house and other ancillary buildings, all surrounded by a high curtain wall which enclosed the level ground just below the summit of the rock. The castle remained relatively intact for around 500 years, playing little part in major military actions but often serving as a prison – King Henry VI may have been briefly incarcerated here after his capture at Brungerley Bridge, below the town, in 1464. During the Commonwealth period, Parliament ordered

The town of Clitheroe was built below the castle but above the river. This is a detail of Bucks' 1727 engraving of the town and castle. The perspective, and the size of hill on which Clitheroe Castle stands are probably not very accurate. Pendle Hill looms over the scene.

that numerous castles, including Clitheroe, should be 'slighted', or rendered unusable to prevent future hostile garrisoning. It is likely that in the case of Clitheroe this order was never carried out – and certainly not completed – since the structure remained largely intact, but neglect and abandonment quickly took their toll and by the early eighteenth century the entire castle complex was in ruins.

The town of Clitheroe grew up a short distance away from the river on higher ground that would not be flooded when the river was in spate, and with its long main street running down the slope from the castle gate in the classic fashion of a medieval 'castle town'. The main river crossing here has always been at Edisford (*Eadig's Ford*), where the remains of a medieval bridge can be seen under the present one. A document of 1339 which sets out the details of pontage (the tolls charged for transporting commodities over the old bridge) survives. For instance, pepper, alum and wax were charged at 2*d* per cwt, wine at 2*d.* per cask, honey at 3*d.* per cask, and herrings ½*d.* per 1,000. It cost 4*d.* to take a cartload of fresh sea fish over the bridge, 2*d.* per sack of wool and ¼*d.* per frail of figs or raisins. The charge for taking a cow, ox, mare or horse over the bridge was ½*d.* each, and for taking a herd of sheep or pigs across 1*d.* per ten.[9] There was a leper hospital, dedicated to St Nicholas, on the north side of the river, close to the bridge; this closed in 1317.

A photograph of Edisford Bridge taken one hundred years ago. Others than the trees, nothing has changed in this view. Note the blocks of masonry in the river beneath the bridge that were part of the medieval bridge.

LRO, QAR 5/14A, REPRODUCED BY KIND PERMISSION OF THE COUNTY ARCHIVIST, LANCASHIRE RECORD OFFICE

EADSFORD   4·X·07

LEFT
Brungerley Bridge.
Before there was
a bridge here
there was a set of
stepping-stones
that enabled the
traveller to pass
with dry feet. It
was at this spot
that Henry VI was
captured in 1465.

RIGHT
Little Ribble is
a superb trout
stream, providing
solitude for the
fly-fisher.

Brungerley Bridge, which carries the road from Clitheroe to Waddington across the Ribble, was built in 1814, replacing an earlier wooden one which had been swept away by floods. In medieval times there was no bridge here, the crossing then being by stepping-stones. The villages of the north side of the river are well away from the main routeway which, for over 2,000 years, has linked the Ribble estuary via the Clitheroe area with Skipton and the gap through to the Wharfe and the Vale of York. This 'natural' route, followed by a Roman road and a key medieval highway, and latterly by a major turnpike road which became the A59, focused trade and commercial activity on the south side of the valley, so that there has never been a direct or convenient route along the north side. This is still very apparent today. The fast road from Preston to Clitheroe and Skipton contrasts with the meandering sequence of country lanes and back roads from Longridge, via Mitton, to Sawley. Partly as a result, no towns developed on the northern side of the valley (until Longridge emerged as a minor industrial centre in the late eighteenth century) and the villages remain small.

However, two of these smaller villages played a brief and unexpected role during the Wars of the Roses. In the spring of 1464 the forces of King Henry

Looking across Little Ribble to the medieval Mitton church and the Tudor Great Mitton Hall.

VI, the last king of the House of Lancaster, who had been deposed by Edward IV in 1461, were defeated at the Battle of Hexham. Henry escaped capture and wandered across northern England enjoying sanctuary provided by his loyal supporters. Eventually he reached the Ribble valley, taking shelter first at Bolton Hall, then at Waddington Hall. However, in July 1465, shortly after leaving Waddington, he was captured by Thomas Talbot of Bashall and his cousin John Talbot of Salesbury close to the stepping-stones crossing the river, where Brungerley Bridge now stands. He was bound tightly to his horse and taken, probably via Clitheroe Castle, to London. Both his captors were given prize-money of £100 and an annual pension for their reward in capturing the fugitive former king. Henry was imprisoned in the Tower but

Great Mitton Hall is a fine building, but much smaller than Little Mitton Hall, on the other bank of the Ribble, that is now a hotel.

his life was spared. In 1470 a counter-coup reinstated him on the throne, but in 1471, after the return of Edward IV, Henry was murdered in the Tower of London.

Mitton is the lowest village on Little Ribble. In his nineteenth-century *Visits to Remarkable Places*, William Howit described how, 'All about us as we ascended [the road from the bridge] were green and whispering trees, and peeps into meadows rich with cattle, and the sound of two rivers came up to us delightfully. Mitton is as singularly as it is sweetly situated. The place is one of the most perfect nooks of the world ...'[10]

There are really two Mittons, Little Mitton (Mitton Parva) and Great Mitton (Mitton Magna). Little Mitton is on the Whalley side of the river, whereas Great Mitton is on the opposite bank that was, until 1974, in Yorkshire. The impressive Little Mitton Hall was built early in the sixteenth century during the reign of Henry VII as seat of the Catterall family. Great Mitton Hall is also Tudor, but architecturally is less ambitious than its 'twin' across the Ribble. Great Mitton also has the church that overlooks bridge and river. Built during the reign of Edward III, it has a dark oak screen, separating nave and chancel, which was made for Cockersand Abbey on the Lune estuary when William Staynford was abbot in 1505–09. It was brought to Mitton church after the Dissolution in 1537 when Cockersand was almost entirely demolished. A leper window in the church is possibly associated with the leper hospital that once stood at Edisford (see page 61). Attached to the church is the private chapel

Stonyhurst is one of the most magnificent buildings in the entire Ribble catchment.

of the Sherburn or Shireburn family. The chapel was built by Sir Richard
Sherburn, who was interred there in July 1594. The Sherburn family also built
nearby Stonyhurst (now a leading Jesuit public school). In a deed from about
1200, land at 'Stanihurst' passed from Hugh de Mitton to Elias de Winkley.
In 1293 the land then became the possession of Walter Bayley and in 1377
Richard Bayley married a Sherburn wife. Instead of her taking his name,
he took hers and became a Sherburn. Richard Bayley's father built the first
house at Stonyhurst and in 1377 was licensed to open an oratory there. Some
stonework in the present complex of building, on which work commenced in
1523, is from that earlier house. The gatehouse was completed by Sir Richard
Sherburn in 1592 and the rectangular ponds, or 'canals' on either side of the
avenue leading to the front entrance of Stonyhurst were built by Sir Nicholas
Sherburn late in the seventeenth century. The same Sir Richard also had
built the original Lower Hodder Bridge (now called Cromwell's Bridge). Sir
Nicholas, who died on 16 December 1717, was the last Sherburn.

The name Mitton is derived from the Old English *mythe-tun*, meaning 'the
farmstead at the confluence', which is very apt as it is here that the Hodder
joins the Ribble. As an old local rhyme puts it,

> Hodder, Calder, Ribble and rain
> Mingle together in Mitton's domain.

So we come to the end of Little Ribble.

Big Ribble

As it flows beneath Mitton Bridge, and before its confluences with the Hodder and Calder, the Ribble is a large stream that, during summer droughts, can be crossed in many places in nothing longer than ordinary wellington boots. Below the two confluences the Ribble is three times bigger, cannot be waded in wellies, and is, logically, referred to as Big Ribble.

The difference in the size of the river is one factor that explains the remarkable contrast in the number of bridges above and below Mitton. Between Settle and the confluence with the Hodder there are ten old bridges plus the very recent Settle bypass bridge, on a stretch of the Ribble which is 35 kilometres long. In sharp contrast, the 18 kilometres of Big Ribble's valley between the Hodder and the crossing at Walton-le-Dale there are only two old bridges. At Ribchester the present bridge was built in 1775–76 to replace one that had been constructed in 1769–70 and had been almost immediately washed away in the Great Ribble Flood of 1771. That was, in turn, the successor of a medieval structure and a four-arched stone bridge which

Calderfoot and the start of Big Ribble. The Calder is the stream flowing into the Ribble from the right of the photograph.

probably dated from the middle years of the seventeenth century. The bridge is close to the site of the Roman ford. The other old bridge over the Ribble carried the Preston and Blackburn turnpike road at the bottom of Brockholes Brow, outside Preston. The original was a temporary wooden structure, built in 1824, and after the collapse of this a new stone bridge was built in 1860–61. Tolls were charged on it for pedestrians as well as road traffic, and for many years it was known as Ha'penny bridge. In addition today there are three separate bridges carrying the M6 and its slip roads over the river next to Ha'penny Bridge, a footbridge at Dinckley, and two aqueducts carrying water pipelines over the Ribble, at Samlesbury and Hurst Green.

Instead of bridges, however, there were formerly at least five ferries (rowing boats) across Big Ribble: at Brockholes, Alston Old Hall, Samlesbury Lower Hall, Osbaldeston Hall and Hacking Hall. All of these are recorded in medieval documents, and their origins may well be even earlier, and they continued into the modern age – that at Osbaldeston operated until the 1940s, and the Hacking Boat survived until the late 1950s.[11] In addition to these, and despite the size and sometimes dangerously high water in the river, there were fords: for example, at Alston it is possible to ford the river at times of comparatively low water even today, though the crossing is certainly not recommended.

Brockhole Bridge, also known as Ha'penny Bridge from the toll once charged for crossing it.

LRO, QAR 5/14A, REPRODUCED BY KIND PERMISSION OF THE COUNTY ARCHIVIST, LANCASHIRE RECORD OFFICE

Along Little Ribble there are six village-pairs close to the river that are linked by bridges: Long Preston–Rathmell, Hellifield–Wigglesworth, Gisburn–Paythorne, Sawley–Bolton, Chatburn–Grindleton, and Clitheroe–Waddington. There are no similar pairings on Big Ribble, but that is primarily because the topography of the valley means that the best sites for settlement have always been on the gentler and better-drained slopes well above and set back from the river. A series of lanes and tracks runs down to the Ribble, with matching lanes on the opposite bank, so paradoxically, in the past cross-river communication was actually far easier than it is today. The role of the river as a formidable north–south barrier to movement is, in many senses, a recent development and, especially a product of the motor age. But the other very apparent feature is that between Mitton and Walton-le-Dale there is only one settlement – Ribchester – which actually stands on the bank of the river.

Big Ribble is a mature river which meanders in sweeping, smooth bends through a straight, flat-bottomed floodplain, almost one kilometre in width, which is bordered by steep bluffs. So wide are the looping meanders that the river flows for 30 kilometres to cover the 18 kilometres between Calderfoot and Walton-le-Dale. Today, on the inside of meanders there is flat alluvial farmland that is almost entirely given over to meadow or pasture. The alluvium deposited by the river is now mainly sand, silt and clay, for Big Ribble carries little in the way of gravel or boulders downstream, even in the most violent of spates. However, beneath the fine alluvium are beds of gravel, mostly deposited at the end of the last Ice Age. In the 1990s gravel extraction began on the floodplain below Red Scar, immediately upstream of the M6 bridges, and gravel-pits – known as Brockholes Quarry – have replaced pasture and meadow. This area, which once witnessed an historic civil war battle in 1648, is now a reserve of the Lancashire Wildlife Trust. On the outside of meanders the river cuts into the bluffs. This may give rise to sheer boulder clay cliffs (as below Old Park Wood, downstream of Ribchester). More often there is a very steep vegetated slope susceptible to landslipping (as at Red Scar, which takes its name from the red clay exposed by a landslip, or at Horseshoe Bend at Balderstone, where major landslips roughly every ten years carry away trees and bushes). These steep slopes have never been cultivated, and substantial stretches are almost impenetrable because of the tangled vegetation and numerous small springs which create extremely wet conditions on the steep clay slopes. These woodlands, clinging precariously to the slopes, are among the most important semi-natural woods in north-west England, with an exceptionally rich ecology. In spring the bluff woodlands are the most beautiful feature of Big Ribble, with their bluebells and other flowers, and the fresh green of the new year's leaves, and the magnificent sweep from Brockholes to Red Scar provides motorists heading north up the M6 with the first great vista since leaving Spaghetti Junction behind.

The landscape of green fields and narrow belts of woodland that we see today on either side of Big Ribble is the result of over 2,000 years of human influence, but much of the detail is the consequence of the colonisation of new agricultural land, by the clearance of woodland, in the early medieval period. Across much of northern England, as indeed in western Europe as a whole, the twelfth and thirteenth centuries were a period of rapid population increase, brought about in part by a favourable climate of warm dry summers and short mild winters, giving a long growing season and a relatively abundant food supply. The increasing population could not be readily accommodated in existing settlements and within the boundaries of the land already exploited for agriculture, so there was a widespread process of 'colonisation', whereby woodland fringes were nibbled away to create new fields, and new farms and hamlets were established beyond the old limits of settlement. In the Ribble valley place-names such as 'Eaves' (as in Bashall Eaves and Wiswell Eaves) often indicate such new settlements – the name means 'the edge of a wood', while the minor place name 'ridding' or variants such as 'rode' or 'rod' reveal the early medieval practice of 'ridding' land of woodland. Such elements are frequently found in the names of fields and farmsteads and are usually a reliable indicator of early medieval colonisation.

The deeds in the archives of local landowning families, and particularly those of the de Hoghtons of Hoghton Tower, give valuable evidence about this period of settlement along the valley. Around 1250, for example, Bruno de Hoghton claimed much of the land around Alston, declaring that 'the

men inhabiting the land will be quit of pannage in the woods'.[12] This record indicates that there were at the time scattered families living around Big Ribble who relied on pannage – the grazing of their swine in the forest – and suggests that de Hoghton intended to oust them. The de Hoghtons steadily accumulated land in and around the Ribble valley during the twelfth and thirteenth centuries. For instance, in about 1230 William de Saumesbury (Samlesbury) gave Adam de Hochtun (Hoghton) a substantial area of land in Alston, in 1259 William de Hudreshale (Hothersall) granted him a smaller property there together with pannage rights in the woodlands, and in 1260 Gerald de Hudreshale granted to Adam part of his land at Alston.[13]

Pannage rights often feature in thirteenth- and fourteenth-century records from the country around Big Ribble, suggesting that extensive tracts were still forested. For instance, on 22 May 1306 at Ribchester, Joan, widow of Thomas Banastre, 'granted that if the animals of Robert de Dilleworthsete escape into her woods or pasture … they shall not be disturbed or claimed except goats

View from the bluff above the De Tabley Arms (SD 661349) looking west to Ribchester. The Ribble meanders between the two bluffs in a broad loop amidst the flat pastures of the floodplain. At Ribchester, 2000 years ago, the river flowed close to this southern bluff, but subsequently it cut north across its floodplain, destroying part of the Roman fort.

all the year round and other animals at mast time.'[14] 'Mast' normally refers to beech (*Fagus sylvatica*) mast; however, because beech has never been a major component of Lancashire woodlands, it is likely that acorns and other tree seeds were included as mast here.

The thirteenth- and fourteenth-century landscape around Big Ribble, as revealed by sources such as these, was thus one of small parcels of pasture and arable land around dwellings and the few villages, with, beyond this, tracts of common grazing land. Further out, towards the margins of each township, there were large areas of scrub and forest ('waste'), but these were being reduced in extent by the processes of 'ridding' and colonisation.

The evidence of contemporary deeds also gives helpful information in the form of boundary descriptions, which record landmarks and give some indication of land use. Thus, in about 1257 Roger de Hodersal (Hothersall) granted a parcel of land to Henry de Ribelcestr (Ribchester), 'beginning at the cloch [i.e. clough: ravine] at the house of Roger, ascending that cloch to Hugh's clearing, across to the first cloch on the east, following it down to the first cloch that descends from the north, going up that cloch northwards to the blazed oak, thence eastwards to the clearing of Thomas, following it on the west down to the torrent, going down to the starting place … With quittance of pannage of his swine and without multure of his corn.'[15] In other words, de Hodersall would no longer put his pigs to feed in the forest, nor would he claim a share (multure) on any corn de Ribelcestr grew on the land. The implication is that de Ribelcestr was being granted 'wasteland' or woodland between the clearings of Hugh and Thomas, for the only other landmarks noted are streams or cloughs, one house and the blazed oak.

Many other parcels of land, both in the valley of Big Ribble and neighbouring areas, were similarly described. In about 1246 Walter Motton of Ribbylcester granted to Roger de Hirste part of his land at 'Turnlegh' [Thornley, near Longridge].[16] The area of land was similarly described in terms of landscape features: beginning at the store house, going eastwards to 'le Smaleclough' (presumably a narrow valley or gulley), then the boundary followed the Smaleclough to the 'Chestirbroc' and followed the Chestirbroc to the blazed oak. Blazed oaks often feature in these land transactions, and were presumably oaks that had a section of bark cut off to give a white blaze that was easily noticed. The boundary now went directly to 'le Blackelache' [Black Lake, which was probably the peaty mire now called Black Moss] and on to 'Chepynlegh' (Chipping), and returned to the starting place by following 'le Risshslade' and 'Bromeslade'.

This is an area of Thornley-with-Wheatley north of Longridge Fell and is perhaps associated with Thornley Hall. However, the area granted to Roger de Hirste was almost certainly too large for one farm, and he would therefore have let out smaller parcels to tenants who would in turn clear and farm the land. The de Hoghton papers refer to one Will Motton who, prior to 1278, 'for three marks silver', granted part of his land in the parish of Ribchester to Adam de Hoghton with a moiety [equal share] of hawk, honey and mill profits (except for the site of a mill at 'Dillewrd' [Dilworth]). This large block of land extended from the Ribble between 'Hudersal' [Hothersall] and 'Alfston' [Alston] to 'Quitinghaym' [Whittingham], 'Queteley' [Wheatley] and 'Thornedley' [Thornley].[17]

Over 70 years later, in 1331, Sir Richard de Hoghton was permitted to bring under his control 'all moors, woods, mosses and other wastes in Grymesargh [Grimsargh] ... but not rights of common pasture'.[18] The landscape for which such a description is given, even though the text is at least in part of standard

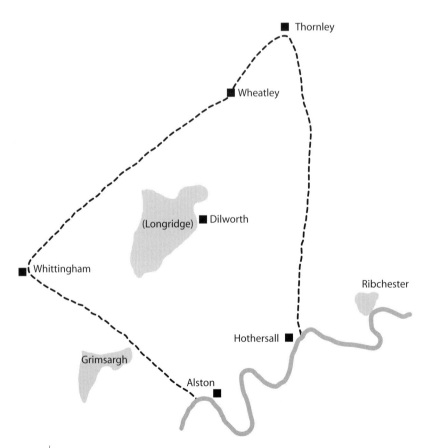

Approximate plot of lands granted to Adam de Hoghton in 1278. Note that Longridge did not then exist.

form of words, is a far cry from the green fields and patches of woodland which surround the village of Grimsargh today. Grimsargh takes its unusual name from the Norse Viking *Grim*, who had a dairy farm (*erg*) here, probably in the tenth century.

Another document among the de Hoghton family papers is an agreement between Sir Alan de Hoghton, Sir Thomas Banastre, William Horneby (rector of Ribchester) – the three wealthiest landowners in that part of the valley – and their tenants at Ribchester, dated 27 September 1357: '… touching the wastes of Dilworth and Riblecestre [Ribchester] they are agreed that the wastes shall not be enclosed by either party and that entrance to them shall be allowed to the beasts of both parties at all seasons of the year.'[19]

The population growth of the twelfth and thirteenth centuries was brought to an end by a serious deterioration of the climate after 1300, which was accompanied by a series of bad harvests, and epidemics of cattle and sheep disease. In north-west England the impact of Scottish raids and incursions between 1316 and 1322 was a further difficulty, and in 1348–50 the entire country was devastated by the Black Death. Population levels, already beginning to

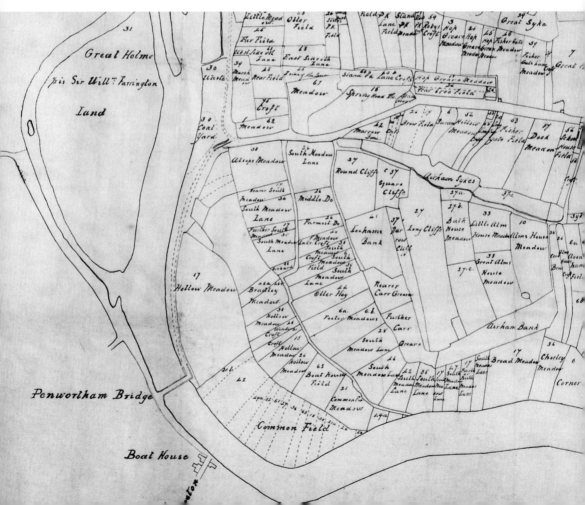

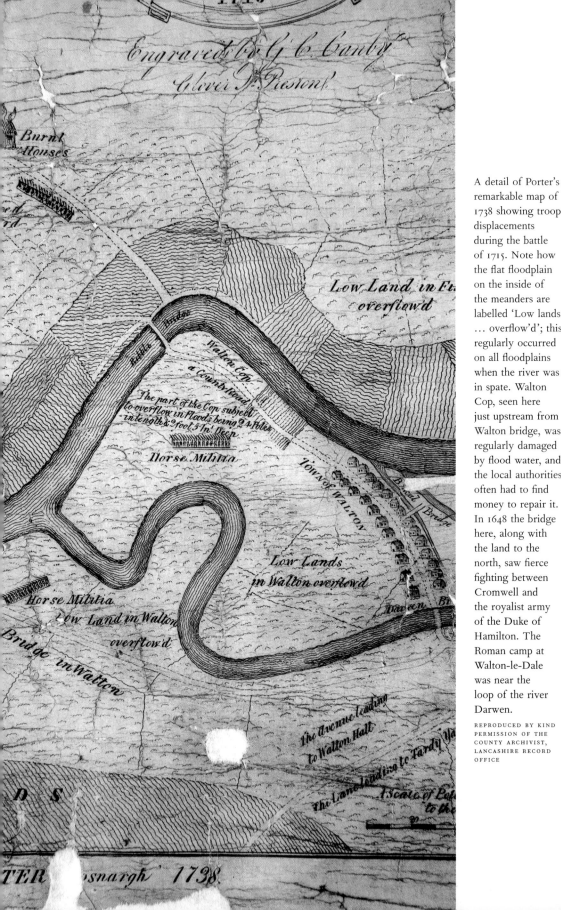

A detail of Porter's remarkable map of 1738 showing troop displacements during the battle of 1715. Note how the flat floodplain on the inside of the meanders are labelled 'Low lands … overflow'd'; this regularly occurred on all floodplains when the river was in spate. Walton Cop, seen here just upstream from Walton bridge, was regularly damaged by flood water, and the local authorities often had to find money to repair it. In 1648 the bridge here, along with the land to the north, saw fierce fighting between Cromwell and the royalist army of the Duke of Hamilton. The Roman camp at Walton-le-Dale was near the loop of the river Darwen.

decline, fell catastrophically, and some marginal land in areas such as the Ribble valley was simply abandoned. However, landowners such as the de Hoghtons and the Banastres were still intent upon extending the profitable agricultural land, so colonisation of waste soon resumed, while from the end of the fifteenth century renewed population growth once more encouraged further exploitation of the margins of settlement. By the end of the fifteenth century considerable areas of the countryside around Big Ribble had been cleared of 'waste' and turned into pasture, meadow and arable farmland.

Maintenance of the cleared land as productive farmland was important, not just to provide food for those dwelling in the valley, but also as a source of income for those owning the land. In the early sixteenth century, for instance, the rector of Ribchester possessed land in the parish which contributed a significant part of his income. By 1540 the rector, Thomas Bishop, had leased those lands to Edward Clayton and Robert Hodersall [Hothersall] for £10 *per annum*, with the agreement that they would keep houses and hedges on the estate in good repair and manage carefully the extensive woodlands. However in 1542 he took action against the two men, claiming that they had let houses and hedges 'go into decay', had cut down large areas of woodland and had not paid the rent due.[20]

Hacking Hall stands close to the Calder/Ribble confluence, with an ancient 'green track' passing by. Built in 1607 on the site of a house built 350 years earlier.

Town fields in the Ribble catchment

From the early medieval period, if not earlier, most villages and manors in the wider valleys of Big Ribble and the Calder and in the better drained areas of the coastal plain (away from the mosses and marshes, and usually on boulder clay) had common arable fields, usually known as 'town fields' but occasionally as 'mean fields' (the word 'mean' indicates that the land was in communal use). The name 'Meanygate' is still used today for certain lanes and tracks south of the estuary (see, for example, page 228), and indicates a road (gate) leading to a 'mean' area, though in these districts the name refers to access routes to common mossland rather than arable fields. It is commonly supposed that all those living in a community would have been entitled to use the town fields, but this was not in fact the case, since manorial tenants and freeholders had preference. R. Cunliffe Shaw, author of *Kirkham in Amounderness* (1949), wrote that, '*The common field in Lancashire was never common to all and sundry*' [his italics][21], and pointed out that 'the mass of people had to use for pasture and possibly for arable plots appendant to "moor" and "carr", or by royal grant the forest launds.' In other words, most people had to eke a living from land that was not as good as the town fields. Shaw demonstrated this from Kirkham where, despite the population of the town growing to over 1,000 in the early years of the eighteenth century, the number paying rent for strips of ground in the town field remained almost static: 25 in 1509, 24 in 1682, 23 in 1736.

The town fields were normally divided into strips, with a family cultivating several strips scattered over the various great open fields. However these fields were not managed in the way that the more famous common fields in midland and parts of southern England were managed. There farmers would have an equal share in all the common fields (often three) and every year one-third of the common fields would lie fallow. The reason for this was that in the warmer and better-drained parts of England wheat was a major crop, and it was sown in autumn. So in year one a crop of beans or peas might be grown on a strip, the autumn that the beans were harvested wheat would be sown and it would be harvested the following summer. The strip would then be left fallow for a year. The fields were managed in such a way that all the farmers had strips growing the same crop or fallow adjacent so that cattle might be tethered on the fallow areas to graze the weeds and scatter manure there.

In contrast wheat was not widely grown in Lancashire. As John Leland put it in the 1530s, 'Whete is not veri communely sowid in thes partes,'[22] and Celia Fiennes explained in the 1690s that 'they have only the summer graine as barley, oates, peas beans and lentils noe wheate or rhye for they are so cold and late in their yeare.'[23] Some have argued that this was not true, and that wheat was widely grown, citing at least three places in the valley with the name Wheatley. But they were probably given that name because they were well-drained corners where wheat could be grown successfully; as such they were exceptional. It has also been suggested that in the sixteenth century the acreage under wheat was close to that under oats. However, records from 1779 indicate that the acreage in the Fylde under spring-sown crops (mainly oats, beans and peas) was more than double that under wheat, and that further east, at Goosnargh and Newsham very little wheat was grown.[24]

By having all crops spring-sown there was no need for one in three years on each strip being fallow. All strips in all town fields were cultivated and sown at the end of March and beginning of April. The harvest was taken in August or September and then those holding land in the town fields would release their cattle so that they could graze on the stubble and stalks and weeds and manure the fields through the winter months. All cattle had to be taken from the fields in March, usually by Lady Day, 25 March (until 1752 under the Julian calendar this was the first day of the year). Often the community would have common meadows where hay could be produced, and beyond would be open grazing and turbaries (peat beds where fuel might be gathered).

The arable strip system had many disadvantages. Often someone ploughing his strip had to trample his adjacent neighbour's strip. There was a waste of land between the many strips. Arguments arose when someone tried to increase the width of his strip or when boundary markers were moved. It was a nuisance when someone held two or more strips widely separated in the same field. And so people began to reorganise by exchanging strips so that they accumulated larger, more manageable blocks of land. The next step was to enclose individual holdings. In some places this began as early as the fourteenth century, at Kirkham about 1550.

A staple diet based on oats, with a few peas and beans, must have been monotonous. According to an unreliable legend, potatoes are said to have arrived at Marshside in what is now Southport in 1565 in a shipwreck and were planted to produce one of the first potato crops in Europe. Regardless of the accuracy of that tale, it is certain that potatoes were being grown in lowland Lancashire by 1640 and had become a major crop by the 1670s. Today, wheat is quite widely grown in lowland Lancashire. These are new varieties, sown in autumn, that can normally withstand our climate (though in the wet summer of 2004 a significant acreage could not be harvested). Today our staples are the humble spud and the wheaten loaf.

The landowners with extensive holdings in the Ribble valley built large houses, almost invariably distinguished by the name 'Hall' and very often situated close to the river and away from the main focus of settlement in the township. From the Mitton downstream to Walton-le-Dale there is a remarkable series of such halls along or close to the banks, often alternating first on the left- and then on the right-hand side – Mitton, Winckley, Hacking, Dinckley, Salesbury, New Hall (near Ribchester), Osbaldeston, Hothersall, Sunderland, Balderstone, Alston Old Hall, Elston Old Hall, Samlesbury Lower Hall, Brockholes, and Cuerdale. Some of these houses are exceptionally ancient, with a recorded history going back over seven hundred years, while others have medieval fabric still surviving.[25]

Hacking Hall, just downstream from the Calder confluence, has roots going back to at least 1258 when it was seat of the de Hakkyng family. Four and a half centuries earlier Hacking was the site of the battle of Billanghoh (Billington) in 798. The *Anglo-Saxon Chronicle* reported that the battle took place on 2 April as Hwaellenge (Whalley), but Simeon of Durham's *Historia Regum* of AD 879 (1885 translation edited by T. Arnold) gives the site of the battle at Billingahoth, at Walalege. In fact, the battle took place just over almost two kilometres from the river on Billington Moor. In 796 Aethelred, King of Northumbria (of which Lancashire was then an outpost), had been murdered. Around this time Northumbria was in great political turmoil, with different families striving to gain control. After Aethelred's death Osbald took the crown but his reign lasted barely a month. Now Eardwulf (sometimes spelt Eardulph) became king, despite his unpopularity. In 791 Aethelred had ordered Eardwulf's execution but the job was botched and monks from Ripon had nursed him back to health. So the power struggle continued. Wada, who

New Hall, built in 1665 by G.T. (George Talbot), is 'new' in that it is younger than nearby Salesbury Hall, that had a licensed chapel in 1371 (though the present Salesbury Hall is a newer rebuild). This is the modern road leading down to the De Tabley Arms and Ribchester Bridge. The Roman road from Manchester to Ribchester was 250 metres away to the west, crossing the Ribble by a ford.

had had a hand in Aethelred's murder, led a force against Eardwulf on the banks of the Ribble just below Calderfoot. The battle was bloody, 'great numbers being slain on both sides', but Eardwulf was victorious. Wada fled with a few survivors.

Traces of this battle have been found, while a tumulus on the other side of the Ribble is supposedly the burial ground of warriors who fell here. The present Hacking Hall was built by Judge Thomas Walmesley in 1607.

Dinckley Hall stands on the left bank of the Ribble between Calderfoot and Ribchester bridge. There is a possibility that there may have been an Iron Age settlement in the vicinity, for *din* is a modified form of the Celtic word for a fort. The first hall was probably built in the thirteenth century and its illustrious list of owners include Roger Nowell who was the local magistrate who interrogated the poor people convicted and condemned as the 'Lancashire witches', the fifteenth-century Talbots who betrayed Henry VI near Clitheroe (see page 63), and the de Tableys whose name is now borne by the hotel close to Ribchester bridge.

The first Osbaldeston Hall, in the lea of the bluff of Flashers Wood, was built by Hugh de Osbaldeston during the reign of Richard I (1189–99). The present hall is on the same site and dates from 1593. Hugh had a son called Ailsi, who had four sons, each of whom took a different surname. The eldest was Hugh Osbaldeston, who retained the family name and the hall, which he inherited in 1245. A second son, William, took the surname

The first Sunderland Hall was built sometime in the thirteenth century by Adam, grandson of Hugh de Osbaldeston. This plaque in the wall of the present Hall shows that it was built in 1596.

Balderstone and built Balderstone Hall some five kilometres downstream of Osbaldeston Hall, again in the lea of a steep bluff. The third son, Adam, took the surname Sunderland and built Sunderland Hall below the bluff on which grows Mercifield Wood and at the head of a sweeping meander. All three of these ancient halls, like others in the valley, occupy a characteristic type of location, at the foot of the steep, wooded bluff which would provide shelter and seclusion, as well as timber resources close to hand. The low-lying land within the loop of the meander provided rich alluvial soils which would provide excellent grazing and arable crops. The fourth of Ailsi's sons took the surname Winckley and built Winckley Hall on the opposite side of the river, close to the Hodder/Ribble confluence.

Hothersall Hall is also an ancient settlement site, but like many halls in the valley the present building is much more recent, the medieval structure having been demolished as fashions changed. In this case the house was completely reconstructed in 1695. In contrast, Alston Old Hall, which is externally relatively modest, contains a very substantial amount of timber-framed work which may date from as early as the late thirteenth century, making it one of the oldest domestic buildings in northern England.

Gospatric de Samlesbury built the first Samlesbury Hall (now called the Lower Hall) by the Ribble early in the reign of Henry II (probably around 1155–60). His great-great-granddaughter Alicia married Sir Gilbert

Samlesbury Hall is a fine timbered building. On the other, western side can be seen some very early hand-made bricks. Indeed, Samlesbury is thought to have been the first building in Lancashire to have brick walls, built in part to support the large chimneys seen here and also to incorporate what is thought to have been a grand window from the dissolved Whalley Abbey.

Southworth in about 1320 and for eleven generations the name Southworth was intimately linked with Samlesbury Hall. Early in the fourteenth century the Lower Hall was sacked by a band of marauding Scots led by Robert the Bruce. It was rebuilt, but in 1325 Sir Gilbert started work on building Higher Samlesbury Hall in secluded woodland away from the river close to a track that eventually became the main turnpike between Preston and Blackburn. The present hall is largely a rebuilding by Sir Thomas Southworth in 1546 and was the first brick house to be built in the county. Debts which accumulated in the second half of the seventeenth century forced the sale of the family's lands in 1676 (for the sum of £318) and the hall was sold to Thomas Braddyll in 1678. In 1824 its setting was transformed, and not for the better, when the new Preston and Blackburn turnpike road was constructed on a direct alignment that passed so close that it almost clipped the corner of the hall itself.

The present Cuerdale Hall, between Ha'penny Bridge and Walton-le-Dale, was built in around 1700 on the site of a much earlier building. In 1582 this earlier house had been purchased by Radcliffe Assheton, a member of one of the leading families of Lancashire. It was on the Cuerdale estate on 15 May 1840 that workmen carrying out repairs to the bank of the Ribble discovered a lead-lined wooden chest containing a total of about 7,500 coins and 1,000 ingots, ornaments and fragments of silver, weighing in all some 40 kg (88 lbs). Of the coins, about 2,800 were Anglo Saxon, 1,000 Frankish and Italian, 3,000 Scandinavian, and others Arabic and Byzantine. The coins were minted between 860 and 905, which was probably the date of burial. Thomas Marsden, the labourer whose spade broke open the hoard, and the rest of the gang pocketed many coins, but before they could leave the site William Assheton's bailiff seized everything and allowed them to keep a coin each as souvenir. Assheton attempted to keep the hoard, for it was found on his land. The coroner declared it the property of the Duchy of Lancaster, and it was then sold by the Crown to museums and private collectors. The most likely explanation for its concealment is that this, the largest hoard of Viking silver ever found in Europe, was part of a treasury brought from Ireland by a large group of Irish-Norsemen expelled from Dublin in 902, and that it may have formed part of the funds to wage a military campaign against their opponents in Ireland. At the time the Ribble valley formed part of a major trade and communication route between the Viking centres of Ireland and York, and Cuerdale lies directly on that route.

The contents of the hoard have been dispersed among a number of museums. An excellent and beautifully illustrated account of the hoard, its discovery and its context is *A Silver Saga: Viking Treasure from the North-West*, published by National Museums and Galleries on Merseyside in 1990.

Ribchester and roads north and west

The conquest of Britain by the Romans began in AD 43, but it was not until the civil war, which broke out in Brigantia in AD 69, forced the Romans to intervene that they became a major presence in Lancashire.[26] In order to assert control they quickly established a network of forts in strategic locations, linked by military roads. By the year 75 the Romans had effectively established their authority as far north as the Tyne–Solway gap, and the construction of permanent forts was well advanced. One of these was at Ribchester (*Bremetennacum*), a strategic location because it was here that the high-level military road from Manchester (*Mamucium*) to Carlisle (*Luguvalium*) crossed the east–west Ribble/Aire/Wharfe axis. Some have argued that there was already an Iron Age settlement called *Ringodunum* (or *Ribodunum*) in the vicinity of what is now Ribchester. Earthworks between the present Ribchester village and Stydd have been interpreted as part of the Iron Age site.

The construction of the first fort at *Bremetennacum* probably took place in 70–71, but there were many subsequent alterations and reconstruction projects, including the possible rebuilding of turf ramparts with stone in the reign of Hadrian (d. 138). The fort was quite compact, 270 metres in length by

Most of the halls in the valley are now farms and have been greatly altered, if not rebuilt. Cuerdale Hall is in the midst of several new buildings, with the Ribble flowing closely by. It was in the bank here that the Cuerdale Hoard was discovered. Beyond the grassy floodplain is the bluff of Fishwick and Brockholes.

The Roman Museum at Ribchester has many 'finds' from the fort including ornate column capitals.

The White Bull at Ribchester with what may be columns of Roman origin around the door.

125 metres in width. It included a temple to the goddess Minerva Belisama and altars 'Deo Marti et Victoriae': to the Gods of Mars and of Victory. Further work into the third century included the building of two large granaries. For almost three hundred years *Bremetennacum* was an important fort, but in the 370s or early 380s, with the gradual loss of Roman political and military control over the outer corners of the Empire, the fort was abandoned.[27]

After the Romans departed their fort was pillaged for building materials (the four columns at the entrance porch of the White Bull in Ribchester village are said to be from the fort), and almost nothing now remains above the present ground surface. Furthermore, during the subsequent 1,600 years the Ribble's meandering has washed away the south-eastern corner of the fort. However, several major archaeological excavations have revealed the footings of many buildings that stood within the fort as well as great 'finds', some of which were taken away to the British Museum, although many others remain in Ribchester's Roman Museum. There is still a great deal of untapped potential for further archaeological work at Ribchester, and over future decades more of its complex and fascinating story will surely be revealed and explained.

For over 700 years there is little clear evidence of what was happening on the site of the village that John Leland called 'Rhibel Chester' (a name which was contracted to the present form, Ribchester). In the period after the Norman Conquest its role as the central place of the Ribble valley was transferred to Clitheroe, which had greater strategic potential. The little chapel at Stydd just outside Ribchester was built in the reign of Stephen (1135–54). It is dedicated to St Saviour, and was a chapel of the Knights Hospitaller of St John of Jerusalem, a foundation that was dissolved in 1338.

St Wilfred's Church, Ribchester, with its tower under renovation, dates back to the thirteenth century. There was an even earlier church here.

The little chapel at Stydd dates from the twelfth century and retains much of its original form (though recently renovated).

The present fabric of St Wilfred's church, by the river in Ribchester village, dates from the thirteenth century, but is on the site of an earlier building which long predated the Norman Conquest. Its dedication to St Wilfrid, one of the most important religious and political figures in seventh-century Northumbria, confirms its antiquity, and it is likely that Ribchester was the centre of the estates on the Ribble which in AD 670 were granted to Wilfrid's abbey at Ripon. On 24 May 1406, Henry IV paid £20 for the founding, and £10 per year maintenance grant, for a perpetual chantry in honour of the Blessed Virgin Mary in the parish church.

Further downstream the Romans had another major site, in the angle between the Ribble and the Darwen at Walton-le-Dale. Despite extensive excavation in the nineteenth and twentieth centuries there is no evidence that there was a fort at this location, and the site is generally accepted to have been an important military depot and supply centre. Its location at the head of the tidal estuary and at the point where the north–south lowland road crossed the Ribble was clearly very advantageous, and is similar to that of the well-known industrial and supply complex at Wilderspool on the southern side of Warrington.

The Roman roads of the Ribble valley have been investigated by historians and antiquarians, and by archaeologists, for over two hundred years, and their basic outline is now familiar. From Manchester a road led northwards through Radcliffe, Turton and Blackburn to Ribchester. The road was designed primarily for military purposes, its course through potentially difficult or rebellious upland areas being one way of exerting control. From Ribchester the road continued on to climb Jeffrey Hill, at the western end of Longridge Fell, and then descended to cross the Hodder by a ford just downstream of the present Doeford Bridge (at SD 656433). The long stretch from Jeffrey Hill to Marl Hill Moor above Browsholme is still clearly visible from the summit of Jeffrey Hill, as a line of hedgerows and lanes running straight as an arrow across the broad valley of the Hodder. On a clear day it is apparent that the Roman engineers took a sight-line from Jeffrey Hill to the tip of Penyghent, which peeps above the skyline as a little pyramid shape in the distance. This is one of the best places in northern England to discern the surveying and design principles followed by the Roman highway engineers. The road re-crossed the Hodder downstream of Newton (at SD 685497) and traversed the eastern Bowland Fells before continuing on to Carlisle and Hadrian's Wall.

This view north-east from Jeffrey Hill reveals a straight line of trees in the distance, in line with the road in the foreground, which indicates the ancient route of the Roman road in this area.

A second road ran north from Middlewich to cross the Mersey at Wilderspool and then headed north through Newton-le-Willows and Wigan (*Coccium*) to Walton-le-Dale, following closely the line of the current A49 road. After fording – or possibly bridging – the Ribble the road continued north to Lancaster before heading up the Lune valley to Overbarrow and then onto Carlisle.

An east–west Roman road started at York and ran along the Wharfe valley as far as Ilkley. It then crossed the watershed into Airedale, near Skipton, and continued through the Aire–Ribble Gap to Ribchester, where it crossed the north–south military road. Beyond Ribchester it continued west, across the higher boulder clay ridges to the north of the Ribble and three kilometres north of Walton-le-Dale, to a fort at Kirkham. There are suggestions that from Kirkham a branch road ran south to a ford over the Ribble somewhere in the vicinity of Freckleton Naze (where a hard surfaced paved ford was seen in the nineteenth century). Place-name evidence also implies that an ancient metalled road existed in the Hutton area in the early medieval period, and some theories propose a Roman harbour or anchorage in Freckleton Pool, which was then a sheltered bay in the middle estuary. A road probably headed north-west from Kirkham to an unknown destination – for centuries it has been argued that an elusive place called *Portus Setantiorum*, shown in late Roman geographies, may have been a port at the mouth of the Wyre, but

St Leonard-the-Less church at Samlesbury dates from 1185, when Gospatric de Samlesbury built a chapel of ease for the monks of Whalley Abbey. The chapel became Anglican after Dissolution and was enlarged. The Victorians added to it, including the stone tower. From the east all three stages in is construction can be seen clearly, including the end wall of the original small chapel. Before the building of the A59 and later the M6, with their bridges at Brockholes, St Leonard-the-Less would have been in a very quiet, secluded spot.

although several substantial hoards of Roman coins have been found in the area of Knott End and Fleetwood no evidence of a settlement site has yet been identified. It is conceivable that, if such a port did exist, it has been totally destroyed by coastal erosion, but it is equally possible that *Portus Setantiorum* was in fact on one of the numerous other estuaries and bays of the coast of north-west England.

The east–west route from Ribble estuary through Ribchester and the Aire–Ribble Gap into the Vale of York was probably used long before the Romans arrived by Neolithic, Bronze Age and Iron Age travellers, and it continued to be used after the Romans had gone. Anglo-Saxons and Danes would have used it when they headed west into Lancashire. Later Norse Vikings, led by Ragnald, used it in 919 as they travelled from the Ribble estuary to seize York from the Danes and establish the Kingdom of Northumbria.

The river becomes tidal at Walton-le-Dale, where the modern London Road bridge spans the waterway carrying a fast and busy urban dual carriageway. This is the latest in a long sequence of bridges, dating back to

Through the 1990s and early 2000s gravel was extracted from the floodplain at Brockholes, resulting in several gravel-pits of varying size. In 2007 the site was obtained by the Lancashire Wildlife Trust as a nature reserve. It will be opened to the public in 2008. It will be the finest still water wildlife site in the valley.

the early Middle Ages. The first bridge was built of wood over the river, and it was this which was crossed by Edward I in 1306 on his way to Scotland, while in 1323 Robert the Bruce reached the bridge from the north when he set fire to Preston. The wooden bridge was severely damaged by ice floes in 1400 and in 1403 Henry IV issued letters patent to permit the construction of a more robust, stone bridge. The bridge at Walton-le-Dale was a vital strategic objective in times of warfare, because of its control of the key north–south route. It was fought over and defended many times. It played a major role in English history on several occasions.[28] In 1487, for example, the Earl of Lincoln, with the impostor and would-be Yorkist puppet-king Lambert Simnel and a band of mercenary troops, crossed the bridge on their way from Dublin to London to overthrow Henry VII. They were routed at Stoke near Newark by the king's army. In 1648 a Scottish and royalist army commanded by the Duke of Hamilton crossed the bridge and engaged Cromwell in bloody battle at Ribbleton. On 11 November 1715, during the first Jacobite Rebellion, an English force led by General Wills marched over the bridge to attack rebels in the streets of Preston. Two days later over 1,500 rebel prisoners were led, in chains, over the bridge. In 1745, during the second Jacobite rising, government troops pursued the retreating forces of Bonnie Prince Charlie as they headed northwards from Derby and Manchester back to Scotland and eventual defeat at Culloden. In 1779–81 that blood-stained bridge, built in 1403–04, was replaced by the present structure at a cost of £4,200, though that, too has several times been widened to cater for increased traffic. This is, arguably the most important crossing on the whole length of the Ribble, though the motorists driving over it today are largely unaware of its historical significance (they are looking out for the speed cameras instead) and the view of the river from the bridge is not particularly impressive, at least for the drivers.

Proud Preston (the Priests' Town) was the successor to the Roman site at Walton-le-Dale and to a short-lived pre-Conquest and immediate post-Conquest centre at Penwortham, on the opposite bank of the Ribble.[29] Preston parish church, which until the sixteenth century was also dedicated to St Wilfrid, is an ancient foundation and may date from the seventh century. The town grew up on an east–west ridge (Church Street and Fishergate, two of the first streets to be laid out in the town, follow the line of the top of the ridge) above the lower reaches of the Ribble, and its excellent location at the head of the estuary and at a crossing of regionally important routeways encouraged its early development. By the twelfth century Preston had eclipsed both Penwortham and Walton-le-Dale. Its first borough charter was granted by Henry II in 1179, giving it the right to a market and also the privilege of a Guild Merchant, a body which had exclusive trading

Preston, Said to arise out of the ruins of Ribble-Chester, is a Borough and Corporation of great Antiquity and Note receiving its first Charter from K. Henry 2.ᵈ which, since hath been confirm'd and additional privileges granted by the succeeding Kings, and Queens. The Body consists of a Mayor, Recorder, Aldermen, &c. The Present Members of P.ᵗ are S.ʳ Henry Hoghton Barr.ᵗ and Daniel Pulteney Esq.ʳ

A view of Preston and the Ribble in 1728, engraved by Samuel and Nathaniel Buck from about SD538275. Then the town was confined to the top of the bluff to the north of the river (now occupied by Church Street and Fishergate), and the only bridge crossing was from Walton-le-Dale, a short distance

rights within the town. The Guild Merchant held celebrations at infrequent intervals, at which the membership rolls were updated. These became the occasion of great festivities and the Preston Guild was, by the early sixteenth century, a major event in Lancashire life. Since 1542 (and probably since 1522) one has been celebrated every 20 years (which has given rise to the saying, 'Once in every Preston Guild', meaning very rarely), save for 1942 when, because of war, it was postponed to 1952. The next Guild will be celebrated in 2012. In 1266 Henry III gave the title of Earl of Lancaster to his second son Edmund (known as Crouchback). The brother of Edward I, Edmund had already, in about 1260, founded a Franciscan friary in Preston. It stood at the northern edge of the town, alongside the road from Lancaster which, as a result, became known as Friargate. Preston already had a small leper hospital, dedicated to St Mary Magdalene and founded sometime in the middle of the

1. { Penwortham the Seat of Henry Fleetwood Esq.

2. Fulcheth.

3. The Boat House.

4. The House of Correction.

5. St George's Chappel.

6. The Town Hall.

7. St Winfreds Church.

8. Avenham Walk.

9. St Edw.d Stanleys.

10. Ribble Bridge.

11. The River Ribble.

12. { Cuerdale, the Seat of Ralph Ashton Esq.r

13. Hoghton Tower.

14. Walton Church.

15. { Walton Hall, the Seat of St Henry Hoghton Bar.t

S. & N. Buck delin.t et Sculp.t 1728.

downstream of the present A6 bridge. Not long before this engraving was made 'Avenham Walk' was laid out as a polite promenade for the genteel folk of this ancient borough to take the air and to admire views of the river.

twelfth century. Fishergate, leads down to the Ribble and takes its name from the fact that it led to the dwellings of the fishermen.

By the fifteenth century Preston had emerged not only as a major commercial and market centre but also as the effective administrative capital of Lancashire, even though Lancaster (from which the county takes its name – Lancastershire) was the original focus of military and political power. Its prime position at the centre of the transport network of north-west England meant that during the industrial revolution it was able to expand very rapidly. From a population of barely 2,000 in 1600 and about 5,000 in 1780, it had grown to 104,012 about a hundred years later (1881 census) and peaked at 133,052 in 1911. The cotton industry, which became established in the town in 1779, survived as its major employer and largest industry until the 1950s. It was a minor estuary port, dealing in coastal trade, until the late nineteenth

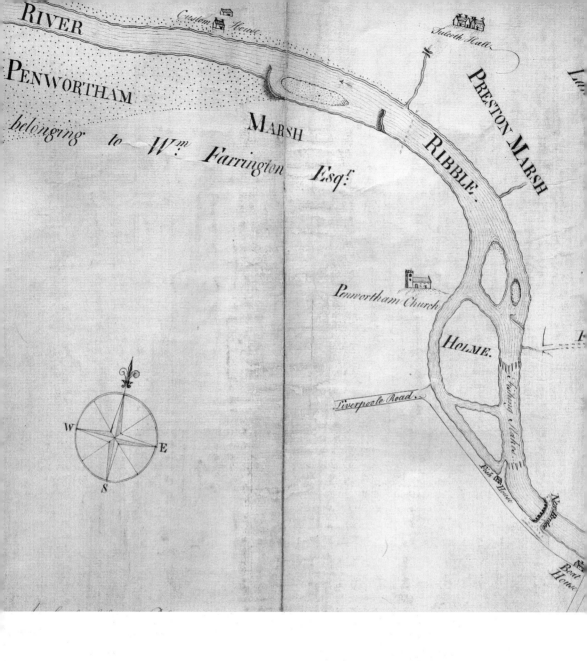

RIVER

PENWORTHAM

belonging to W:^m Farrington Esq:

MARSH

Custom House

PRESTON MARSH

Tulcoth Hall

RIBBLE.

Penwortham Church

HOLME.

Liverpoole Road.

Fishing Hutts

Fish House

Boat House

W — E
S

century, when the Corporation paid for an ambitiously large new dock (the largest single wet dock in the country) and the canalising of the 30 km of estuary out to the open sea. From the opening of the dock in 1892 until the its closure in 1981 Preston was therefore a port of some significance, though it was never without major problems – most notably, the constant silting, and equally constant dredging, of the river. The town also developed an important engineering industry, with the celebrated Dick Kerr works producing thousands of tramcars exported all over the world from the 1890s onwards; the works on Strand Road were later taken over by English Electric,

LEFT
The Ribble
between
Penwortham
and Preston in
the eighteenth
century. Until
1820 there was no
bridge connecting
Fishergate directly
with Liverpool
Road, and the
river was split by
four islands, one
of them known
as Penwortham
Holme. Preston
Marsh was
reclaimed and
is now crossed
by Strand Road.
When the huge
Albert Edward
dock was
constructed the
Custom House
was demolished;
and during the
excavation work
for the dock
many prehistoric
finds were made,
including dug-out
canoes.

and produced military aircraft and then aerospace components before their closure in 1993. Since the 1970s, as Greater Preston has grown apace (in part as a result of its designation in 1970 as the focus of the Central Lancashire New town) an ugly and often unnecessary sprawl of industrial units and vast estates of 'executive homes' has covered green fields with tarmac and concrete. In 1961 I watched and listened to a male corncrake (*Crex crex*) displaying to a female in a meadow north of Fulwood. Today corncrakes are extinct in Lancashire and the building which produces the *Lancashire Evening Post* covers that very meadow.

Preston has a fine natural setting on its ridge-top location above the river, with views to the fells and the moors of Bowland and Winter Hill, and across the Lancashire plain. Travellers approaching the town by train from the south see its impressive skyline, admittedly marred by 1960s tower blocks, but with churches and the public buildings of the town centre set against a backcloth of dark hills and green slopes. The view from the North Union Railway viaduct of 1836, as the train arrives at Preston station, also looks along the length of the Ribble and the wooded slopes to the south of the centre. Two other bridges can be seen – the long East Lancashire Railway viaduct (1850) and the Old Tram Bridge, a concrete and girder replica of a bridge built in 1803 to carry a horse-drawn tramroad which ran from the northern end of the southern portion of the Lancaster Canal at Walton Summit, to the southern end of the northern portion of the canal at Lune Street in Preston town centre! There was a gap in the canal, and this reminds us of one of the great might-have-beens of Lancashire, and Ribble, history. The Lancaster Canal, designed to link south Lancashire and the Wigan coalfield with north Lancashire, was

Penwortham Old
Bridge (1759)
replaced an
earlier (1755) one
that was washed
away. This was
the lowest bridge
across the Ribble
until, following the
canalisation of the
river downstream
(see p. 246), it was
possible to built
a bridge from the
foot of Fishergate
to Penwortham.

built in the late 1790s but ran out of money. The canal was to have crossed the Ribble valley from Preston to Bamber Bridge by a splendid aqueduct, which would have been the longest and most impressive in England. Had it been built, Preston would have had one of the outstanding transport structures of the eighteenth century. Instead, though, the horse-drawn tramroad was constructed to link the two halves pending financial recovery and the building of the aqueduct … and that, unfortunately, never happened.

The tidal stretch of the river at Preston remains surprisingly unspoilt and, remarkably, only a few hundred yards from the middle of one of northern England's largest and most thriving cities, there is a broad, untamed waterway that rushes over its rocky bed with shoals and rapids and plenty of real character. The Ribble ends its life not as a sluggish, sleepy, slow and slovenly river, but as a lively, bright, fast-flowing and sparkling water, within sight and sound of the city centre but still reminding us of its origins high in the dales and moors of Yorkshire. On the south bank there are broad open meadows where cows still graze within view of the tower blocks, and from the riverbank real countryside is easily visible. Contrast this with the Lune and Lancaster or the Mersey at Warrington, where long stretches are lined by factories and fast roads, and Preston's rare good fortune is clear.

From the North Union Bridge the river passes under the delightful Penwortham Old Bridge of 1759; then the huge Penwortham New Bridge (1915); and finally the high-level bridge of 1985. The old Penwortham bridge

The end of Big Ribble and the start of its estuary is crossed by the West Coast main line railway bridge.

The overgrown motte and bailey Norman castle at Penwortham. There was a similar castle at Tulketh, on the other side of the river.

was the first fixed crossing of the river below Walton-le-Dale. A short-lived predecessor, built in 1755, collapsed while the vicar of Preston was riding over it: his Anglican supporters pointed to his deliverance as a sign that God was on their side, his Catholic and Nonconformist opponents saw the accident as a damning verdict from on high! Before the bridge was built a ferry plied across the river at higher water, from Broadgate to the Penwortham bank just below the present Bridge Inn: there are records of ferrymen here as early as 1338, but the ferry itself was undoubtedly much older than that. Below the ferry a long ford crossed the river (which was then very much wider) at the foot of Fishergate, using the islands and gravel banks of Penwortham 'Holme' as stepping stones in the channel.

Penwortham itself is a site of great historical interest, and the river has played a crucial part in its history. Until the early tenth century the lands between the Ribble and the Mersey were loosely under the control of the kingdom of Northumbria, but to the south lay the kingdom of Mercia which was gradually extending its territory and influence. Mercia was constantly under threat from Scandinavian incursions and aggression, and in the years from 920 (when many Vikings were expelled from Dublin and came to Lancashire) the threats increased. The Mercians took steps to defend the northern frontier, first by building a chain of fortifications along the Mersey valley from Chester to Manchester and then, in about 920, moving into south Lancashire and trying to secure the Ribble as a new outer defence line. It seems likely that they came to Penwortham and there built some sort of defended camp or outpost, situated on the low but prominent hillock above the bluffs on the south bank of the river, at the point where two separate routeways crossed the marshes and riverside flats and forded the river. One was the east–west route from Preston, the other a south–north track which ran from the Leyland area, and on the north bank headed out towards Fulwood and the Lancaster direction.

The Mercian *burh* or fortified place is mentioned by implication in the Domesday Survey of 1086, when Penwortham is described as a borough. The Normans built a motte and bailey castle (an earthen pudding-shaped mound, surmounted by a wooden stockade and tower, and surrounded by earth ramparts) on the site, which was immediately above and commanded the fords, and then constructed a second castle, at Tulketh on the north bank of the river. The twin castles not only controlled all traffic on the cross-river fords, but also guarded the vulnerable head of the estuary, a possible access point for invaders from Scotland or Ireland. Penwortham's castle mound still survives, tree-covered and tucked away at the back of the churchyard of St Mary's parish church, but Tulketh castle was, most regrettably, levelled to make way for terraced housing in the mid-1840s. In the early 1140s a Benedictine priory, a daughter house of Evesham Abbey in Worcestershire, was founded here by Warrin Bussel, Baron of Penwortham. It was always small and dependent upon the mother house, and at the Dissolution it housed only the prior and one other monk. There is now no trace of it. From the eleventh century to late in the nineteenth Penwortham was the site of a major salmon netting station and on one day in June 1768 3,384 salmon and sea trout were taken in one sweep of a net.

Had the Romans continued to develop and maintain their fortifications and roads in this region, instead of abandoning the area in the fourth century, and had the kingdoms of Northumbria and Mercia not treated the Ribble valley and southern Lancashire as a frontier to be fought over but rather a place to settle, there is no doubt that the draining of the coastal plain (see page 222) and the clearance of 'waste, forest and moor' further inland would have occurred centuries earlier. It is, for instance, highly unlikely that the Romans would have allowed their road between Wigan and Walton-le-Dale to get into the condition that Arthur Young described in 1770: 'I know not in the whole range of language terms sufficiently expressive to describe this infernal road [now, the A49]. Let me most seriously caution all travellers to avoid it as they would the devil, for a thousand to one but they break their necks or their limbs by overthrows or breakdowns. They will meet with ruts, which I actually measured, four feet deep, and floating with mud, only from a wet summer. What therefore must it be after a winter. The only mending it in places receives is the tumbling-in of some loose stones which serve no other purpose but jolting a carriage in the most intolerable manner. These are not merely opinions, but facts, for I actually passed three carts broken down in these eighteen miles of execrable memory.'[30]

Little Ribble and Big Ribble: character and wildlife

Below Long Preston Deeps, as the river flows from its confluences with Wigglesworth and Long Preston Becks and then under the gritstone span of Cow Bridge, the Ribble becomes once more a series of slow, deep pools separated by shallow, boulder-strewn, bubbling riffles. This character continues to Hodderfoot, though the river does increase a little in size as it receives water from several small streams including Stock Beck (which flows through the small industrial town of Barnoldswick and has, in the past, brought polluting cyanide to the Ribble), Skirden Beck, Swanside Beck and Bashall Brook. At their confluence the Ribble and the Hodder are of roughly the same size, and one might expect them to have a comparable natural history, but in fact the characters of the two rivers are quite different.

In its 24 kilometres between Dunsop Bridge and Hodderfoot, the Hodder falls by 75 metres (3.125 metres per kilometre), whereas the Ribble falls 70 metres in its 39 kilometres between Cow Bridge and Hodderfoot (1.8 metres per kilometre). The Hodder is therefore a more turbulent and quicker-flowing river. The Hodder has only three small villages and no town on its course: Dunsop Bridge, Slaidburn, and Newton, and there is also Chipping on a tributary, the Loud. In contrast Little Ribble and its tributaries have 12 villages (Long Preston, Rathmell, Wigglesworth, Hellifield, Paythorne, Gisburn, Bolton, Sawley, Grindleton, Chatburn, West Bradford, and Waddington), and three towns, Settle, Barnoldswick and Clitheroe. More humans mean more human waste: the Hodder has only three very small sewage works whereas Little Ribble has seven (and those at Settle and Clitheroe are relatively large). The Hodder flows through the expanse of Gisburn Forest and to the west of the river the land rises quickly to the heather moors of Bowland and Longridge Fell; there is pasture close to the river, but much is sheep-grazing. In contrast, along almost the entire length on either side of Little Ribble the countryside is given over to pasture or silage-meadow, much of it intensively managed for dairy cattle. From Whitewell downstream the Hodder mostly flows through a steep-sided and well-wooded gorge. On Little Ribble, save for a section between Bolton and Gisburn, pasture and meadow reaches the waterside in most places. The Hodder flows over a bed consisting of large boulders, gravel, coarse sand and much bedrock; the bed of Little Ribble is mostly compacted silt, sand or gravel.

Big Ribble, below Calderfoot, has a similar character to Little Ribble. It flows sedately, falling about 30 metres in 30 kilometres (1.0 metre per kilometre) over a bed of compacted mud, sand or gravel, with very deep slow pools alternating with shallow swifter runs. As with Little Ribble, leached fertilisers reach the water from the pasture and meadow on either hand. But the water flowing down Big Ribble is further enriched with water from the Calder, which carries very high concentrations of nutrients (see Chapter 4).

These differences in character are reflected in the natural history of Little Ribble, Big Ribble and Hodder. The most obvious difference can be seen on a hot sunny summer day after a few weeks with little rain. Large areas of the bed of the Ribble will be smothered by the fine, filamentous green alga called blanket-weed (*Cladophora*), whereas on the bed of the Hodder blanket-weed may be absent or growth very sparse. The reason is that blanket-weed thrives under warm, bright conditions in water that has a high phosphate and nitrate concentration. The leaching of fertilisers, put on waterside pastures to encourage lush growths of grass, and treated sewage effluent released into the river, means that the waters of the Ribble have very high concentrations of these plant nutrients. I have been paddling in the Ribble since 1958 and have witnessed the tremendous increase of blanket-weed in both Little and Big Ribble, especially since the 1970s. Before then, at places such as Sawley and Ribchester, it was possible, in July and August, to stand knee-deep in the

Moorhens are commoner along Ribble than Hodder.

The aquatic nymphs of stoneflies and mayflies are very susceptible to pollution.

However their adults can fly (though not strongly) so they can colonise waters as they become cleaner.

A male sedge warbler proclaiming its territory.

river and see the riverbed clearly. Today it is often impossible even to see one's feet for the green slimy mass, let alone the riverbed! Two aquatic mosses also reflect the difference in water quality between Ribble and Hodder. In the Hodder, one of the commonest mosses that grow on underwater boulders and masonry is *Rhynchostegium (Eurynchium) riparoides*; a second moss, *Leptodictyum (Amblystegium) riparum*, that can tolerate a degree of pollution, is absent. Both mosses can be found on rocks in Little Ribble, but in Big Ribble *Leptodictyum* is dominant and *Rhynchostegium* is absent.[31]

The effects of the blanket-weed growth on other plants and the invertebrates in both Little and Big Ribble are marked. Up to the early 1980s, *Ranunculus penicellatus*, a water-buttercup (or water crowfoot) which thrives only in clear limestone streams, dominated Little Ribble and *R. fluitans*, a similar species that can tolerate a degree of pollution and more acid water, dominated Big Ribble below Calderfoot. Every year, in early summer the shallows above Sawley Bridge and almost the entire river between Paythorne and Cow Bridge were a mass of their flowing fronds and white blooms. The last year of such a growth of water-buttercup was 1983. A succession of hot summers, accompanied by growing concentrations of fertiliser and effluent flowing down the river, generated a thick blanket of blanket-weed that choked the water-buttercup. More recently, in the relatively wet summers of 2000, 2001, 2004 and 2007, the blanket-weed failed to smother the riverbed, but only small clumps of water-buttercup grew in a few sites. The next hot summer and drought will see them choked. Only when the scattering of excessive fertiliser on fields is stopped and all sewage works have 'scrubbers' fitted to remove nitrates and phosphates from effluent will the scourge of blanket-weed be removed.

The effect of blanket-weed on water-buttercup is obvious. Its consequences within the riverbed on the invertebrate populations are not so easily seen. They are there, nonetheless. In 1982 the riverbed at five sites on Little Ribble between Paythorne Bridge and Cow Bridge held nine species of stoneflies (Plecoptera) and 17 species of upwinged flies (mayflies: Ephemeroptera). In 1996 only three species of stoneflies and 12 species of upwinged flies could be found there. This contrasts with 12 species of stonefly and 17 species of upwinged fly in the Hodder in 2000. Blanket-weed, choking the riverbed and starving it of oxygen on warm summer nights, had suffocated these sensitive insects. By contrast the blanket-weed was supporting massive populations of midge larvae (Chironomidae), together with small populations of lesser water-boatmen (Corixidae), freshwater shrimp (*Gammarus pulex*) and water hog-louse (*Asellus aquaticus*), groups that are more tolerant of low oxygen levels in the water. There were even reports of fish mortality in the hot summers of the early and mid-1990s, when during the night in prolonged low water flows and hot weather the oxygen level on the riverbed fell more or less to zero. One report was that a few small trout and grayling and salmon parr were found dead near West Bradford and above Mitton, but the true mortality may have been greater as scavengers such as gulls and herons rapidly remove dead fish from the river.

In Big Ribble both stoneflies and upwinged flies were very rare during the 1960s and early 1970s, mainly because of the effects of pollutants carried into the Ribble by the River Calder that flows through Burnley and enters the Ribble below Mitton (Chapter 4). During the 1990s, as the sources of pollution in the Calder were cleaned up, populations of four upwinged flies and one stonefly immediately became established. There is, however, no doubt that without the negative effects of blanket-weed larger and more diverse stonefly and upwinged fly populations would have developed here.

It is interesting to contrast the mayfly and stonefly species occurring in Little Ribble, Big Ribble and Hodder. I have records of 22 species of mayfly and 11 species of stonefly from Little Ribble, but only 8 species of mayfly and five of stonefly from Big Ribble. By contrast, 22 species of mayfly and 23 species of stonefly have been recorded from the Hodder (see pages 294–7). This indicates the cleanliness of the Hodder and why Hodder water is in great demand for human consumption and use (see pages 143–5).

One striking feature of Little Ribble and Big Ribble that contrasts with the headwaters above Settle and with the Hodder is the water and waterside bird community. Excluding the Deeps (see above), in 1999–2000 and 2002, there were two pairs of mute swans, at least 43 pairs of mallard, 15 pairs of moorhens, six pairs of coot, 11 pairs of reed buntings and four pairs of sedge warblers along Little Ribble, and three pairs of mute swans, two pairs of tufted duck (*Aythya fuligula*), 27 pairs of mallard, 11 pairs of moorhens, three pairs of coot and two pairs each of sedge warbler and reed bunting along Big Ribble. The equivalent figures for the Hodder are: no swans, coots or sedge warblers, 17 pairs of mallard, six pairs of moorhens and three pairs of reed buntings. These species either require weed in their diet, and the Ribble has more than the Hodder, or they require tall waterside vegetation (willows and reed canary grass *Phalaris arundinacea* occurs commonly by the Ribble, less so on the Hodder). In contrast bird species that feed on insects or tiny fish are more abundant on the Hodder. In 2005, Little Ribble had four pairs of goosanders (*Mergus merganser*), 10 pairs of common sandpipers, two pairs of kingfishers *(Alcedo atthis)*, 13 pairs of grey wagtails and six pairs of dippers along its 39 kilometres, whilst the 30 kilometres of Big Ribble had only three pairs of common sandpipers, two or three pairs of kingfishers, four pairs of grey wagtails and no dippers. These are much lower densities than on the Hodder (see page 148).

Fish

Thirty-four species of fish (excluding marine species that may be found in the outer estuary) have been recorded from the Ribble, its tributaries and in ponds and lakes in its catchment. All have appeared since the last Ice Age, when the area was frozen and inhospitable to fish.[32]

Many species colonised the river from the sea after the ice melted, for they can tolerate salt water and may spend part of their lives at sea: these are sea lamprey (*Petromyzon marinus*), river lamprey (*Lampetra fluviatilis*), brook lamprey (*L. planeri*), sturgeon (*Acipenser sturio*), allis shad (*Alosa alosa*), twaite shad (*A. fallax*), eel, salmon, brown and sea trout, smelt (*Osmerus eperlanus*), three-spined stickleback (*Gasterosteus aculeatus*), nine-spined stickleback (*Pungitius pungitius*), bass (*Dicentrarchus labrax*), thick-lipped mullet (*Chelon labrosus*), flounder (*Platichthys flesus*) and probably the miller's thumb.

Of these the sturgeon and the shads are very rare vagrants. Sea lamprey appear to be rare but have been recorded in recent years spawning between Walton-le-Dale and Salmesbury, and close to Hodderfoot. River lamprey is probably overlooked: in 1981 I found post-spawning corpses at Mitton. Brook. Lampreys are widespread but are frequently unnoticed because they hide away in the riverbed. Eels are very common, and many travel overland to reach isolated lakes. The sticklebacks are best known as the inhabitants of

Little Ribble is an excellent trout stream.

Grayling are now common in both Little Ribble and Hodder, and slowly spreading into the Calder and Big Ribble as they have become cleaner. Unlike trout and salmon, that spawn in early winter, grayling spawn in spring.

weedy ponds, but the three-spined can be found on saltpans on the estuary saltmarshes and brackish pools at Birkdale. Bass, mullet and flounder are primarily saltwater species that may penetrate freshwater in the estuary, with the flounder occurring as far as Samlesbury and occasionally even higher up Big Ribble. Miller's thumb are common in clean water where there are boulders under which they can hide and lay their eggs; they are most abundant in the Hodder and the Ribble upstream of Settle.

The Ribble system has long been an important fishery for salmon, trout and sea trout (brown trout that run to sea to feed and grow). Following the Norman Conquest the most important fisheries in the estuary and Big Ribble close to Preston were under the control of religious houses. Cockersand Abbey and the priories at Lytham and Penwortham had the rights to the greater part of the estuary fishing. Whalley Abbey had netting stations at Walton-le-Dale and Cuerdale, Sawley Abbey at Sunderland Hall. These fisheries were highly prized. In 1320, for example, an agreement was reached whereby the Priory of Penwortham would send, every year to Evesham Abbey, in time for the feast of St Egwin (30 December), fifty salmons. This is a curious agreement, for 30 December is after salmon have spawned and before the first runs of fresh fish in early spring. Presumably these fifty salmon were kelts that had recently spawned. To us they would have been almost inedible, but in 1320 they were prized as a source of protein.

Following the Dissolution the fisheries came into the hands of wealthy landowners who exploited the fisheries as far as they could, though fortunately there were close seasons to protect the stocks of spawning fish. The earliest of all close seasons was established here by Richard II in 1389–90 who decreed that 'no young salmon be taken or destroyed by nets, as milldams or in other places, from the middle of April till the Nativity of St John the Baptist [26 June] … from the waters of the Lone [Lune], Wyre, Mersee [Mersey], Rybble and all other waters in the County of Lancaster.'[33] This protected the salmon and sea trout smolts heading downstream to the sea. The decree continued, '… no salmon can be taken from Michaelmas Day [29 September] to the Purification of Our Lady [2 February] … because that salmons be not seasonable in the said water in the time aforesaid.' This protected fish from just before spawning and allowed the survivors (kelts) to get back to sea without danger of being caught. It would have also put an end to the eating of salmon on St Egwin's Day at Evesham.

We have very few early records of catches. On 31 March 1732 one draught of the net at Penwortham produced 3,190 salmon and sea trout, two further sweeps realising another 800 fish. One day in 1823, 116 salmon weighing almost 1,000 pounds were carried up Fishergate and sold in Preston market. Later in the nineteenth century records increase, but they trace the decline

A detail of Porter's map of the Ribble from the middle of the eighteenth century, showing the area around Walton bridge. Several banks of fishing stakes can be clearly seen upstream of the bridge.

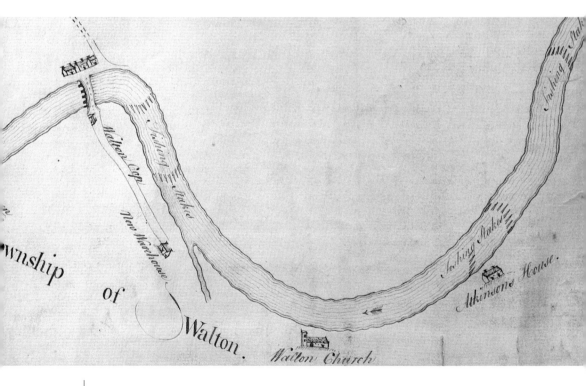

of the salmon and sea trout. In 1867 the total catch was about 15,000 fish, in 1892 only 926 and in 1897, 470. By 1900 salmon and sea trout had virtually disappeared because of blocking of the river and tributaries with milldams and as a result of increasing pollution, especially from the Calder (see page 167).

However, following the Salmon and Freshwater Fisheries Act of 1923 a Fisheries Board was funded to allow fish-passes to be built on milldams and weirs, the building of a hatchery to raise young salmon, and the introduction of bye-laws to protect the fish (the first of these regulations prohibited netting in the estuary upstream of Freckleton Naze). From 1931 to 1950 the annual rod and net catch steadily increased from 206 to 1,995 and the number of redds (salmon nests) counted in the river increased from 175 to 2,290.

From 1951 the numbers of salmon running the Ribble fluctuated widely, with a feeling amongst both those trying to catch salmon and those managing the fishery (now the Environment Agency) that overall the population was in decline. In 1996 831 salmon were caught and 767 redds counted, while in 1997 only 411 were caught and 303 redds counted. However, in 2004 there was a sudden upturn in the numbers of salmon running the river, 1,737 fish being caught by rod or net, the largest number since 1950. We can see the increase clearly from three year averages: 1944–46, 112 salmon caught; 1954–56, 120; 1964–66, 225; 1974–76, 543; 1984–86, 391; 1994–96, 638; 2004–06, 1,197 *per annum*. It may be that work undertaken in recent years by the Ribble Valley Conservation Trust and Hodder Consultative to enhance the riverine habitat for salmon and trout is paying dividends.

Of the other species of fish found in the Ribble catchment, we know that rainbow trout (*Oncorhynchus mykiss*) and speckled char (*Salvelinus fontinalis*) were introduced from North America. They are mainly found in stillwater fisheries, and not often in the rivers, though in recent years numbers of rainbow trout have escaped into the Hodder over Stocks reservoir dam. We also know that the barbel (*Barbus barbus*) was introduced illegally in 1971 to the Ribble at Samlesbury, since when it has spread upstream as far as Settle (and in 2002 one was reported from the Hodder upstream of Winckley weir).

The remaining species were probably introduced, perhaps by the Cistercians who were great fish-breeders and had a fish-farm at Whalley (see page 173): pike (*Esox lucius*), grayling, carp (*Cyprinus carpio*), crucian carp (*Carassius carassius*), chub, dace (*L. leuciscus*), roach (*Rutilus rutilus*), rudd (*Scardinius erythrophthalmus*), minnow, bream (*Abramis brama*), gudgeon (*Gobio gobio*), tench (*Tinca tinca*), stone loach, perch (*Perca fluviatilis*) and ruffe (*Gymnocephalus cernuus*).

Pike occurs in Long Preston Deeps and in the larger pools of Big Ribble. Up to 1975 grayling was found only in the Hodder, Little Ribble and the

Eels feed and grow in the river but migrate to the Sargasso Sea to breed.

headwaters upstream to Stainforth, but since the cleaning of the Calder it has also colonised the lower reaches of that tributary and is spreading down Big Ribble. Until the late 1970s Big Ribble was noted as a wonderful fishery for chub, dace, gudgeon with lesser quantities of roach and perch. The populations of these have declined or (in the case of dace and gudgeon) collapsed. The reason is not clear. The Environment Agency has attempted to support these species in both Ribbles as well as Calder, Darwen and Yarrow (see Chapter 4) with hatchery raised fish. Minnow and stone loach are abundant in Hodder and Little Ribble and are increasing in the other tributaries.

The other fish in this category are primarily stillwater species (they have been introduced to ponds and some lakes), though there are carp (with specimens to nine kilograms) and bream in Big Ribble between Walton-le-Dale and Balderstone.

Chub are one of the commonest fish in the Ribble, though they are not native and were probably introduced here by medieval monks.

Flounders are primarily estuary fish, but they do move upstream into Big Ribble. Known as 'flukes' in Lancashire, they have long been acclaimed as a source of protein.

On either bank

The farmland on either side of Big and Little Ribble has long been ideal nesting territory for wading birds and for ground-nesting passerines. Pastures and meadows that are poorly drained and have stands of rushes have the highest densities, and in recent years drainage of these meadows, the increasing use of fertilisers, and ploughing followed by re-seeding with monoculture grasses have led to declines. This can be seen from surveys made in 1983, 1992, 2002 and 2004 over an area of 11 square kilometres between Gisburn and Nappa:

| | Number of pairs | | | |
	1983	1992	2002	2004
Oystercatcher	1	3	4	4
Lapwing	94	63	59	51
Snipe	14	6	8	4
Curlew	63	30	34	35
Redshank	7	3	1	0
Meadow pipit	15–20	–	5–7	about 5
Yellow wagtail	2	0	0	0
Skylark	about 480	–	320	about 270

With the exception of the oystercatcher (*Haematopus ostralegus*), which has increased nationally as a farmland bird, all these ground-nesting species have declined and two, the redshank and yellow wagtail, have become extinct in the area. In 1965–66 the Big Ribble floodplain downstream of Ribchester, below Hothersall Hall, at Elston and at Higher Brockholes held nine pairs of redshank and 22 pairs of yellow wagtails. In 1997–2000 fieldwork for the *Atlas of the Breeding Birds of Lancashire and North Merseyside* found only one or two pairs of redshank in that part of the valley and only one pair of yellow wagtails on Big Ribble, at Balderstone. In 2001–04 there was not one pair of yellow wagtails in the Ribble valley. This is entirely because of pasture and meadow 'improvement' and the early cropping of grass for silage, an action that destroys eggs and chicks. Compare these with the fortunes of the pied wagtail, which nests in holes in dry stone walls and farm buildings: in 1988 11 pairs nested on five farms around Paythorne and in 1999 there were 13 pairs.

We have also almost lost the barn owl (*Tyto alba*), once a common sight as it glided silently over the meadows of the flood plain in a winter's dusk, and screeched eerily from Ribchester churchyard at dead of night. Seven barns

Oystercatchers colonised the Ribble valley in the late 1950s. This chick relies on its camouflage to escape the eyes of predators.

in the valley that had barn owls nesting in the 1960s have been converted to human homes.

The extensive woodlands found on the bluffs in the Ribble Valley are mainly oak and sycamore, with some ash, elm, beech, lime, hazel, bird cherry and elder (*Sambucus nigra*). Alder and willow are often at the waterside. Crab apples (*Malus sylvestris*) occur in the woods and by the river; between Paythorne and Nappa one of Little Ribble's pools is named after an old gnarled crab, the fruit of which makes delightful jelly! In spring, before the leaf canopy cuts out sunlight and prevents it reaching the woodland floor, there is often a fine flora including snowdrop (*Galanthus nivalis*), lesser celandine, primrose, dog's mercury, bluebell, wood sorrel (*Oxalis acetosella*), wood anemone (*Anemone nemorosa*), lords-and-ladies (*Arum maculatum*) and wild garlic (ransoms). At the woodland edge or where the sun does reach the woodland floor the flora may include wood sedge (*Carex sylvaticus*), wood club-rush (*Scirpus sylvaticus*), hairy and great wood rush (*Luzula pilosa*, *L. sylvatica*), three woodland grasses *Poa nemoralis*, *Festuca altissima* and *Bromus ramosus*, green helleborine (*Epipactis helleborine*), baneberry, common and woodland violets (*Viola riviniana* and *V. reichenbachiana*), herb bennet (*Geum urbanum*), wood stitchwort (*Myosotum nemorum*), tufted and scarce wood vetches (*Vicia cracca* and *V. sylvatica*), bellflower (*Campanula latifolia*), figwort (*Scrophularia nodosa*), wood speedwell (*Veronica montana*) and wood woundwort (*Stachys sylvatica*).

The woodlands by Big Ribble have a very high concentration of badger setts and many fox earths, though neither species is seen often. In the 1960s, Preston naturalist Philip Thompson found that Ribble valley badgers loved honey on their toast! Red squirrels (*Sciurus vulgaris*) vanished from the Ribble valley woodlands in the early 1960s and today grey squirrels (*S. carolinensis*) abound. Roe occur throughout the valley, though the feral sika deer (*Cervus nippon*) occurs in woods between Gisburn and Ribchester and the tiny muntjac (*Muntiacus reevsi*) has very recently been reported from around Hodderfoot, Ribchester and Alston. Hedgehog (*Erinaceus europaeus*), common and pygmy shrew, woodmouse and bank vole, stoat (*Mustela erminea*) and weasel, and Daubenton's (*Myotis daubentoni*), pipistrelle (*Pipistrellus pipistrellus*), noctule (*Nyctalus noctula*) and long-eared bats (*Plecotus auritus*) are widespread through the valley. The dormouse (*Muscardinus avellanarius*) was recorded long ago from Cuerdale and Samlesbury, but is now extinct here. The only reptile to be readily seen in the valley is the slow-worm (*Anguis fragilis*); it occurs on the wooded bluffs and sometimes blue-spotted males may be found.

The Big Ribble woodlands appear to have lost several species of bird in recent years, including marsh tit (*Parus palustris*), lesser redpoll (*Carduelis*

flammea), wood warbler (*Phylloscopus sibilatrix*) and hawfinch (*Coccothraustes coccothraustes*). The latter, always a secretive bird, bred at Brockholes and in late summer one or two family parties gathered in nearby Preston cemetery to feed in the cherry trees there. There have been gains. Nuthatches (*Sitta europaea*) and pied flycatchers (*Fidecula hypoleuca*) colonised the woods of both Big and Little Ribble during the 1980s and 1990s.

The valleys of both Little and Big Ribble are incredibly beautiful, especially in late spring when the variety of shades of green is endless and the place echoes to the cries of displaying lapwing and curlew. There is, however, a major problem. It is a problem brought about by agricultural practices forced upon farmers by the European Union, our own government and by supermarket giants who seek to pay farmers as little as possible for their dairy products. It is not a problem brought about by the farming community that has, since the 1980s, been forced to do all in its power to survive. Farmers have had to

The field geranium, along with many other wild flowers, was once a familiar feature of hedge banks around valley meadows. Now it is much scarcer: plants like this do not appreciate herbicides! And why spray them anyway?

sell barns for barn conversions to help fund their farming. They have had to open their own farm-gate shops. One I know drove daily to Manchester to make a little extra profit by selling some of his dairy produce to small specialist retailers.

The problem is the way farmers have been forced to manage their meadows. Wild flower meadows have been ploughed up so that today we have grass monocultures. We have lost the flowers and insects that live in the traditional Ribble valley meadows. The meadows are cut for silage in May or early June instead of for hay in July. We are losing the bird species that nest in meadows simply because their eggs and chicks are mown with the early cut of grass. We have lost all the yellow wagtails and most of the snipe and redshank. Soon, perhaps, the place will no longer echo to the cries of displaying lapwings and curlews.

Every year, to increase the quality and quantity of the grass vast quantities of fertiliser is scattered over the meadows and lots of it end up in the river where it generates massive 'blooms' of blanket-weed. That horrible alga has, since the late 1970s, destroyed the natural river flora and threatens the clean water animal life in the river.

No dairy farmer in the valley could manage his farm as it was managed in the 1950s and 1960s without going bankrupt. It is only by a reversal of political decisions that led to modern agricultural practices, by offering financial incentives to farmers to manage their land in a wildlife friendly way, and by the supermarket shopper to accept that they must pay the true cost of milk and milk products that these problems will perhaps be overcome.

CHAPTER THREE

The Hodder

The beautiful River Hodder, famous for its umber,* rises near the
Cross of Greet, and passing through the parish of Sladeburn intersects
the forest and forms the only ornamental scenery of a track otherwise
bleak and barren, by its deep and fringed banks.

Dr Thomas Whitaker, History of Whalley, 1801.

The headwaters

A narrow lane leads in a north-westerly direction from Slaidburn and after
a short distance becomes a track that traverses the Bowland fells to the Lune
valley. The moorland crossed by this track is called Salter Fell and the track
is Salter Fell Road. This road originated as a Roman military highway, part
of the high-level route, built in the years around AD 70, which ran from
Manchester via Ribchester to Burrow in Lonsdale, and then through the
Lune Gorge to the Eden valley and Carlisle. Its more recent name has often
been interpreted as indicating that the road was used by salt traffic, involving
packhorses laden with salt from Cheshire, but recent research suggests that
the name (and that of the four farm or settlement sites called Higher, High,
Mid and Lower Salter in Roeburndale, on the north side of Bowland) is in fact
derived from the 'salters' or places where the deer of the Forest of Bowland
were fed. The word is almost certainly from the early medieval technical
term *salterie*, a deer-leap.

A second lane leaves Slaidburn in an almost due northerly direction to
cross the easternmost Bowland Fells. It eventually reaches Bentham in the
Wenning valley. Today this is a metalled road. The summit is at Cross of

---

* Umber, an old English name for the grayling, is a characteristic fish of both
Hodder and Ribble (see page 103).

Greet on Lythe Fell (at 427 metres), where there still survives the gritstone base of a medieval cross with a rectangular mortice hole into which the stone cross itself would have fitted. To the south-west of this point the moorland continues to rise for two kilometres to the summit cairn of White Hill (544 metres) and from this extensive slope several tiny streams flow in a north-easterly direction and meet at the roadside close to the Cross of Greet. The meeting of these rills is the source of the river Hodder, one of the most beautiful rivers flowing through one of the most beautiful valleys in the British Isles. This is not a new opinion, for the name of the river is derived from the British *Hod-dubro*, lovely or pleasant river.

The first three kilometres of the Hodder's course is down a steep-sided clough of crag and heather moor to the Cross of Greet Bridge. This is red grouse country. Indeed, this is the eastern expanse of the most famous grouse moor in the world, extending westwards into Wyresdale and with Abbeystead in its centre. On 12 August 1915 eight guns shot 2,929 grouse in six drives over 4,800 hectares of these moors. The next two days produced a further 3,042 grouse and, in the entire season, over 17,000 grouse were shot on 6,900 hectares. This is the record grouse bag, for both day and season, on any moor.[1] In recent years bags have been very much lower and in some years (such as 2005) the population has been too low for any shooting.

The moors are carefully managed to encourage the production of as many grouse as possible, for without the income from grouse shooting they would

The base of the Cross of Greet (Cross of Grit or Stone). This marked the point on the track, now road, where the traveller passes from Hodder to Wenning catchments.

The source of the Hodder.

either have been afforested or turned into over-grazed sheep-walk (as have been the West Pennine moors, see page 181). However, this management system does more than just foster and encourage the grouse, with its unmistakeable clucking 'go-back' call. The regular burning of the heather destroys leggy growth as well as rank grasses in favour of shorter, denser heather and bilberry. One consequence is that these Bowland fells are one of the finest heather-bilberry moors and are a mass of purple in late summer.

The headwaters of the Hodder flow through some of the finest heather-grouse moor in the world. To maintain top-quality heather patches of moor are burned every year.

Short-eared owls
(*Asio flammeus*)
nest on the moors
high in the Hodder
valley.

Another is that the cover provided by these short shrubs attracts high densities of meadow pipits and field voles that provide food for merlins, short-eared owls and (the emblem of Bowland) the hen harrier (*Circus cyaneus*). Sit quietly by the Cross of Greet or slowly walk along Salter Fell Road, and you are likely to see all three of these. The hen harrier is the most spectacular. Extinct in Lancashire from the mid-nineteenth century until 1969, when the first pair nested here and raised three young, by the beginning of the twenty-first century up to ten pairs bred (11 pairs in 2006; 11 pairs in 2007 raising 22 young), then the only regular breeding population in England.[2]

The heather moorland habitat has several other breeding bird species. Wheatears build their nests among piles of gritstone boulders and in drystone walls. Ring ouzels nest usually on heather-clad steep clough sides. Where there are a few scrubby gorse or hawthorn bushes and patches of bracken, whinchats and, after a series of mild winters, for one hard winter will exterminate them, stonechats may be found. In spring cuckoos are attracted by the high density of meadow pipits, and many a pair of pipits raise a solitary cuckoo (*Cuculus canorus*) in their nest instead of a brood of their own kind. In recent years ravens (*Corvus corax*), exterminated in the past by gamekeepers, have returned, and once more they may be seen perching on the boulders of Raven's Castle. Climb away from the stream onto the moorland tops and you will find the two characteristic waders of Pennine moorlands, golden plover and dunlin.

The Ordnance Survey map can tell us something of the natural history of this area. The name of Catlow Fell, which overlooks Cross of Greet Bridge, is derived from *catt hlaw* or wild cat hill, since centuries ago wild cats had their lairs on the boulder-strewn moor. On the opposite side of the infant river, Stag Holes reminds us that in Norman and medieval times Bowland was a deer forest. Close by, Snout Berry Hill once had enough cloudberries (*Rubus chamaemorus*) to make it worthwhile gathering them. Snoutberry is an ancient name for the cloudberry, a creeping arctic form of the blackberry but with orange-yellow fruits. Today the plant is fairly scarce here and its fruits rarely seen. Badger Moss, Fox Holes, Fox Clough, Weasel Clough and Hare Clough need no explanation. To the west of Salter Fell Road, Wolf Hole Crag reminds us that Europe's largest predator, long extinct in the British Isles, once hunted here.

Yet there is more than heather, bilberry and birds on these moors. Heather and bilberry flowers are visited by two species of bumblebees, *Bombus jonellus* and *B. lapponicus*. A dark blue-green shield-bug *Zicrona caerulea* and a green mirid bug *Orthotylus ericetorum* feed on heather. Several species of beetle are closely associated with heather. *Carabus nitens* is a small beetle that appears at first sight to be black, but on closer inspection its back (elytra) reflects dark metallic green with metallic copper borders. *Carabus* hunts lesser insects in the heather cover, but the green tiger beetle (*Cicindela campestris*) seeks its prey in the open. The heather weevil (*Micrelus ericae*) is tiny — two millimetres in length at most — and is black with a red rostrum (long snout) and legs. Sometimes the heather will appear red-brown and be dying back. This damage is caused by the heather beetle (*Lochmaea suturalis*), a seven millimetre dark brown or blackish insect, which sometimes occurs in plague numbers.

Heather and bilberry are also host to the larvae of many moths. The northern eggar is a close relative of the lowland oak eggar as indicated by its scientific name *Lasiocampa quercus callunae*. The moor carpet moth (*Entephria caesiata*) is often abundant. So too are the mottled-brown common heath (*Ematurga atomaria*), the mottled-grey narrow-winged pug (*Eupithecia nanata*) and the beautiful yellow underwing (*Anarta myrtilli*), which is tiny with grey-brown-purple forewings and hindwings that flash yellow when the resting moth is disturbed. In some years the drab buff fox moth (*Macrothylacia rubi*) can be so numerous that black-headed gulls nesting on the island in Stocks Reservoir flock to the moor to gorge on them. The larvae of the emperor moth (*Saturnia pavonia*), that start out as tiny black caterpillars with orange spots but grow into fat green caterpillars before pupating, feed on both heather and bilberry; the adult is the most conspicuous of moorland moths.

As elsewhere in north-west England, the number of species of butterflies and dragonflies found in the Hodder valley is relatively small. Yet there are some interesting ones. The small skipper (*Thymelicus sylvestris*), whose caterpillars feed predominantly on the grass Yorkshire fog, colonised the upper Hodder Valley in 1997. There are several small colonies of the green hairstreak on the drier heather and bilberry 'edges', and there is a population of the small pearl-bordered fritillary (*Clossiana selene*). The large heath is a species of butterfly that has declined in some parts of northern England because of the drainage of its bog habitat. It remains in the upper Hodder valley wherever its main larval food-plant cotton-grass is abundant and where there is plenty of cross-leaved heath to provide nectar for the adults.

Of dragonflies, the large common hawker will often be seen in the upper Hodder valley. However, two very local species can also be found here. The golden-ringed dragonfly (*Cordulegaster boltonii*) – well named from its gold-ringed black body – breeds in at least three peaty moorland runnels that trickle down to the Hodder, and the black darter (*Sympetrum danae*) breeds in bog pools on the open moor.[3]

Of other insects, the heather fly (*Bibio pomonae*) sometimes occurs in huge numbers in late summer. Glossy black, with trailing hind legs, the leg bases are distinctly red.

Below Cross of Greet Bridge the valley widens, and upland pasture, grazed by sheep from the highest farms of Catlow, Lamb Hill, Kenibus, Higher Clough and New House, replaces heather-bilberry grouse moor. Although meadow pipits are common and short-eared owls occasional nesters in rushy pastures, several moorland birds are lost by the change in habitat. This is prime curlew and lapwing country. Many people think of curlews as being moorland birds, but they occur in much higher densities on damp pastures below the moor. Snipe and redshank, species that have become scarce breeding birds throughout much of the British Isles, still nest here in the poorly drained wet pastures, although numbers have declined in the last forty years. Pied wagtails abound, nesting in holes in drystone walls or barns and feeding on flies attracted by cattle and sheep. Below the junction of the infant Hodder and Near Costy Clough, close to the bridge, are the highest breeding pairs of common sandpipers, dippers and grey wagtails in the valley.

Stocks-in-Bowland

Keasden and Hasgill Becks drain the moorland of Bowland Knotts and flow into the growing river Hodder upstream of the head of Stocks reservoir. The reservoir takes its name from the village that was drowned when the area was flooded. The name Stocks is from the Old English *stocc*, and it means

The small green
hairstreak butterfly
is common on the
moors wherever
bilberry is
abundant.

Stocks reservoir
was filled with
water for the first
time in September
1931. Its catchment
was planted with
mostly foreign
conifer forest,
though today
much conifer
plantation is being
felled and replaced
with native mixed
or broad-leaf
woodland.

'dairy farm'. In 1180 Robert de Lacy granted lands here to the Cistercian
abbey of Kirkstall near Leeds, and Rushton grange, a large commercial farm,
was established on the estate, providing grazing for 160 brood-mares and
200 cows with their calves. Further grants of land were added to the grange
up to 1235, but at the Dissolution the property was sold by the Crown and
became a private farm. The small village of Stocks-in-Bowland developed

St James's church,
Stocks-in-Bowland,
was rescued from
the flooding of
Stocks reservoir.

around this nucleus and by the beginning of the twentieth century there
were five farmsteads (including the original grange), several cottages and a
chapel. In 1923, however, the Fylde Water Board obtained planning consent
to dam and flood this part of the valley to create a reservoir to provide water
for Blackpool and the growing holiday towns of the Fylde coast. During
the construction Rushton and the farms of Stocks were demolished and the

Large numbers of
black-headed gulls
nest on the island
in Stocks reservoir.

chapel was moved to a new site by the road close to the eastern shore of the reservoir. In September 1930 a 400-metre long dam was completed and by the end of the 1930–31 winter almost 100 hectares of upland pasture and the village site were submerged.

As well as the Hodder, much of the water that enters Stocks reservoir flows down Bottoms Beck, a stream which drains over 1,600 hectares of what was, before the reservoir was built, upland pasture and moorland. Early in the twentieth century water authorities were concerned that their reservoirs would suffer pollution from human and animal wastes. To reduce the risk here, Fylde Water Board cleared 26 farms and planted 1,500 hectares with conifers. Today this woodland, known as Gisburn Forest, is a major amenity area with car parks, forest walks and picnic sites, and as conifers have been felled, broad-leaved trees have been planted. Since 1985 Stocks reservoir has itself been developed into a major commercial trout fishery. So whilst the construction of the reservoir irreversibly damaged the river Hodder by reducing flow downstream of the dam (see page 143), it added two previously missing wildlife habitats to the valley: a large lake and a forest.

Stocks reservoir is a regionally important inland wintering site for waterfowl, including up to 45 cormorants (*Phalacrocorax carbo*), 570 wigeon, 360 teal (*Anas crecca*), 925 mallard (*A. platyrhynchos*) and 70 pintail (*Anas acuta*). Canada geese breed here, their numbers peaking at up to 700 during June. Teal also nest on the moor close to the reservoir. Since 1957 one or two pairs of red-breasted mergansers (*Mergus serrator*) have raised broods on the reservoir. The island in the middle of the reservoir has a breeding colony of up to 1,400 black-headed gulls (*Larus ridibundus*), and during the 1990s and 2000s Stocks became one of the very few British sites with nesting Mediterranean gulls (*Larus melanocephalus*). Each spring ospreys (*Pandion haliaetus*) pass through on migration and, as the osprey population continues to spread in Britain, it is not likely to be long before a pair stops and breeds here. Occasionally even rarer birds are found by the reservoir: for instance, in November 1996 an Isabelline shrike (*Lanius isabellinus*), which breeds no closer than Greece, killed and devoured robins and blue tits in the hawthorn scrub near Hollins Bay.

The pine forest around Stocks attracts many woodland species of birds, including buzzard (*Buteo buteo*), goshawk (*Accipiter gentilis*), sparrowhawk (*A. nisus*), woodcock (*Scolopax rusticola*), tree pipit (*Anthus trivialis*), treecreeper (*Certhia familiaris*), goldcrest (*Regulus regulus*) and jay (*Garrulus glandarius*). In recent years siskins (*Carduelis spinus*), formerly only winter visitors to northern England from Scotland and Scandinavia, have remained to nest. And in the early springs following previous late summer eruptions from Scandinavia, crossbills (*Loxia curvirostra*) have nested here. One bird that has become extinct here is the black grouse (*Tetrao tetrix*). In the *Journal of Nicholas Assheton of Downham* the diarist records killing three here on 23 December 1617. Black grouse survived in the forest around Stocks until at least 1985; the last recorded in the area were five, on Waddington Fell, on 22 September 1991.[5]

The conifer plantations around Stocks and elsewhere in the valley have had a considerable effect on the deer population. In the Forest of Bowland substantial populations of red and fallow deer (*Cervus elaphus* and *C. dama*) were protected for hunting until the start of the seventeenth century. However, from the reign of James I onwards the enclosure of the open lands of the forest and the development of agriculture, as well as the lifting of the forest laws which protected the deer resulted in these two species becoming extinct here. Similarly the roe deer (*Capreolus capreolus*) became extinct throughout north-west England during the eighteenth century. Late in the nineteenth century, following the planting of conifer plantations in Cumbria, roe deer began to spread south from the Scottish borders and they recolonised the area. The first appear to have returned to the Hodder valley sometime in the 1920s or 1930s, and today they are common throughout wooded areas of both Hodder and Ribble valleys as far downstream as the outskirts of Preston, in the wooded parts of the Calder and Darwen valleys, and in the Douglas valley to the source at the well-wooded Anglezarke/Rivington reservoirs. Outside the winter months (when groups of four or five may be observed) the monogamous roe deer are usually seen in pairs or as a small family group. Rutting occurs in July and August, calving in June, and does are often seen with twin fawns from late summer.

In 1907 Lord Ribblesdale released a small number of sika deer near Gisburn and formed the Ribblesdale buckhounds to hunt them. In the Lancashire and Cheshire Fauna Committee Report for 1959, it was stated that 'the deer can be seen in the Ribble Valley between Ribchester and Bolton-by-Bowland. I do not imagine that there are more than 50 in the whole area – if that number.' Today sikas can be found throughout the wooded areas of the middle Ribble and Hodder valleys. Observations have shown that they are not pure Japanese sika deer (in which the stags have black velvet on their growing antlers and reach 80 centimetres at the shoulder), but a cross between Japanese and Manchurian sikas (the stags have apricot velvet and reach 100 centimetres at the shoulder). The hinds gather in small herds of up to eight through August and September, prior to the rut in October and November. After the rut the sexes remain separate in small herds. Calving occurs in late May and June, and each female produces only one calf.[6] In recent years the muntjac (*Muntiacus reevesi*), a small Chinese species of deer, has been reported from the middle Ribble and lower Hodder.

The Forest of Bowland and Lower Hodder

The river Hodder flows through the middle of the Forest of Bowland, an Area of Outstanding Natural Beauty, and the villages of Slaidburn and Whitewell downstream from Stocks have long been the major centres in the forest. The origin of the name Bowland has been the subject of some controversy. Margaret Greenwood and Father Charles Bolton name the forest Bolland in their book *Bolland Forest and the Hodder Valley* (1955). This is its traditional pronunciation, still used by many local people, and Greenwood and Bolton argue that the name comes from the Old Norse *bu* for cattle and *bol* for a shippon or byre. 'Bolland' thus becomes 'the land of cattle'.[7] However, the name is in fact derived from the Old English *boga* and Old Norse *bogi* meaning 'bow'. In the twelfth century, when the forest was defined, the name appears as *Boelands* (1102), *Bouland* (1140) and *Bochlande* (1194) and simply means 'land in the bow or bend of the river'.[8] Greenwood and Bolton say that they 'know of no such bend', but the Ribble flows south from Settle to Halton West and then bends round sharply at Nappa to flow to the south-west past Clitheroe and on to Preston. Bowland is within that bow of the river. Alternatively, the name may originally have applied to a much smaller area, such as the land within one of the large bends of the Hodder in the vicinity of Slaidburn and Whitewell, and then gradually been used to designate a larger upland area.

While most of Bowland is within easy reach of a road, parts are still fairly remote.

Leagram is now well-treed farmland; 700 years ago it was an important deer park.

New Laund, close to Whitewell, is now a farm. 700 years ago it was managed as a secluded grazing area for deer.

The Forest of Bowland was a deer forest covering about 18,000 hectares, established following the Norman Conquest by the de Lacy family.[9] By virtue of marriage connections it became part of the estates of the earls of Lancaster in 1311. In 1351 the earldom was upgraded to a dukedom and in 1397 and 1399, on the death of John of Gaunt and the accession of his son as Henry IV, the dukedom became one of the titles of the sovereign. However, the duchy estates have always been held managed entirely separately from the Crown estates. The term 'forest' can cause some confusion for the area is not, and never was, wooded to any great extent. The name comes from the medieval Latin term *foris*, which has the same origin as our word 'foreign' and in this context means land which was outside or set apart from the normal pattern of landholding and legal process, an area to which special laws and conditions applied. In medieval England a forest was an area where there was a mix of open country and woodland, where deer were hunted on horseback by huntsmen and hounds, and where special forest laws were enforced. The forest was nominally administered by a master forester and his deputy (whose alternative title was 'bowbearer'), who held the right to hunt as well as being paid an annual salary of ten marks (a mark was worth 13s. 4d., that is two-thirds of £1). The post of master forester was in reality a sinecure, and the hard work was done by underlings. In 1469 Richard, Duke of Gloucester, was appointed to the post, and from 1556 to 1594 Sir Richard Shireburn, who

Whitewell was once the centre for hunting in Bowland. Now there is the inn and chapel.

built Stonyhurst, was master forester. Although Bowland was a hunting chase of the duchy of Lancaster, the only monarch known to have hunted there in person was James VI and I, the same king who famously 'dubbed' the Sir Loin at Hoghton Tower.

There were originally two deer parks within the forest, one at Leagram near Chipping (the present farm is at SD 625441) and one at Radholme near Whitewell (SD 666459). In 1340 Leagram Park extended over much of the land bounded by the rivers Loud and Hodder; its name possibly comes from Old Norse *Lathegrin*, meaning a slash made on a tree to mark a track. Radholme, now a farm like Leagram, also comes from the Old Norse, and probably means 'hill with roe deer'. Both parks produced red and fallow deer and were enclosed by a ditch and a bank with a wooden fence on top to keep the deer in. The bank at Leagram was at least ten kilometres in length, and the fence required huge quantities of timber, not only for the initial building, but for repair. Within each park were special areas called launds where trees and scrub was cleared to encourage quality grazing for the deer. In winter extra fodder was brought to the launds to sustain the deer.

Deer were released before a chase in the four designated hunting areas (wards) at Bashall, Slaidburn, Harrop (above Grindleton) and Chipping. Each ward had a keeper and assistant keepers who were appointed by the master forrester. The hunting was organised from a lodge at Whitewell, built at the end of the fourteenth century by Walter Urswyck, the site of which is now occupied by the Inn at Whitewell. In 1422 the monks of Whalley Abbey founded a chapel at Whitewell; the present nineteenth-century chapel is on the same site. Forest laws forbade people killing deer or from felling trees without permission, and those breaking the law were tried in a forest court at Whitewell.

Yet the forest was not uninhabited. Outside the launds the land was divided in to seven (in 1258) or eight (in 1442) vaccaries, or dairy farms, at Battris, now called Beatrix Farm (SD 664514), Browsholme (SD 684452), Burholme (SD 661485), Eshknot (SD 693482), Greystonleigh (SD 646457), Hareden (SD 641505), Lickhurst (637459) and Stapleoak (SD 652505). By 1564 many other vaccaries had been established, including Denglegrene (Dinkling Green at SD 64469), Thorneholme (SD 613500), Trogh (Trough House at SD 633528) and Sykes (SD 630515). And while the size of each vaccary remained constant through the time that Bowland was a deer forest, they were increasingly subdivided into smaller farms. Sykes vaccary at the foot of the Trough of Bowland, on the flat land where Langden and Losterdale Becks meet, is a good example. In 1498 it was one farm, worked by one Thomas Bond for an annual rent of 106s. 8d. By 1527, however, there were nine farms on the same land, at a combined rent of 131s. 7d. Eventually these subdivided and

fragmented holdings were no longer viable, and as the rural and agricultural population began to decline in the early nineteenth century the process was reversed. Thus in 1845 what had been Sykes vaccary, and then became nine separate holdings, had been reduced to just five farms and today there is only one. Similarly Battris (Beatrix) vaccary, which in 1442 was a single farm, had, by 1498, been divided into two farms, by 1527 five, by 1539 seven and by 1664 eleven farms. Today, once more, there is just one Beatrix Farm.

There is evidence that in the medieval period some pre-Norman settlements in the Hodder valley were abandoned, either because of the impact of the forest or because of changing social and economic circumstances. For instance, east of Newton the township of Easington (SD 710508) appears in the Domesday Survey of 1086 as a small village. Today, however, there is only a single farm there, called Robinson's after the man who built it during the seventeenth century. Easington (the 'town at the edge of the wood') seems to have been populated until about 1379 but was then deserted, with its site marked now in the grassy fields by the outlines of buildings and old field boundaries from that time. Another abandoned settlement may lie by the Hodder close to Bashall Eaves (at SD 683426), where terrace-like lynchets, some ridge-and-furrow strips and old field boundaries can be picked out. The rest is long gone.

In the fourteenth century Easington seems to have been a thriving village, but it was abandoned in about 1379. Today there is a farm and a few cottages.

Henry VII ordered a survey to be made of his estates in Bowland, as a consequence of which, in 1507, he repealed several forest laws, thus making life easier for those trying to eke out a living in the forest. For instance, they could now freely gather timber for fuel or for building, and they could scare away deer that were eating their crops. Another survey was carried out in January 1556 by Sir Thomas Talbot, Thomas Catterall and John Braddyll, on command of Queen Mary I, 'to view the state of the woods and underwoods there and of the game and "deare", what kind of wood and underwood there is, the state of the "pale" [fence] about the said park, what store of trees and timber there is in the park for the continual maintenance of the "pale," etc., etc.'[10]

During his brief reign (1547–53) Mary's predecessor Edward VI had already 'disparked' Leagram. The 1548 Duchy Court records relate how Sir Arthur Darcye, let the herbage, or grazing, in Bowland to Richard Grenakers, and in the following year Rauf Grenacres and Thomas Cattrall were summoned to attend the court over the occupation and profits they had made from eight Bowland farms.[11] The duchy records tell us that the three investigators in 1556 found Leagram to be almost devoid of trees (there were about 30 old oaks near Leagram Lodge and 30 more scattered about the park), and the fences in a state of 'underfull and great decaye'. As for the deer, 'there ys non at all' in Leagram Park. There was insufficient wood in Bowland to provide new fences for Leagram and, if any were used to repair the deer park, then those who had built farms and corn mills, and the queen's manors and lodges in and around the forest would not have enough reserves of timber for their repairs to be carried out. The survey also revealed that, whilst there were parcels of arable and pasture, much was overgrown by carr or wet scrub ('carrishe ground'), bog ('evill mossyd grownde'), a mixture of carr and bog ('carre and marraysshe') or wet heather moor ('heth and mossyd ground'). In Leagram Park there was a 'deppe and wete carre', overgrown with scrub including holly ('hollins') and hazel ('hassilles').

The Hark to Bounty Inn, Slaidburn, was a court as long ago as the thirteenth century. The curious name comes from a foxhound called Bounty that was barking outside the inn. 'Hark to Bounty!' said someone, and the name stuck.

The Crown began to sell off small parcels of land. Yet much of Bowland was still 'waste' of bog, woodland, scrub and open moorland and it was not until Elizabeth I and James I positively encouraged the conversion of this waste into productive farmland that Bowland began to look something like the landscape we see today.[12] For instance, in 1621 James set up a committee to divide up 3,100 hectares of land to be cleared in the years 1622–30. Besides increasing the area of farmland, this marked the beginning of extensive enclosure in Bowland as hedgerows were planted and stone walls built to keep livestock in and predators out. Altogether in the period 1560–1630 approximately one-third of Bowland was reclaimed from forest into farmland, and in the period 1527–1662 the population of western Bowland (that is, the area which was always within Lancashire) more than doubled as people settled the land as farmers.

Some 'new' land was awarded to villages. Slaidburn is one of the oldest villages in the valley. The name was originally that of the stream which is now called Croasdale Beck, and from its early forms (such as *Slateborne* and *Slaytburn*, both recorded in the thirteenth and fourteenth centuries) it is clear that it means 'stream by the sheep-pasture'. It has had a parish church since at least the eleventh century and, from the middle of the thirteenth century, what is now the Hark to Bounty Inn was the ward court (the last courtroom can still be seen in the inn). In 1507 the parish of Slaidburn had only 56 households, but by 1664 this had increased to 98. By contrast the nearby village of Newton (the 'new settlement') was founded by nonconformist farmers in an area of enclosure of former forest lands. Following the Act of Toleration of 1689, the dissenting community opened their independent chapel there in 1696.

Other land was granted to individuals. In the fourteenth century Peter de Alancotes was a park-keeper in Bowland but on promotion to the post of 'bowbearer' he changed the family name to Parker. When Henry VII began to relax the forest law in 1507 the family built the first Browsholme Hall from timber and wattle-and-daub. In 1604 Thomas Parker, who had purchased the Browsholme vaccary from James I, began the construction of the present magnificent Browsholme Hall (the grand gateway was completed in 1682). As well as some stained glass which, it is claimed, was taken from Whalley Abbey after the Dissolution, the Hall has some items recalling the days of the old forest. The most interesting, perhaps, is a gauge. When Bowland was a deer forest it was illegal for people living there to have a dog large enough to hunt deer. So a suspect dog was stood in the gauge and, if it was too tall it was either killed or its legs broken so that it could not chase the deer.

The farms called Lees, a mile south-west of Browsholme, are particularly interesting. In 1464 there was a Legh or Leghes Farm within the duchy forest and by 1567 it was known as Lees Farm. It became Higher Lees (SD 664448)

Mason's Farm is typically late sixteenth or early seventeenth century, though if you look carefully you can see more recent extensions. Many of these lovely old farmhouses were demolished and new ones built early in the twentieth century

when, following further clearances, another house, Lower Lees was built (at SD 654443) in 1596. By 1652 enough woodland had been felled for the area to support a third farm, Middle Lees (SD 661444). Many farms in the Hodder valley date from this late sixteenth- and seventeenth-century era of forest clearance, and while some are named after those who built the farm (for instance, Marsden's, Mason's and Proctor's), many hark back to their origins. Buckthorn was perhaps an area of scrub frequented by deer. The name of

Cow Ark has its roots going back to Norse settlements of a thousand years ago. The name should be 'cow erg': a summer pasture for cows.

Chipping has roots going back about 1200 years, its name signifying that it was a market ('chepyn') in Anglo-Saxon times. The oldest buildings today date from forest clearance in the late sixteenth century on.

Buckstall farm relates to a type of deer trap, a 'buck stall' which was a large strong net for catching the beasts. Buckden Farm was built on a known haunt of deer. Cow Hey and Horse Hey were both clearings (*hey*) which provided grazing. Higher Woodhouse Farm was built where today there is no wood, and linked to Slaidburn by Woodhouse Lane. The name of Cow Ark, a farm close to Browsholme, possibly includes the Old Norse *erg*, meaning a shieling or summer pasture. Another curious name in the valley is Armrydding, which translates as 'a hut in a clearing surrounded by forest'. Aigden Farm was built in a valley (*dene*) with lots of oaks (*aig*). Nearby Sandalholme is built on top of the bluff overlooking the river, and means a sandy water-meadow. Boarsden was where the wild boar hid, whereas Swinglehurst was a wood with swine; both have roots going back to when wild boar roamed Bowland. Of villages in Bowland, the Old English name of Bashall Eaves most closely describes its position in the forest: *beac*: back, *scelf* = of a shelf (overlooking the Hodder), *efes* = in the eaves or edge of the forest. Some Hodder farms predate the Normans, with names that indicate Norse roots. One is Dunnow Hall, between Slaidburn and Newton, that was built on Bathar's Byre, a tenth-century Norse farm. Today this old name is still in use as the name of a solitary barn, Battersby's Barn.

Not all clearance of waste and setting up of farmsteads was done in an organised manner. Henry VII's relaxation of forest law in 1507 encouraged impoverished families to practise 'encroachment'. They would move into an area that was still wild forest, build a crude hovel in which they would live, and clear an area around where they might grow a crop of oats and beans and graze a few pigs or goats. Before 1507, when an agent of the Crown discovered such a family, they would be expelled and their possessions confiscated. After 1507 they would merely be fined and, once the fine had been paid, they could keep the land as 'copyholders' for a fair rent. Encroachment, and thereby forest clearance, was thus encouraged. Between 1522 and 1624 court rolls list about 250 cases of encroachment in Bowland, with a peak of 76 in 1577.

Some existing farmers, wishing to increase their legally held farms and happy to pay the initial fine and new rent, also encroached onto wasteland. For example the Swinglehurst family, who first appear in the records as farming half of the Burholme vaccary in 1498, made encroachments at Newton and Slaidburn for which they were fined in 1583. They sub-let the encroachments so that tenants would pay the rent to the Crown, but by 1592 they were farming the land themselves.

In most communities there were extensive areas of common pasture and grazing land beyond the perimeter of the enclosed farms. On the higher ground the common pastures and moors of different communities would adjoin, the boundaries being indicated by boundary stones or by natural features such as streams or moorland ridges. A tenant was permitted to put out onto the common grazing in summer the number of livestock that could be

Doeford Bridge, photographed in 1907: a bridge built over a ford used by roe deer. Winter.

Many seventeenth-century farmhouses were built attached to barn, shippon (byre) and other buildings. Less masonry was needed (end walls were shared), and the lagging of barn against farmhouse provided some insulation in the long Bowland winter. Such farmsteads are sometimes called Laith or Laithe, an ancient name for a barn.

supported on the farm during the winter. A tenant could also gather stone for walling, heather for thatching and peat for burning from the open moor of the village. However, as the number of small farms grew and villages expanded, there was a demand to extend individual holdings onto the common lands. For instance vaccaries had been split up into farms that could barely support those who lived on them, yet the sons born there also wanted their own farms. So, for example, in 1586 the villagers of Grindleton petitioned the Duchy of Lancaster to permit 'some reasonable part and portion of the best and most fruitful part of the said commons might be enclosed and fenced in and in some reasonable manner apportioned and divided amongst freeholders and copyholders'. By 1630 many areas of Bowland common were thus enclosed around Slaidburn, Newton, Bashall, Waddington, Grindleton, West Bradford and Champion. The same pattern of forest clearance and the development of farmsteads occurred elsewhere in Lancashire and Yorkshire, wherever deer forests were abandoned as places to hunt.

The final stage of forest, scrub and 'waste' clearance came with the Enclosure Acts, which were mostly imposed here in the early nineteenth century. They removed all rights of common grazing and ensured that the land was controlled by individual farmers who could afford to enclose according to law and who would farm the land profitably. Those who could not afford

Bowland in winter from Burholme Bridge.

Looking downstream from Doeford Bridge in summer. The Roman ford across the Hodder (page 86) was just downstream of the distant bend in the river.

'Cromwell's' Bridge. It seems impossible that his entire force of 8,000 could all have crossed this bridge on their way to the Battle of Preston. Most surely would have forded the shallow river.

Hodder means 'beautiful river', an apt name even in the middle of winter.

to enclose lost their land. Despite the earlier phases of enclosure, a significant extent of common remained to be tackled. For instance, when the Enclosure Act for Chipping and Thornley was passed in 1840, 533 hectares out of 3,585 hectares in the two townships were still open, common land. In the Hodder valley, much land is still owned by large estates which rent out their farms to tenants (the Duchy of Lancaster remains the largest landowner). Some of the farmhouses are the original buildings and date from the sixteenth and seventeenth centuries. Others retain some parts of the original farmhouse, but many have new farmhouses built, often early in the twentieth century, on the site of the earlier one.

As for the deer forest, as farms increasingly took over the open forest, cleared trees and scrub and constructed deer-proof fences, deer numbers fell sharply. The January 1556 survey of Leagram Park reported that 'there are no deer abiding or bred within the said park and there has not been any for many years past'.[13] In 1570 the Whitewell court heard that 273 deer had died from starvation the previous winter and in 1596 it was estimated that only about 800 red and fallow deer survived. By 1652 only about 20 deer were reported in the remaining forest, though some must have been overlooked. The last red deer was killed in Bowland in 1805.

Despite the clearance of the forest and the farming of the valley, the Hodder valley has the appearance of being relatively unspoilt. One reason for this is that the moors around the valley are well-managed grouse moors and provide a wild backdrop to the scene. Another reason is that there is no significant industry, so the valley is green, with limestone drystone walls and buildings. A third reason is that the river from Burholme Bridge above Whitewell down to the confluence with the Ribble flows through a steep-sided limestone and shale gorge that is heavily wooded, mostly with deciduous trees. In winter the scene is of stark silhouettes of trees and branches. In spring the scene is dominated by bluebells and the lime-green of opening buds. In summer there is cool olive-green. And in autumn drab green turns to golds, and yellows and reds and the sky can be full of falling leaves.

Because of the nature of the river there are few bridges. Burholm Bridge crosses the Hodder downstream from its confluence with Langden Beck and upstream of the start of the deep gorge. Doeford Bridge crosses in a gap in the gorge just below the Hodder's confluence with the river Loud, a small silty stream that flows from marshy pastures around Chipping. Then there is Higher Hodder Bridge (which still has iron rings in its stone parapet to which your horse can be tethered while you gaze over the bridge to spot a salmon). Downstream is Lower Hodder Bridge, built by Macadam in 1826, which is only a few metres upstream of the Old Lower Hodder Bridge, popularly known as Cromwell's Bridge. This is a superb and graceful packhorse bridge, one of the finest in northern England, which replaced an earlier wooden one which had been swept away in a flood. It was completed in 1562 by Sir Richard Sherburn at a cost of £70. Its popular name of Cromwell's Bridge derives from the occasion on 16 August 1648 when a parliamentarian army of about 8,000 men crossed the river here before going on to defeat the Duke of Hamilton and royalist troops at the battle of Preston the following day.

Wildlife around the lower Hodder

FARMLAND

We have seen how the farmland here was won from what was then called 'forest, moss, mire, moor and waste' mainly during the sixteenth and seventeenth centuries, and all was enclosed by the early decades of the nineteenth century. It would, however, be wrong to conclude that the pastures and meadows that we see today in and around Bowland are as they were in former times. Few are. Almost all, for example, have been drained; many have been sprayed with herbicides. Even today some farmers spray the smallest patches of nettles simply because the nettles are there and without appreciating that the humble nettle is an important wildlife niche, harbouring insects such as the small tortoiseshell butterfly and the seven-spot ladybird (*Coccinella 7-punctata*). Only two days before these words were written a farmer in the valley was spraying a clump of jack-by-the-hedge (*Alliaia petiolata*), probably because he had a few minutes to spare. Jack-by-the-hedge does no harm and is an important food plant of the orange tip (*Anthocaris cardamines*), one of the most beautiful butterflies in the valley. Even worse from the wildlife point of view is the ploughing up of semi-natural grasslands and replacing them with 'more productive' strains of rye grass. Such fields may be green, and raise fat lambs and produce fat-rich milk and cream. Otherwise, they are dead.

There are a few records of the plants which ought to flourish in a Hodder valley meadow. For instance, referring to this area, the nineteenth-century notes of J. F. Pickard state that 'most of the moist meadows yield Primula farinose [birdseye primrose], Valeriana dioica [marsh valerian], Pinguicula [butterwort], Triglochin [arrow-grass], Habenaria conopsea [fragrant orchid, now in the genus *Gymnadenia*], Sagina nodosa [knotted pearlwort], Pedicularis sylvatica [lousewort] and Equisetum sylvaticum [wood horsetail].'[14] Today there are a few, very few, small corners that drainage, herbicides and the plough have not reached that can remind us of what the rest was like before the government sought to improve food production in the 1940s or the European Union Common Agricultural Policy was imposed in the 1970s. Contrast the following with what we have today.

The orange tip butterfly was rare in the Ribble catchment 50 years ago, but it is now a common sight in late April and May.

Lady's smock is a common flower in meadows that have not been sprayed or ploughed. It is not as common as it was.

Besides those species noted by Pickard, and a wide range of grass species, including timothy, crested dogstail, common bent, soft brome (*Bromus hordaceus*) and yellow oat-grass (*Trisetum flavescens*), the following were also found in ancient Hodder meadows well into the 1970s[15]: red and white clover, meadow vetchling (*Lathyrus pratense*), dandelion (*Taraxacum officinale*), several species of buttercup including meadow buttercup and creeping buttercup (*R. repens*), daisy (*Bellis perennis*), ox-eye daisy (*Leucanthemum vulgare*), lady's bedstraw (*Calium verum*), field mouse-ear (*Cerastium arvense*), water avens (*Geum rivale*), lady's smock (*Cardamine pratensis*), great burnet (*Sanguisorba officinale*), ragged robin, cowslip (*Primula veris*), hardheads (*Centaurea nigra*), curled dock (*Rumex crispus*) and early marsh and spotted orchids.

Lose the flowers and you lose the insects that feed on the flowers. In the 1950s and 1960s meadows were alive with the buzzing of bees and flies, and night-flying moths fluttered away with flashes of orange and yellow hind wings as one waded through the knee-high mixture of grasses and herbs found in every Hodder meadow. Today the meadows are mostly silent of insects buzzing, and disturbed moths are rare sights.

The wildlife problem with the meadows is not only one of grass monoculture, or fewer plant species growing there. There has been a major change in which the meadows are managed. Up to the early 1960s the fields may have been limed, they may have had manure spread on them, and in early spring they may have been rolled. They were then left, from April to late June or July, giving birds such as the lapwing, yellow wagtail and skylark plenty of time to raise a brood. The meadows were mown in early summer (this coincided on a farm where I gave a hand with the start of the school summer holidays in the second week of July) and the hay crop dried in the sun and was then carted to the barn. Today the meadows receive a large dose of inorganic fertiliser in March or early April and the first crop of silage is taken about the second or third week in May, just in time to crush eggs in nests or mangle growing chicks which cannot fly away. The consequence is that we have lost not only plant diversity, but also many breeding birds. One, the yellow wagtail, is now extinct here (see also page 108).

Yet it is not only in the grassy fields that a decline in wildlife has been noted. In the lower Hodder valley, enclosure was achieved mainly by planting hedges, mostly of hawthorn and blackthorn, but also including other shrubs such as holly (*Ilex aquifolium*) and elder. Such hedgerows, which can harbour a great community of animals, require maintenance: layering to prevent them becoming 'leggy' and develop holes through which stock can escape, and clipping so that the hedge has a good and dense shape. This is labour-intensive. Today flails fitted to tractors are used to control hedges and, as gaps appear or the hedge dies, barbed wire replaces hedge. The consequence is clear: the animal life of the hedgerows slowly disappears.

Very few animals have not suffered from the decline of the grasslands. One which has survived and flourished is the brown hare (*Lepus capensis*), a very common species in the lower Hodder valley. In March 2002, 17 mad hares cavorted in one monoculture meadow.

WOODLAND

In contrast to the farmland, the quantity and quality of woodland in the Hodder Valley have never been better since, perhaps, Norman times. Besides the conifer plantations above Stocks (page 128), in the Dunsop valley and on Longridge Fell, broad-leaved woodlands have been encouraged to grow on the steeper banks of the river and alongside streams flowing down to the river. There are two main reasons for the latter. The first is that the woodland cover slows down soil erosion on the steep slopes. The second is that the Hodder valley is prime pheasant-shooting country, and the birds fly high and fast over the guns from the wooded slopes.

The broad-leaved woodlands are not natural. They were planted or have regenerated following earlier planting. The Worsley-Taylor family records from Bashall Eaves, for instance, include the planting of over one million trees on their estate in the early 1800s.[16] We can see this from the high proportion of non-native tree species among the native oaks, beech and ash in the woodlands. The sycamore, a native of central Europe and probably introduced to Britain by the Romans, is abundant and may have been specially planted close to farmsteads as a fuel, for it grows very rapidly and burns readily when green. In Lancashire it was also traditionally used, from the seventeenth century onwards, to create shelter belts around farmsteads in more exposed places. Horse chestnuts (*Aesculus hippocastaneum*) occur naturally nowhere nearer than the Greek mountains, and were introduced for their beauty. The copper beech does not grow from seed; instead a bud of the copper 'sport' must be grafted onto a root of the native beech. Several fine specimens of copper beech can be seen in the valley. So too can a few turkey oaks (*Quercus cerris*), a species introduced from southern Europe in the eighteenth century. Understoreys are dominated by seedlings and saplings, hazel and holly. Ivy (*Hedera helix*) grows up many tree trunks, which also support thick growths of mosses, lichens and ferns such as the polypody (*Polypodium vulgaris*).

In general the woodland floor is devoid of vegetation other than grasses and sedges except for springtime when, for a few weeks before the leaf canopy reduces the amount of light, several flowers complete their annual cycle. Clumps of snowdrops (*Galanthus nivalis*) are the first to appear in February. They are followed by dog's mercury (*Mercurialis perennis*), primrose and wood anemone from March onwards. Then from April to June the woodland floor is carpeted in places with bluebells, in others wood sorrel, or lesser celandine or wild garlic that gives the still air a heavy garlicky perfume. Where the sun strikes the ground there may be dog-violets and in shaded corners cuckoopint. By late June their blooms are faded and seeds set for yet another year.

The woodlands harbour roe and sika deer (see page 121), fox and badger, rabbits (*Oryctolagus cuniculus*), wood mice, bank voles, common shrews, stoats and weasels. Some Hodder stoats turn ermine-white in winter, and resemble paper bags being blown by the wind as they bound across the snowless country. During the 1950s red squirrels were common, but they are gone. The now ubiquitous American grey squirrel has ousted them. The woodlands are also home to bats including Daubenton's, which can often be seen before dusk hunting along the edge of the wood, the noctule, a large bat that can sometimes be seen flying high over woodlands at dusk, and the almost strictly nocturnal pipistrelle and brown long-eared bat. However, the most frequently seen bat in the valley is probably the Natterer's (*Myotis nattereri*), for this sometimes emerges as early as mid-afternoon to feed on flies over the river.

Forty-seven species of bird have been recorded nesting, in recent years, in woodlands in the Hodder valley. Goshawks are the rarest, having bred here only since the 1990s. Watching goshawks displaying in early spring or hunting woodpigeons is exciting. But it is equally thrilling to watch male woodcock

A mayfly rests on a Hodder bluebell. A spring sight. The Hodder has a rich population of mayflies and stoneflies.

Redstarts nest throughout the Hodder woodlands.

roding on a warm early summer evening, for they are secretive birds and not often seen at other times of the year. This is one of the few areas in northern England where all three species of woodpeckers can be seen in one day – great spotted (*Dendrocopos major*), lesser spotted (*D. minor*) and green (*Picus viridis*) – though the lesser spotted is difficult to spot! There are five species of warblers. The blackcap (*Sylvia atricapilla*) and garden warbler (*S. borin*) occur where there are lots of bramble, hawthorn and other shrubs, usually in a glade or at the edge of the wood. Willow warblers (*Phylloscopus trochilus*) are also woodland edge and scrub birds, whereas the chiffchaff (*P. collybita*) occurs in taller trees and the scarcer and decreasing wood warbler occurs in the tallest trees and seems to prefer pure oak and beech stands. The pied flycatcher and redstart (*Phoenicurus phoenicurus*) are summer visitors and nest in holes in trees. Both occur in the valley using natural holes (fortunately the Hodder woodlands are not heavily manicured so that crevices in timber are common) and nest-boxes put up to attract them. They compete for holes with the resident tits, one of which – the marsh tit – is a scarce species through much of Britain and decreasing here in Lancashire. Treecreepers are common. So too is the nuthatch which colonised the Ribble and Hodder and Calder valleys during the 1970s (it first bred at Padiham in 1973) from Airedale to the east.

The River Hodder and its tributaries

The Hodder below Stocks dam has a flow which is reduced by the reservoir. Today a legal minimum 'compensation' of 15 million litres per day flows from the dam. This is – or should be – quickly swollen by inflowing tributaries. Croasdale Brook enters the river at Slaidburn, and the river Dunsop (which is itself formed by the confluence of the rivers Brennand and Whitendale) and Langden Beck join the Hodder at Dunsop Bridge. They drain about 80 square kilometres of Bowland's heather moors immediately west of the source of the Hodder itself. The only other major tributary is the Loud, a slow lowland

This is 'compensation water' being released from the bottom of Stocks dam. It is vital for the river below the dam, for in long droughts it is the river's main source of water, the other tributaries being over abstracted to the point of running almost dry.

The Brennand and Whitendale both have crystal clear water. Perfect for the water industry!

stream that rises from springs in the boulder clay farmland around the village of Chipping and enters the Hodder close to Doeford Bridge.

H. B. Rogers noted that, '... for more than a century, few streams in east and central Lancashire have contained soft water, except in their moorland courses; their lower reaches have long been better than industrial sewers, and a great hardness is the inevitable consequence of pollution.'[17]

It is not surprising, therefore, that the industrial towns south and west of the Ribble have looked to the crystal clear Hodder and its tributaries (the Loud excepted, for it carries a lot of red clay in suspension after heavy rain) as a source of water. Under the Blackburn Water Act of 1885, water intakes were built on the Brennand and Whitendale. Today, United Utilities (formerly North West Water) are licensed to abstract a maximum of 45 million litres per day from these sources, and during low water conditions both streams and the river Dunsop, which is formed by their confluence, run dry or almost so, with just a few shallow pools remaining. Further intakes were also constructed subsequently on Langden Beck and its two tributaries, Losterdale and Hareden Becks. From these an average 11.7 million litres per day is abstracted, and these becks also run almost dry in summer. Thus the main river has a flow that is much less than it was before the beginning of abstraction; my own estimate is that the annual flow is down by 78 per cent on what it was before Stocks reservoir and abstraction points on the tributaries were built. Thus, in times of drought, large areas of shingle, which ought to be habitat for fish and aquatic invertebrates, are exposed.

United Utilities are unable to take their licence quota from Brennand and Whitendale during dry summer weather, and average only 30 million litres instead of 45 million litres per day. The company had planned (in 2004) to build another abstraction point on the main river from which they could have taken their full quota. They would then have closed the intakes on the two tributaries in periods of drought, so that the Brennand and the Whitendale would always have had some flow. In 2004, however, the government body Ofwat declared that the scheme was too expensive, so the existing intakes must continue in full-time use and in future summer droughts the headwater streams will almost be dry shingle. What is particularly galling is that a significant percentage of the abstracted water is lost from leaks in the pipework carrying the water away, and that a high percentage of the water that reaches the consumer is used for flushing lavatories, cleaning cars and watering grass!

The village of Dunsop Bridge developed, following the abandonment of the deer forest, as a centre for tree forestry and as the hub of the Duchy of Lancaster estate.

The Hodder is a major game-fishing river, especially for salmon, sea trout and grayling.

ABOVE
A sea trout caught in a short summer night.

LEFT
A grayling taken from the icy flow in mid-winter.

Though some
hen salmon may
survive the rigours
of spawning and
make it back to
the sea, invariably
the cock fish die.
In January many
can be found dead,
washed up on the
frozen bank of the
river.

And if these streams had a constant flow? Then the streams would have thriving populations of dippers and kingfishers, salmon and sea trout.

If the Law of Best Practice were followed, all abstraction from the Hodder would take place at Hodderfoot, just above the confluence with the Ribble. United Utilities would benefit by taking its full quota, and the entire river and its wildlife would benefit from its natural flow. It would then be possible to take away the eyesores of abstraction points on the feeder streams, eyesores which should have no place in an area designated an Area of Outstanding Natural Beauty.

The lower Hodder has a large and diverse population of aquatic invertebrates, including 22 species of mayflies (Ephemeroptera), 23 species of stoneflies (Plectoptera) and about 60 species of caddisflies (Trichoptera). It also has thriving stocks of salmon, sea trout, grayling and several other fish species (see page 102). Such bare facts confirm that the water flowing downstream is of the highest quality.

Otters (*Lutra lutra*) disappeared from the valley in the 1960s, partly through pesticide pollution and partly because of persecution. At about the same time,

American mink (*Mustella vison*) arrived in the valley as a consequence of escapes and deliberate release from fur-farms. The otter returned to the Hodder in the late 1980s (I watched one at Bashall Eaves in 1985 and saw a family above Sandalholme in 1988) and in recent years the mink population appears to have declined (I have not seen one by the river since 1991).

Goosanders first bred in the Hodder valley in 1980 and about eight females nest here each spring. Oystercatchers arrived in the 1951 and, while a few pairs nest on shingle in the gorge downstream of Whitewell and below Stocks dam, the main centre of population is between Burholme Bridge and Dunsop Bridge with about ten pairs. Common sandpipers are much more numerous than they seem, for where there appears to be just one pair there may, in fact, be three or four pairs nesting close together. The Hodder population (excluding Stocks) is about 30 pairs. The river is one long chain of about 20 dipper territories, with one or two pairs on the tributaries. Grey wagtails have smaller territories and total about 32–35 pairs. In contrast kingfishers are missing from some stretches and the river usually holds about eight pairs (though following the extremely severe 1962–63 winter there was none).

Despite all the problems created by the twentieth century, the Hodder and its environs are still a most beautiful area, but this is a very fragile environment. We must ensure that it continues to be beautiful, and try to protect its future.

CHAPTER FOUR

The Calder, the Darwen and the Douglas

> There were eight watchers by the beacon on Pendle Hill, in
> Lancashire … Dreary was the prospect on all sides, black moor,
> bleak fell, straggling forest, intersected with sullen streams as black
> as ink, with here and there a small tarn, or moss-pool, with water of
> the same hue. These constituted the chief features of the scene. The
> whole district was barren and thinly populated.
>
> Harrison Ainsworth, *The Lancashire Witches* (1845)

Big Ribble is a dividing line on the map of north-west England. To the
north there is the open country of moorlands and sparsely populated dales
stretching away to the Scottish border. If you follow the ancient A6 road north
from Preston you will pass through fewer than a handful of sizeable towns
– Lancaster, Kendal, Penrith and Carlisle – before crossing the border.

By contrast, south of the Ribble far more the present-day landscape has
been shaped and moulded by industrialisation and the associated extensive
urban growth, and has been dramatically altered by more than 250 years of
intensive development. The built-up areas of small country market towns
have sprawled until they are now great commercial cities, and adjacent
towns have merged and coalesced so that, on the ground though not in the
perceptions of their inhabitants, they are hard to distinguish. Where does
Colne become Nelson, Nelson Brierfield, Brierfield Burnley, or Burnley
Padiham? From the air it is very hard to tell. Accrington and Oswaldtwistle
almost meet Blackburn, which, to the south, leads into Darwen with barely a
field separating them. The built-up area of Preston now crosses the Ribble and

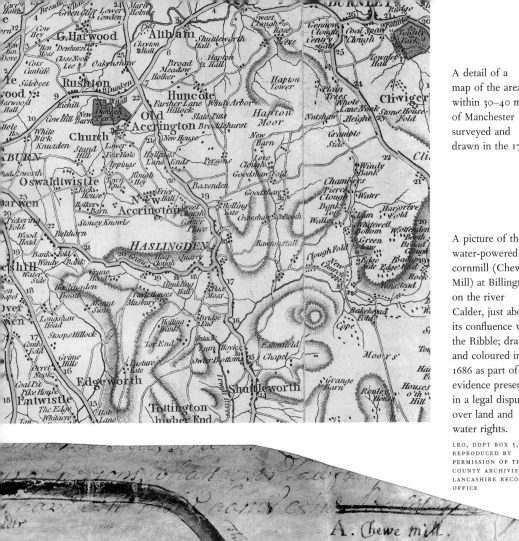

A detail of a map of the area within 30–40 miles of Manchester surveyed and drawn in the 1790s.

A picture of the water-powered cornmill (Chew Mill) at Billington on the river Calder, just above its confluence with the Ribble; drawn and coloured in 1686 as part of the evidence presented in a legal dispute over land and water rights.

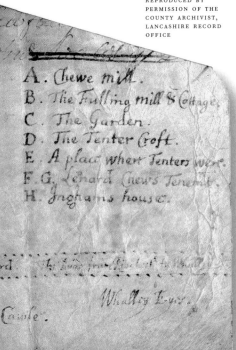

A. Chewe mill.
B. The Fulling mill & Cottage.
C. The Garden.
D. The Tenter Croft.
E. A place where Tenters were.
F. G. Lenard Chews Tenent.
H. Inghams house.

embraces Penwortham, Bamber Bridge and Walton-le-Dale, and it has almost reached Chorley and Leyland. From Chorley there are only a few patches of green before Adlington is reached, and that small town (it is hardly a village today) is a mere skip from the former railway town of Horwich where we leave the Ribble catchment. The urban sprawl continues, without a break, through Bolton, Farnworth and on into Manchester. Or, from Chorley, our urban journey might continue, with only a few fields interrupting, through Coppull to Standish and then to Wigan. South of Wigan we leave the Ribble catchment again, though the blanket of industry, shops, retail parks, terraced streets and estates of new 'executive homes' continues, linking St Helens, Haydock, Ashton-in-Makerfield and Leigh. Take a slight detour from these broad routes and you may come across countryside, but not for long. Here, south of the Ribble, the lower-lying land is mostly town with occasional patches of countryside, although once the hills are gained the open country is extensive and very distinctive in character.

This dividing line between the largely rural and the largely urban is most vividly seen on a cloudless night from the window of a plane flying from Glasgow to Manchester. On the first part of this short flight blackness, with small patches of light from villages or the string of lights along the M74/M6 motorway, is all you can discern as you cross the Southern Uplands and the Lake District. Then, as the Ribble is crossed and the plane begins its descent, the ground is illuminated by the jigsaw of towns, with only the occasional black patch signifying the uninhabited moorland tops. To stress the point, it is claimed that the two parts of the world which suffer most from light pollution at night are the Los Angeles area of California and the belt of northern England between the Ribble and the Mersey and extending east to the former woollen towns of the West Riding.

The main reason why the area north of the Ribble has been relatively unaffected by urbanisation is clear. The northern edge of the Lancashire coalfield extends from Trawden and Colne, through Barrowford and Padiham, to Rishton and Blackburn, before turning south-west towards Chorley. South of that line there is a lot of coal (though none is mined today), and very little to the north – just a few outliers in the Ingleton area and the lower Lune valley around Quernmore and Halton. The close and direct relationship between coal and the later phases of the industrial revolution, when steam power superseded water power, meant that the most conspicuous and pervasive effects of industrialisation took place in the lands south of the Ribble. There are plenty of examples of water-powered industries to the north, in areas such as Calder Vale, Chipping and Knowle Green, but once water power was eclipsed, the divergent destinies of the two halves of the Ribble catchment were inevitable. New towns, such as Nelson, emerged more or less from nothing; villages such as Oswaldtwistle and Brierfield grew into sizeable towns; and existing country market centres such as Blackburn and Burnley became industrial cities of global significance.

However, the importance of the Ribble as a boundary long predates the period of industrialisation. In the pre-Conquest period it formed the southern boundary of the lands which were directly controlled by the Anglo Saxon kingdom of Northumbria, although the Northumbrian kings exercised a loose authority over the lands south of the river as far as the Mersey. It was also the southern limit of major Scandinavian influence. This cultural and political division is reflected in, for example, place-names. North of the river the term 'fell', derived from the Old Norse, is very commonly used for a hill (for instance, Wolf Fell near Chipping and Birkett Fell above Slaidburn), but it does not occur south of the Ribble (Longridge Fell being the southernmost). Northwards from the Ribble a small stream is usually known as a 'beck', again from the Old Norse, but south of the river they are called 'brook' or 'water' or, occasionally, 'burn' (as in the dark-coloured stream which gave Blackburn its name). This is one of the most significant linguistic boundaries in Britain, and even today it is clearly reflected in the local dialects which long ago produced these place-name terms. The river was a dividing line in other senses. From the pre-Conquest period until 1541, when the diocese of Chester was created, it formed the boundary between the immense and sprawling diocese of Coventry and Lichfield to the south (extending as far as the edge of Banbury in Oxfordshire) and the no less huge diocese of York to the north (for Lancashire beyond the Ribble, and much of south Cumbria, came within the jurisdiction of the latter). Even after the creation of the new diocese of Chester in the reign of Henry VIII the largely self-governing archdeaconry of Richmond was north of the river, that of Chester to the south.

Culturally, politically, economically and visually, therefore, the Ribble is a boundary river. So we may contrast the Hodder – flowing from the north through an outstandingly beautiful landscape along its entire length – with the three tributaries described in this chapter – entering the Ribble from the south – where towns and industries and environmental damage have been a dominant theme. Nowhere on the course of the Hodder remotely resembles the town centres of Wigan (on the Douglas) or Burnley (on the Calder and Brun), or Ewood Park football ground (by which the Darwen flows) on a winter Saturday when Blackburn Rovers are playing Manchester United.

The Calder

> The grounde is baren for the moste part of wood and corne, as forest
> grounde ful of lynge, mores and mosses with stony hilles.
>
> J. Leland, Itinerary, 1535

Pendle dominates the view from much of the Ribble valley. From the estuary
at Lytham or Marshside its characteristic triangular form seems to brood over
Preston, even though Pendle and Preston are almost 30 kilometres apart.
Yet in terms of the Pennines as a whole, the altitude of Pendle (557 metres)
is not particularly high. It simply seems higher and more imposing than it
really is. In the early seventeenth century Michael Drayton considered, in
his *Polyolbion*, that:

> Majestic Pendle's hoary crest
> In grandeur soars above the rest.

And in 1786 Thomas Hurtley estimated Pendle's height at precisely 3,411 feet
(1,023 metres)![1] Yet the Celts and Angles who settled here knew that Pendle

Pendle Hill is a
focal point in the
Ribble catchment.

I discovered
this lovely
old packhorse
bridge quite by
accident when
going to watch
trout spawning
in a stream near
Downham. It is
not shown as such
on the Ordnance
Survey map. The
Ribble catchment
has many hidden
jewels.

was a hill and not a mountain. *Pen*, the first syllable, is the Celtic word for 'hill', and the second syllable comes from the Anglo-Saxon or Old English, *hyll* also meaning 'a hill'. So Pendle literally means 'hill-hill', and to add yet another Hill, as in Pendle Hill is doubly tautological!

Pendle seems much higher than it is because it is isolated from other upland areas. Steep slopes lead upwards for roughly one kilometre from a necklace of encircling lanes to a summit plateau of barely three square kilometres. Here there is some heather, and consequently a small red grouse population. There is also some wet, black, peaty blanket-bog, where a pair or two of golden plover nest in cotton-grass. There are merlins, and a diminishing population of the mountain linnet or twite (*Acanthis flavirostris*). Yet because of its small area and isolated situation Pendle lacks the wildlife importance of the Bowland fells around the Hodder or the limestone moors of Ribblehead. Its greatest interest is either as a vantage point from which to view the surrounding landscape or, for birdwatchers, to observe the trip of dotterel (*Eudromias morinellus*) that stop off here every spring to refuel on their migration from North Africa to the northern Highlands of Scotland or Scandinavia.

Like Bowland, Pendle was an area set aside as a hunting chase in the medieval period, and the Forest of Pendle extended over the hill itself and substantial tracts of the lower slopes and adjacent lowland margins. Early in the twelfth century the Forest of Pendle and its hunting rights belonged to the de Lacy family, Earls of Lincoln and Lords of the Honours of Clitheroe and Pontefract. Their estates also included the adjacent Forests of Trawden and Rossendale. Pendle was part of the huge parish of Whalley, the second largest in England after Halifax, though Burnley and Colne, then small market towns, had their own chapels which were subordinate to the parish church of Whalley.[2]

Within the Forest of Pendle in the thirteenth century the de Lacy family established two vaccaries, or commercial cattle farms, in each of the forest's six booths, or subdivisions (Reedley, Higham, Goldshaw, Barley-with-Wheatley, Roughlee and Barrowford) and had their deer fenced in launds around Pendle Water where there was excellent grazing. The village of Fence probably takes its name from this process of enclosure. The vaccaries were eventually subdivided into smaller farming units, as direct management of the estates gave way to sub-letting. The de Lacy estates eventually passed by marriage and inheritance to the duchy of Lancaster, and hence to the *de facto* possession of the Crown. When Henry VII had the chases in what was then known as Blackburnshire surveyed in 1507, each of the Pendle booths had up to thirteen separate farmsteads. The tenants of these farms were made copyholders, giving them the right to pass on the land that they farmed to their children, in return for the payment of an entry fine normally equivalent to one year's rent, every time a property passed to a new tenant. This had the advantage of making farming a more long-term prospect, and that was reinforced by the fact that rents did not rise significantly during the sixteenth century. At the beginning of the reign of James I in 1603 Pendle rents were almost identical to those that had been charged in 1507. James did not increase rents, but to compensate he required that the entry fine should be set at the equivalent to twelve years rent. The effect of the copyhold system and the inheritable tenancies was to allow ordinary tenants to accumulate greater wealth and rise to the ranks of yeomen and freeholders.

As was the case in the Ribble valley, the more prosperous farmers in Pendle increased their holdings by buying out the less prosperous, or they exchanged plots of land to make their holdings more compact. For instance, Ellis Nutter, who farmed at Reedley between Burnley and Barrowford, had land 'lying and being in Salterforth in the Countie of Yorke wich I have latly pourched of John Ellis of Coulne [Colne] Acourding to a diede or Indentuere bearing date the tenneth daie of Aprill in the yeare of our Lord God 1654 and being of the yearely Rente to the Lord of the Manor there of thiretie eyght shillings.'[3]

Other Pendle farmers increased their holdings by extending the area of cultivation into parcels of land reclaimed from the open moor. This process, which was extremely common throughout the Lancashire Pennines in the sixteenth and seventeenth centuries, was known as 'intacking', or 'taking in'.

For instance, in 1652 John Hargreaves of Higham enclosed two fields, one called the Great Intacke (Intake), the other the Little Intacke.[4] Such intakes (some are still so called on modern Ordnance Survey maps) were turned into reasonable farmland by liming, manuring and tilling. The process required the approval of the manorial lords and was actively encouraged by the Duchy of Lancaster, primarily because the income from rents for the newly enclosed lands greatly exceeded the financial returns available from the unenclosed waste. As the area of farmland in Pendle increased during the seventeenth century, the number of individual farms rose rapidly, although many of them were smallholdings of limited extent. Hunterholme had 3 farms in 1608, 13 in 1662. Goldshaw Booth had 15 farms in 1608; by 1662 there were 41. In 1608 there were 27 farms at Barrowford and 16 at Barley; by 1662 the numbers had risen to 48 and 27 respectively.[5]

Today the countryside of Pendle and the adjacent Forest of Trawden is dominated by sheep and cattle pasture. In the seventeenth century, however, cereals were widely grown, for then the farms were mixed arable/livestock. Oats predominated, with a little rye, for only a very few farms in ideal conditions were capable of growing a good crop of wheat (see also page 76). Some are still named from that attribute: Wheatley Lane at Barrowford, Higher Wheathead at the foot of Burn Moor, and Wheatley Farm near Gisburn. The grain produced was for local consumption and processed in mills in the area.

Pendle's real fame comes from its association with the Lancashire witches. Early in the seventeenth century most people were far more superstitious

Roughlee, once home to the so-called witch Alice Nutter, dates from the demise of the deer forests when land was cleared for agriculture.

than they are today and, encouraged by their new king James I, they vigorously pursued witch-hunts. In his book *Demonology* James insisted that, 'All persons involving any evil spirit, or concealing, covenanting with, entertaining, employing, feeding, or rewarding any evil spirit; or taking up dead bodies from their graves to be used in any witchcraft, sorcery, charm, or enchantment; or killing or otherwise hurting any person by such infernal acts, shall be guilty of felony without clergy, and suffer death.'

In 1612, twelve witches were taken from around Pendle to the autumn assizes at Lancaster. Among them was an old illiterate widow called Elizabeth Southernes, nicknamed Old Demdike. She had lived at Malkin Tower, a kilometre east of the hamlet of Blacko. Elizabeth Device was known as Young Demdike; she and her three children Alizon, Jennet and James were among the accused. The blind and about 80-year-old Ann Whittle was known as Mother Chattox; she was accused of murdering Robert Nutter and John Device, husband of Young Demdike, and of being capable of making butter from skimmed milk. Her daughter, Ann Redfern, was accused of aiding her in her witchcraft. Of all the witches Alice Nutter was the most unlikely, for she was wife of Richard, the wealthy owner of Roughlee, a grand house on the road between Barley and Barrowford. The Devices swore that she had attended a coven at Malkin Tower on Good Friday 1612, and later she was also

Wycoller is a Pennine hamlet frozen in time. The hall was built in 1595 and extended in the seventeenth century and is now a ruin. It is not far over the moors to Haworth, and it is thought that in *Jane Eyre* Charlotte Brontë based the mansion of Fearndean on this building.

Three ancient bridges have been built across Wycoller back, two of them strangely close to a very shallow ford in the centre of the hamlet. One is a packhorse bridge, the other a clapper bridge similar to others found in Dartmoor and, not too far away, over the Aire at Hanlith. There are arguments as to the ages of these bridges, but they are probably no older than the late sixteenth century, when the deer forests were opened up and Wycoller was built.

accused of bewitching and murdering one of the gaolers at Lancaster Castle. Old Demdike died after making a confession (probably from the effects of torture). The others were found guilty and executed.

Two local families were closely linked to the events surrounding the Lancashire witches and both built houses on the lower slopes of Pendle that stand today. Little Mearley Hall, on the western side of the hill and overlooking Clitheroe, was built by Christopher Nowell in 1557. Some of its windows were taken from the recently dissolved Sawley Abbey. The following year the Assheton family built Downham Hall in the centre of Downham, most beautiful of Pendle's villages. Some of the masonry also came from the ruined Sawley Abbey.

Most of the small valleys on the slopes of Pendle, and in the area south of Colne and Nelson, contain reservoirs. Unlike those in, for example, the Rivington area, or at Stocks, these are modest in size. They were built not by major water companies or the great municipal water undertakings, but were the local response to the lack of fresh clean drinking water in the separate industrial towns of the area during and after the second half of the seventeenth

century. Each of the towns had its own waterworks department, and each looked to its nearest suitable valley for reservoir sites. Money was limited, so no grand schemes were feasible, and there was no attempt at pooling resources to undertake larger projects. Thus, Pendle Water flows from the south side of Pendle summit to the two Ogden reservoirs and then on to the lovely village of Barley. Here, Barley Water, its flow reduced and controlled by the two Black Moss reservoirs, joins Pendle Water. Five kilometres downstream, Pendle Water passes into urban East Lancashire at Higherford before flowing through Barrowford, Nelson and Brierfield, beneath the M65 motorway bridge, and reaching Wood End sewage works. The largest reservoirs in the area, at Foulridge, Whitemoor and Higherford, were actually built not to supply drinking water but to maintain water levels on the summit reaches of the Leeds and Liverpool Canal (a large amount of water being required to replenish the level each time a lock was used). What would have been the most extensive reservoir was never built – on several occasions in the late nineteenth and early twentieth centuries Nelson Corporation proposed to construct a sizeable reservoir on the Wycoller Beck above Laneshaw Bridge. The scheme was eventually authorised, and the village of Wycoller was partly depopulated, but the work on the dam and reservoir was never undertaken. Wycoller became a semi-deserted community, declining into partial dereliction

The head of the Thursden valley with Boulsworth Hill (517 metres) beyond. Thursden Brook becomes the River Don, which flows into the River Brun close to Burnley (Brunley).

before restoration and rehabilitation produced the delightful oasis which we see today.

The Pennine moors that separate the Lancashire cotton towns of Burnley, Nelson and Colne from the Yorkshire woollen towns of Haworth, Keighley, Hebden Bridge and Todmorden are not very high. Ickornshaw Moor reaches 443 metres on Wolf Stones, Boulsworth Hill 517 metres and Black Hambledon 479 metres. These moors are quite unlike those of Ribblehead, Bowland or even Pendle, for they lack any outstanding features. They have long and comparatively flat summit plateaux, bleak expanses of smooth upland, covered with blanket bog. The wetter areas are white with the fruit-heads of cotton-grass in late spring, whereas in early autumn the drier slopes are purple with heather. These gritstone uplands covered with deep deposits of peat that in places are three metres deep are the northernmost outliers of the much better known Dark Peak that begins in Derbyshire. Walkers on the Pennine Way flounder at the beginning of their 400-kilometre trek across Kinder, Bleaklow (Old English: *bleak hlaw* or bleak hill), Black Hill and Blackstone Edge and finish this part of their journey along the watershed on Ickornshaw Moor before descending to the firm footing of the Ribble–Aire Gap and limestone country. By the time they reach Airedale the feet of Pennine Way walkers are ingrained with peat.

Cliviger and the upper Calder valley. The Long Causeway runs along the top of the distant ridge, now desecrated by wind turbines. It was used by the Romans (who dropped coins there) and is probably of Iron Age origin.

The Iron Age fort of Castercliffe was on the low flat mound in the centre distance.

Despite the inhospitable nature of the tops of the moors stretching northwards from Worsthorne to the east of Burnley through the Forest of Trawden, the better drained west-facing slopes attracted populations of Neolithic and Iron Age farmers since about 1500 BC. This area has yielded a greater concentration of remains and 'finds' (including many flints[6]) from these periods than any other in the Ribble catchment, with a stone circle, ring stones and an ancient track known as the Long Causeway on Worsthorne

Moor. The latter track, now a tarmac road, leads from Burnley on easy gradients high above Cliviger Gorge towards Hebden Bridge. It was certainly used by the Romans (whose coins have been found by the Causeway) and may be of Iron Age, if not earlier age.[7] A few kilometres away to the north is the Iron Age fort at Castercliffe, overlooking Nelson and Colne. The large numbers of flint tools and other finds (many are on display at Wycoller and local museums) suggest a small but thriving community lived there between 750 and 500 BC.[8]

Worsthorne was a village whose economy was based on handloom weaving. It was also a packhorse centre, being at the hub of several tracks, some of them modern roads. One leads across the Pennines to Hebden Bridge, another led, via the Long Causeway, to Todmorden, and a third, (now called the Brontë Way) eventually reached Ripon.

In spring and early summer these wet moors are nesting grounds of a special community of bird species. Meadow pipits are most abundant. Merlins feed on them and cuckoos lay their eggs in the pipits' nests and let them care for their young. Ring ouzels nest on the steeper heathery slopes, wheatears wherever there are rock outcrops or scattered boulders. The drier areas of moor have field voles, and short-eared owls feed on them. In years when the vole population is low the owls lay few eggs (only two or three) and may raise no young, whereas when the vole population is huge the owls may lay clutches of eight or more eggs and raise all the young that hatch. Lapwings, curlew, redshank and snipe all breed or used to breed here, mainly on the wet meadows and pastures leading down into the valleys. Redshanks are gone, snipe now rare, and even the curlew and lapwing appear to be in decline. On the grassy moor above Worsthorne in the 1950s and 1960s Burnley naturalist Ken Spencer and author of *The Lapwing in Britain* (1953) ringed

Hurstwood Hall was built, according to a carving over the door, in 1579 by Barnard and Agnes Townley. The infant River Brun, its water swallowed by Hurstwood and Cant Clough reservoirs, trickles by the back door.

large numbers of lapwing chicks; in 2005, he told me, there were none there. The new system of making an early cut of silage in May on these upland meadows has destroyed the nests and chicks of nesting ground birds and their populations have crashed. Some survive on the open peat moorland, where the vegetation is dominated by heather, crowberry, bilberry and cotton-grass, but the most characteristic waders of the wild moors are golden plover and dunlin. With the Black Peak, these moors are the most southerly significant

After forest clearances, there were several small farms on the lower slopes in the foreground. Now there is only the one, Dyneley Farm (see also Sykes Farm, page 126). Burnley is in the middle distance, with Pendle beyond.

breeding grounds of golden plover and dunlin in the world. The plaintive call
of the plover and purring trill of the dunlin are as evocative of these moors
as is the almost constant whistling of the wind. In winter these birds move
away to milder climes and only one species remains, the red grouse, which
is carefully protected for shooting.

Several streams drain westwards from these moors and pass through the
Forest of Trawden. The headwaters of the River Laneshaw are trapped
by Laneshaw reservoir, high on the Yorkshire border, and then join the
Wycoller Beck to become the Colne Water, which flows into Pendle Water
at Barrowford. Thursden Brook rises on Boulsworth Hill and, just before
reaching Burnley, becomes the river Don. The river Brun drains Worsthorne
Moor, but Hurstwood and Cant Clough reservoirs take most of its water. The
Don and the Brun join at Rowley Hall. The River Calder flows from Cliviger
Gorge in a north-westerly direction through the parkland of Towneley Hall
and on to Burnley town centre. Here it receives water from the Don and Brun,
and at Wood End Pendle Water joins the Calder. Now the Calder is a river
of some substance, though not the 'violent stream' that one interpretation of
the name's Celtic origin suggests, for 15 reservoirs have abstracted much of
its flow. In fact, much of the flow below Wood End originates in and around
towns, with the moorland water taken away, consumed by the townspeople

The Calder as
it flows beneath
Altham Bridge,
leaving industry
and the urban
environment in its
wake.

and industry, and later returned to the river after treatment. From Wood End the Calder passes on to Gawthorpe Hall and then Padiham. Close to Altham sewage works the Calder is joined by the Hyndburn, a stream that drains the barren moors above Oswaldtwistle and Accrington and then passes through the urban sprawl of Great Harwood and Clayton-le-Moors. About 10 kilometres downstream, and having flowed past the small town of Whalley, the Calder joins the Ribble about one kilometre below Hodderfoot.

All these rivers, therefore, have courses which are heavily urbanised and, particularly in the nineteenth century, became intensively industrialised. Their waters provided power for the first phase of industrial development,

The Calder
upstream of
Whalley. Portfield
Iron Age fort
was on top of the
wooded bluff in the
distance.

as waterwheels drove machinery in early mills and factories, and the rivers
also provided the water supply for dyeworks, tanneries and other water-
based processes. The inevitable consequence was disastrously high levels of
pollution, so by 1914 the Calder, the Hyndburn and other rivers in this part
of the catchment were among the most polluted watercourses in the world.
The effluent from a myriad industrial concerns was poured untreated into
the waterways, and the sewage from tens of thousands of homes flowed in
to produce a noxious stream of filth. No wonder the municipal authorities
had to look high on the moors and remote valleys for pure drinking water
catchments. At the same time, as towns grew along the banks and factories

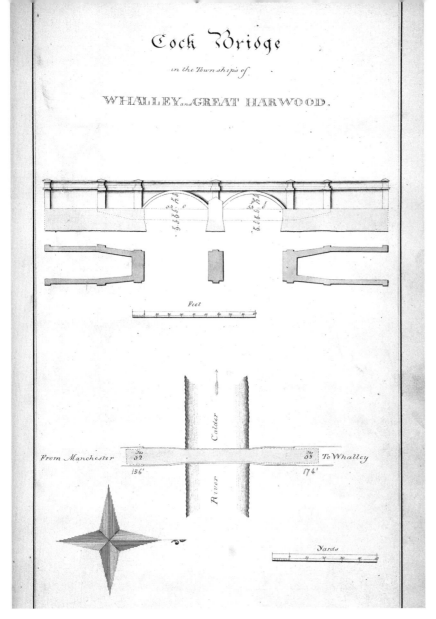

Cock Bridge

in the Townships of

WHALLEY and GREAT HARWOOD,

Cock Bridge carries the road between Whalley and Great Harwood over the Calder. It was widened in 1921 to accommodate the increasing number of infernal, internal combustion engines!

were built on the water's edge, the rivers and streams themselves began to disappear from view. Their prime location in the middle of urban areas meant that the space they occupied could be better used, while because of their filthy and disgusting condition 'out of sight, out of mind' was a widespread if rarely expressed maxim. Sections of, for example, the Calder and Brun in Burnley, or the Blackwater in the middle of Blackburn, were culverted and forced to run in dark foetid tunnels, while elsewhere the tall walls of mills and factories pressing along the bank created a canyon-like landscape, in which the dirty waters flowed sluggishly and almost invisibly in a dark slot. To take just one example among many, in 1895 a one-mile stretch of the Hyndburn, where it flowed through central Accrington, was lined with nine cotton mills, three timber yards, a brass foundry, cornmill, gasworks, dyeworks, tallow works, sawmill and six other industrial premises, while 300 yards of the river had been concealed in a culvert beneath the market hall. Such watercourses could be forgotten about, until they spectacularly revealed their presence – torrential rains on the high summits and bleak moors would inevitably be followed by these rivers bursting out of their prison-like confines and pouring filthy water through the streets, as though in protest. In February 1907, for example, the Blackwater flowed six feet deep through the streets of central Blackburn.

The problem was that urbanisation and industrialisation in the belt of Lancashire running from Darwen and Blackburn north-eastwards through Great Harwood and Accrington, then on to Burnley and Padiham and terminating at Nelson and Colne took place very quickly. Well into the eighteenth century places such as Blackburn, Accrington, Burnley and Colne were villages with small populations. One estimate put the population of Burnley as no more than 2,000 in 1790 and of Blackburn 8,000 in 1783.[9] Nelson did not even exist as a place in the eighteenth century, for it gained its name in Victorian times when the villages of Little Marsden, Great Marsden and Barrowford had spread and covered the countryside in between.

Like many rivers to the south of the Ribble, the Darwen has changed much over the last two hundred years … The large arch supports the Ewood aqueduct of the Leeds and Liverpool (built 1813–16); at this time the arch was almost circular. A century later the road was built through the centre of the arch and the poor river Darwen (right at the bottom) was culverted and hemmed in by banks of concrete.

The start of the ten-year national censuses in 1801 coincided with the tremendous growth of population, so that we can see its scale and rate. In 1801 Burnley had a population of only 5,200, by 1891 58,751 and by 1921 103,186. In 1801 the villages that became Nelson had a population of 5,529; ninety years later the town had 22,700 inhabitants. In 1801 there were about 3,500 people living in Darwen; by 1901 the population was 38,000. From a village housing about 2,000 in 1801, Accrington's population peaked at 44,975 in 1921. In the 1801 census, 11,980 people were registered as living in Blackburn; by 1891 Blackburn's population had increased ten-fold to 120,064 and the town had gained the reputation of being the cotton weaving capital of the world.

A close inspection of this detail of the 1893 Ordnance Survey map of the centre of Blackburn reveals just a tiny stretch of the river Blackwater (centre left) visible above ground. Industrialisation on an epic scale.

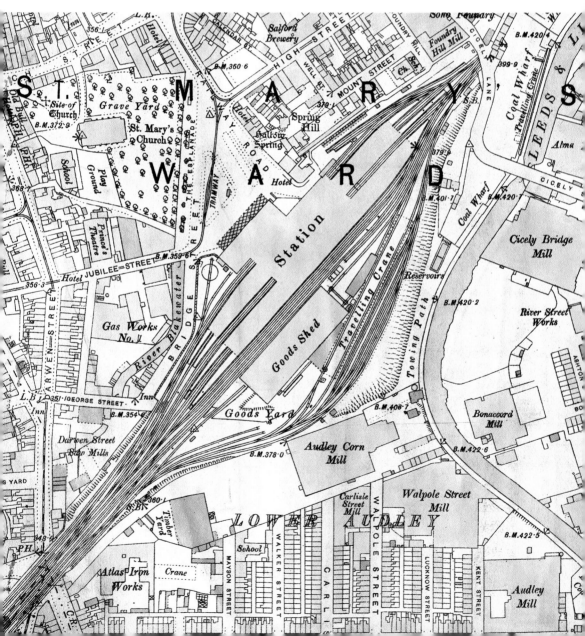

Crosses in Whalley churchyard are from the late ninth or early tenth century, indicating that a Christian place of worship was here long before the Normans began to build the present church.

Little wonder, therefore, that in this belt of Lancashire the urgency to build polluting mills and high densities of terraced houses outstripped the development of means to treat foul effluents. The consequence was that the Calder became one of the most polluted rivers in the British Isles. Yet head downstream below Padiham and Altham the river still flowed through a delightfully green valley, with pasture and woodland on every hand. Well into the second half of the twentieth century the casual watcher of the river from the bridge in Whalley would never have suspected that the flow could be so noxious that it killed fish and other clean-water wildlife far below its confluence with the Ribble.

Whalley is an ancient place in a strategically important position close to the confluences of the Ribble with the Calder and the Hodder.[10] Just outside the town, on a bluff overlooking the Calder and close to the Whalley–Padiham road, are the earth ramparts of Portfield, an Iron Age hillfort dating from the first millennium BC, and there have been numerous Roman finds in the vicinity of the town. Whalley became a centre of importance in the early Anglo Saxon period, and it is popularly claimed that the church was founded

2

in 627 by St Paulinus, when he visited north-west England on a mission to convert the heathens. The place appears in the *Anglo Saxon Chronicle* of 798 as Hwaelleage, from *waelle*, a stream, and *leah*, a meadow. Although the fabric of the church is medieval, the churchyard includes the magnificent Whalley crosses, two tall carved stone pillars which show combinations of Christian and Viking symbolism and are believed to date from the late ninth or early tenth centuries. They are some of the finest pre-Conquest sculpture to be seen *in situ* anywhere in northern England. In 1283 Henry de Lacy, Lord of Clitheroe, agreed to grant lands at Whalley to the monks of Stanlow Abbey, on the shores of the Mersey in Cheshire. The site of Stanlow was damp and prone to flooding, and the community wanted to relocate. The formal transfer to the new site was made on 4 April 1296 and the foundation stone of the great church was laid two months later by Henry de Lacy himself.

Whalley Abbey following the Dissolution, an original engraving by S. and N. Buck, dating to the 1720s. All valuable items such as vestments, silver and gold were confiscated. Furniture and windows were removed and either sold or used in other 'official' buildings such as parish churches of the halls of gentlemen (such

as at Samlesbury).
Roofs were removed for the lead and stone, and the stonework of the walls was carted off to be used in new building. Part of the old abbey was rebuilt as a grand house by the Assheton family.

LRO, DP189/14, REPRODUCED BY KIND PERMISSION OF THE COUNTY ARCHIVIST, LANCASHIRE RECORD OFFICE

The abbey was consecrated on 28 April 1306, although the buildings were not completed until the early fifteenth century. Whalley Abbey must have been a magnificent sight, exhibiting the highest level of workmanship. Today we can walk round the ruined gateways, chapter house, cloister, refectory, kitchen and mill. They give a taste of what once was, although almost no trace now remains of the great church itself. This was a major religious centre. In its heyday there were at least 30 monks, up to 90 servants and large numbers of visitors. They consumed 130 cows, 60 calves, 120 sheep and 30 lambs *per annum* (that is, in the 235 days when meat was allowed). The consumption of fish was not restricted. Salmon and trout were netted from Ribble and Calder; their appearance was seasonal, so to provide a constant supply, special fishponds were dug on the Calder floodplain. Wooden-sided channels were dug between them and the river to allow a through flow of clean water. The

THE CALDER, THE DARWEN AND THE DOUGLAS | 173

Whalley Abbey:
well-preserved
remains.

Ribble system has several species of fish that cannot pass through saltwater and so could not naturally colonise the river after the last Ice Age (see page 102). Although we have yet to discover contemporary documentary evidence, it is likely that the monks, who were great pisciculturists, had species such as carp, bream, pike and grayling brought here to stock their fishponds.

The last abbot of Whalley was John Paslew. He was renowned for his extravagance and had been accused of financial irregularities during the 1520s, but his fate was sealed not by this but by his involvement with the Pilgrimage of Grace, the northern rising against Henry VIII in the autumn of 1536. He, and William Haydock and Richard Eastgate, two other monks of Whalley, were tried at Lancaster for treason in March 1537, together with William de Trafford, the abbot of Sawley. Paslew and de Trafford were hanged on Lancaster Moor on 9 March, while Haydock and Eastgate were executed at Whalley. The abbey and a sizeable part of its estates eventually passed into the hands of the Assheton family, who demolished the church and some of the other buildings and converted the remainder into a fine country house. Today this is owned by the diocese of Blackburn and is used as a conference centre and retreat house.

Today Whalley is a small dormitory town, linked by railway to Manchester and kept fairly quiet by main road bypasses. Visitors come here to see the ruins of the abbey, or the medieval church and its superb pre-Conquest crosses. They may also see Whalley's other great architectural monument, the immense red-brick viaduct which carries the railway to Clitheroe high above the meadows and the waters of the Calder by 48 massive arches. The viaduct, opened in 1850, is very close to the ruins of Whalley abbey itself – the central section has curious 'gothic' arches, designed, with conspicuous lack of success, to blend in with the medieval context!

The Douglas and the Darwen

> … the greate river of Duglas, the ffinney pooles, and the river of Yarrowe overflowinge the way for all the most p[ar]te of the winter tyme.
>
> Anon., early seventeenth century

THE HEADWATERS

The television station with its eight tall masts on the summit of Winter Hill (456 metres) dominates the eastern skyline from much of west and south Lancashire. From a series of springs close to the TV station rises the river Douglas. For its first three kilometres it flows quickly down the steep slope of Rivington Moor, through crowberry, moor-grass, rush and bracken. Then, on the outskirts of Horwich, the Douglas leaves wild moorland, flows through

Winter Hill, source
of the Douglas.

Tiger Clough
and the Douglas
headwater.

the wooded Tiger Clough, and is consumed by Lower Rivington reservoir. Before the reservoir was built, Knoll Bleachworks took water from the infant Douglas. Close by was an illicit pub that brewed its own ale (these were not rare in Lancashire and were known as 'hush-ale shops'). Over the pub was a sign showing two tiger heads and it was this that gave the narrow clough its name.

The largest of the Douglas tributaries, the river Yarrow, rises on Hordern Stoops on the Anglezarke moors. It flows westwards through drab brown

Thunderbird 3 on Darwen Moor? The gritstone tower at the northern edge of Darwen Moor (SD 679216) was built to celebrate the golden jubilee of Queen Victoria in 1887. The view from here takes in much of the course of the river Darwen.

sheep pasture and, immediately after its confluence with Limestone Brook that drains from the moor before flowing through Lead Mines Clough, it is swallowed by Yarrow reservoir.

The river Darwen has several sources draining the northern West Pennine Moors including Stepback Brook, Duckshaw Brook and Waterside Brook. These meet to form the river Darwen close to the town of Darwen. The Darwen's main tributary, the Roddlesworth, drains the moors to the west of the Darwen's source. It avoids urban Lancashire, flowing northwards to a confluence with the Darwen downstream of Blackburn. Like Douglas and Yarrow, however, both these streams first are gathered into reservoirs.

RESERVOIRS
The first reservoirs to be built in the Douglas/Yarrow headwaters was only four hectares in area; it was constructed to supply nearby Chorley with water

under an 1847 Act of Parliament. However the growing city of Liverpool had been looking in this direction for its water supply and in 1850–57 this small reservoir was incorporated in the construction of Upper and Lower Rivington reservoirs, the two being separated by a causeway, now a road, called the Horrobin Bank. Almost as soon as these were completed a third, Anglezarke reservoir, was built above Upper Rivington, these two being separated by the Knowsley Bank. These three reservoirs cover a large area but are fairly shallow and soon Liverpool's growing demand was outstripping their ability to supply. So, above the chain of three reservoirs were built High Bullough and Yarrow reservoirs (the latter was the last, in 1875). In the same period that Liverpool was developing its Rivington complex it was also exploiting the river Roddlesworth in the north, the water from which would naturally flow to the Darwen. Here three dams were built to create Rake Brook, Roddlesworth and Upper Roddlesworth reservoirs (the last, in 1865). The water from these now flows through an artificial channel, the Goit, west and then south to top up Anglezarke reservoir. Water from this entire complex, which was designed by the eminent Victorian architect Thomas Hawksley (1807–93), eventually reaches Lower Rivington reservoir where, after filtering, it flows to storage reservoirs at Prescot. There it is treated before being pumped to the Liverpool consumer.[11]

Anglezarke Moor, source of the river Yarrow. Anglezarke comes from a mix of Old English (*Anlaf*) and Norse (*Erg*), meaning a hill pasture belonging to Anlaf. But habitation here goes further back, for Bronze Age people dwelt here. The moor was farmed until Liverpool Corporation constructed their Rivington/Anglezarke reservoirs, when those living in the farms were evicted.

Smaller reservoirs take water from other smaller streams in the West Pennines. For example, there are seven small ones on Dean Black Brook below White Coppice, while Earnsdale and Sunnyhurst Hey reservoirs take water from the Darwen headstreams for the town of Darwen.

So, only a tiny fraction of the rain that falls on these sodden moors flows to the sea through the rivers Douglas and Darwen and their tributaries. The rest is drunk, used for washing or in industrial processes, flushed down the loo, used to water gardens, or wasted.

The countryside here has a long history. From the late Neolithic/early Bronze Age period of about 4,000 years ago there survive the Pike Stones chambered long cairn and the saucer tumulus of Round Loaf on Anglezarke Moor and several scattered cairns and other tumuli.[12] From about AD 650 Angles, and from about 1000 Norse colonists settled here, although little remains other than farmstead and village names. Anglezarke is the *airgh* or

Relicts of the lead mines are displayed in Lead Mines Clough.

farm belonging to an Angle called Anlaf and first appears in print in 1224 as Anlauesargh. Rivington is the *tun* or town close to the *hreof-ing* (written in 1325 as 'Rouyng') or rough place.[13]

Blackrod, which overlooks the source of the Douglas from the south, has been claimed as the site of an Iron Age settlement, and of a Roman camp, though there is no real evidence for either supposition. Its name comes from the Old English word *blaec* combined with the early medieval term 'rode', meaning an area cleared of woodland: it was a black clearing. Nearby Horwich, spelt 'Horewych' in 1254, was 'the boundary to the forest with wych-elms'. Hordern, at the source of the Douglas, comes from *har* and *dene*, meaning a grey valley, and is the pass between Rivington and Belmont. As is very often the case, the names of the rivers have much older origins, with Celtic or even earlier roots. Douglas was *dub-glassjo*: a black stream, Yarrow was *garwo*: a rough stream, and Darwen was *derventjo*: a stream flowing through oak woodland.[14]

Following the Norman Conquest, landowning families gradually accumulated extensive estates in the district. The most prominent were the de Hoghtons, who became significant property-holders in the township of Hoghton as early as the twelfth century, and by the sixteenth century held numerous estates in that area and beyond, including parts of the Ribble valley. The present Hoghton Tower, on its prominent and defensible hilltop, was built from the mid-sixteenth century on the site of an earlier fortified house (it was largely destroyed by what was considered an accidental explosion during the civil wars of the mid-seventeenth century). Some lands in the area between Chorley, Blackburn and Walton-le-Dale had passed into monastic hands in the thirteenth century. Much of this property was eventually acquired by the de Hoghtons after the Dissolution. Abbey Village, close to Rakes Brook Reservoir, takes it name from the fact that Whalley Abbey once held land in the vicinity, although the village itself was only built in the 1840s and is a particularly fine example of a planned industrial community. Beneath the moors are some lead-bearing mineral veins, together with some small copper and coal seams. The rights to mine the metal ores were granted to the Knights Hospitaller of St John of Jerusalem in 1152 by King Stephen. Mining was undertaken sporadically around Lead Mines Clough for over 600 years, though it was never on a significant scale, and in the 1930s all remaining shafts were filled in. During the 1980s excavations took place so that some of the surface workings can be seen by walkers using the paths along the clough.

Between the late fifteenth and mid-seventeenth centuries many lower areas of moor were cleared and farmsteads built. Here sheep and cattle grazed the rough pastures. However, following the Liverpool Corporation Act of 1902, all the land in the catchment of the reservoirs was compulsorily purchased and cleared to remove all risks of pollution. One such was Old Rachel's farm, on the slope leading down to the Yarrow below the Rivington–Belmont road. Cleared in 1903, the farmhouse was used for target practice by tanks during the Second World War so that only a small part remains, together with sycamores planted there for shelter and for firewood. Today these upland pastures are waterlogged rush and purple moor-grass grassland that, for most of the year, colours the scene a drab brown.

In recent years the body responsible for producing clean drinking water (now United Utilities) has realised that the risk of pollution from people living in or visiting a reservoir catchment is very slight. So today the area around the Rivington/Anglezarke reservoirs, like that around Stocks in the Hodder valley, is one of the most popular of tourist 'honey-pots'. In 1900 William Hesketh Lever, Lord Leverhulme, purchased the Rivington estate for £60,000. The son of a Bolton grocer, he had made an immense fortune from soap and other manufacturing. He remodelled the landscape of Rivington, building gardens, reconstructing the house, laying out miles of roads, paths and trackways, and planting huge numbers of trees and shrubs to soften the bareness of the open moorland and the steep slopes above the reservoirs. On his death in 1945 much of the land was made available for public access, even though in 1902 large parts of the area had been closed off under the Liverpool Corporation Act. People may now walk the moors and climb Rivington Pike where, in 1588, a beacon was prepared to pass on the news that the Spanish Armada was approaching the English coast (the present beacon tower was built in 1733). And after their exertions on a Bank Holiday Monday or summer Sunday, folk throng to Rivington Hall Barn for refreshment.

Up to 1914 the Darwen, Anglezarke and Rivington Moors above the old farmsteads were managed heather-grouse moor, but a combination of circumstances largely put an end to this system. The landowners in the Winter Hill area, such as the Ainsworths of Smithills Hall, lost interest in the shooting (which was never of top quality) and eventually moved away; the restrictive actions of the water authorities gradually reduced access; and the First World War itself caused major disruption as gamekeepers were sent off to fight the Germans. The result was that, as the numbers of grouse declined, sheep-grazing took over from grouse-management, and this eventually resulted in over-grazing of the heather, which was replaced by tough grasses and unpalatable crowberry. There are still a few patches of heather and bilberry (locally called whimberry or whinberry) and a small area of managed grouse moor supporting about 200 pairs of red grouse. Bilberry is still reasonably abundant in the Roddlesworth valley, on the margins of woodland and in open glades in wooded areas. A few pairs of short-eared owls and merlins breed locally, and in recent years hen harriers have been seen. There are a few pairs of golden plover and dunlins on the wetter moors; lapwing, snipe, and curlew breed in the rushy grasslands. Skylarks and meadow pipits remain abundant, but the numbers of the once common twite have declined to only a few pairs because herbicides and the earlier mowing of the high meadows has taken away the weed-seeds on which they feed their young.

With the exception of Stocks (page 118), the nine pumped-storage reservoirs around Longridge and Grimsargh, and the holding reservoirs of Guide, Fishmoor and Parsonage at Blackburn (which get their water direct from the Hodder through an aqueduct), all the reservoirs in the Ribble catchment are on upland tributaries and take their water from the inflowing stream. In these reservoirs there is a general pattern of fluctuation of water level. In the winter months rain fills the reservoirs and during summer droughts the level falls. In long summer droughts the level may fall very low. For instance, in the March–October 1995 drought the level in all the reservoirs fell to 20 per cent or less of their capacity.

The consequence is that in summer the shallow margins dry out and aquatic plants are unable to colonise. The sparseness of plant food, linked to the exposure of the reservoir bed and the purity of the water results in very small populations of aquatic invertebrates. And this leads to slow growing fish stocks. Most of these reservoirs have a wild brown trout population, with a

Parsonage reservoir, in the hills above Blackburn, usually has its level maintained so that weedbeds develop and insect life is rich.

small average weight of around 100 g, and with few attaining 500 g. Many are now stocked annually with rainbow trout, and the poor feeding sometimes results in one kilo stocked fish falling to 500 g in a couple of months. Over 90 per cent of food taken by some reservoir trout consists of land-bred insects that have been blown onto the water from surrounding conifer plantations or the open moor. The breeding bird community of such reservoirs is similarly sparse. Most have a pair of great crested grebes (*Podiceps cristatus*) that feed on the diminutive trout (or other fish that have been stocked to the water such as rudd or ruffe). If there are mallard or coot nesting by the reservoir, a large proportion of their diet consists of bread provided by generous humans! In winter these waters can support only tiny populations of tufted duck, goldeneye (*Bucephala clangula*) and goosanders.

Since 1997 the water level of Parsonage reservoir, in the hills above Blackburn, has been maintained by pumping water in from the Hodder. Here weedbeds (including Canadian pondweed) have developed in the shallower areas. The insect populations are large and diverse, with huge hatches of midges, at least 18 species of caddisfly (including the 3 cm long *Phyganea grandis*) and a large spring hatch of the upwinged fly, the sepia dun (*Leptophlebia marginata*) and in spring through to late summer of the lake olive (*Cloeon simile*). In late summer the margins are crammed with shoals of three-spined sticklebacks and rudd fry. Brown trout here are mostly stocked at a small size but grow quickly: some stocked at 20 cm length in the summer of 2001 were in the range 35–40 cm a year later. Great crested grebes, coot, moorhen and mallard nest here. In spring ospreys stop off to refuel. And in winter the coot and duck populations of this small reservoir are greater than all those in the huge Rivington/Anglezarke complex combined. For instance, a count made in November 2001 gave:

	Parsonage reservoir	Rivington/Anglezarke
Great crested grebe	2	5
Coot	51	7
Mallard	18	30*
Teal	4	0
Wigeon	16	0
Tufted duck	9	3
Goldeneye	6	8
Goosander	3	2
Total	109	55
Numbers per hectare of lake surface	6.9	.025

* A flock of mallard is attracted by bread-throwing humans!

Some fine tracts of predominantly broad-leaved woodland were planted, mostly in the eighteenth and nineteenth centuries, on the lower slopes of the reservoir catchments and around the reservoirs themselves. The Tockholes and Roddlesworth plantations and the strips and blocks of mainly oak woodland around the Anglezarke/Rivington reservoirs are particularly attractive. In the former instance the stretch of the Roddlesworth above the top reservoir is one of the few relatively unmanaged and natural sections of river in the area, with an impressive rocky bed, vertical cliffs up to 10 metres high, waterfalls, and a very variable flood regime. It gives a small taste of the character of many of the West Pennine watercourses before water catchment strategies and reservoir-building interfered so extensively with the landscape after 1850. There are also some sizeable blocks of conifer plantation established through the twentieth century. Roe deer have colonised these in recent years (see page 121). Goshawks prospected in 2001 and nested in 2005. Green, great spotted and lesser spotted woodpeckers occur, though the latter is difficult to locate other than in early spring. Tree pipits nest in open woodland on the fellsides. Woodcock, redstart, garden warbler, blackcap, wood warbler, chiffchaff, willow warbler, goldcrest, spotted flycatcher (*Muscicapa striata*), pied flycatcher, nuthatch and treecreeper breed in the woods where, in winter, flocks of brambling (*Fringilla montifringilla*) feed on seeds and beechmast and fieldfares (*Turdus pilaris*) and redwings (*T. iliacus*) on haws.

THE URBAN EFFECT ON THE DOUGLAS SYSTEM

Below Rivington the river Douglas passes beneath the M61 motorway and then heads in a northerly direction to Adlington. There it swings westwards, flows in a culvert beneath the Leeds and Liverpool Canal, and then veers

Many stretches of the Douglas between Wigan and Tarleton were canalised to allow coal barges to pass.

south-west to disgorge what little flow it has gathered since Rivington into Worthington reservoirs. The outflow is at the southern end of this chain of three lakes, close to the small town of Standish. Now the Douglas meanders its way south through the centre of Wigan, with sections hidden from view in a culvert buried beneath brick, tarmac and concrete, though with other sections open enough to sprout supermarket trolleys, beer cans and polystyrene fast-food boxes. At Poolstock the river comes alongside the Leeds and Liverpool Canal, and both waterways leave the town heading north-west through a steep-sided valley that has industrial Lancashire on either hand almost as far as Gathurst viaduct, which carries the M6 across river, canal and Wigan–Southport railway.

But then, to the west of Gathurst, river and canal pass into green and well-wooded countryside extending as far as Parbold. This secluded stretch of the river shows the imprint of several phases of transport development. At the beginning of the eighteenth century the growth of the Wigan coalfield,

Before the rage for building canals as we now know them began in the late eighteenth century many rivers or 'navigations' were improved to allow boats to travel further inland. One early such example was the river Douglas which allowed the more efficient carriage of coal from the Wigan coalfield. Various parts of the early workings can still be seen, particularly at Sollom, not far from Tarleton.

and the new demands for fuel created by the rapid expansion of Liverpool, encouraged schemes to improve access for coal to the city. Overland routes were extremely expensive and inefficient, and projects for making the Douglas navigable emerged. In 1721 a scheme to create a river navigation from Wigan to the sea was authorised by Parliament and, although progress was disappointingly slow, the project was eventually completed in 1742. The impact was immediate: coal traffic could now head down the Douglas to

Tarleton and then via coastal vessels to Liverpool or the northern basin of the Irish Sea, including Ireland itself. Thus, river flats crossed the Ribble estuary to unload on the shore at Lytham and Freckleton. This river navigation was relatively unambitious: a few short new cuts were made, and locks built, but the engineering works were modest. The construction of the Leeds and Liverpool Canal along the valley between 1770 and 1774 meant that the navigation (based on the old river channel) was abandoned. Some of the old locks and artificial cuts became backwaters as all traffic then used the canal.[15] Subsequently, the railway line from Wigan to Southport followed a course very close to the canal, using the convenient gap through the hills, so that today the old navigation, the 1770s canal and the railway are parallel for several kilometres. The opening of the navigation and canal encouraged the exploitation of the mineral resources of the valley. A series of collieries opened on the north side, linked to canal wharves by short horse-drawn

Lathom Chapel and the row of almshouses were built at the end of the eighteenth century.

tramroads of which some traces may still be seen, but much more impressive were the great stone quarries on Parbold Hill. These supplied building stone, and particularly paving slabs, to south Lancashire from the early nineteenth century until after the Second World War and they provided the stone for the construction of the shipping channel through the estuary (page 247). Then, after a period of abandonment, some of the largest quarries were re-used as household waste landfill sites, so that today the landscape has undergone further dramatic change as the huge excavations have been filled in.

From Parbold the canal continues on to Burscough and then Liverpool, with a branch heading north past the ancient village of Rufford and on to Tarleton. The Douglas flows northwards from Parbold through a wide, flat floodplain called Low Meadows, formerly edged by extensive tracts of mossland (such as Hoscar Moss). The mosses, and the valley bottom, were drained in the eighteenth century, and today have become rich market-gardening land and improved pasture. Below Rufford the river once meandered widely but with the construction of the branch of the Leeds and Liverpool Canal after 1770

Rufford Old Hall lies close to the Douglas and the Rufford branch of the Leeds and Liverpool Canal. Home to the Heskeths since Tudor times, it was given to the National Trust in 1936.

its flow was canalised. The original channel south of Sollom is now only a hollow with a ditch at the bottom of it, but north of Sollom the Rufford branch of the Leeds and Liverpool Canal took the old river channel as far as the A59 bridge close to the Lilford family seat of Bank Hall (see page 273). From there the now tidal Douglas takes over its natural course to the Ribble estuary at Hesketh Bank, though with embankments on either hand to prevent flooding of surrounding farmland during spring tides. The Rufford branch of the canal enters the Douglas at Tarleton through a set of lock-gates. Now only pleasure craft pass through the lock and out to the Ribble beneath the clay-ridge of Hesketh Bank, but with the opening in 2000 of the Ribble Link canal at Preston, which connects the river with the northern section of the Lancaster Canal, traffic has grown steadily and the waterway is now busier than it has been for over 100 years.

A main tributary of the Douglas is the Tawd, which rises on the western slopes of Ashurst Beacon and in the former mosslands north of Rainford, and flows through Skelmersdale. Until the 1840s this was a tranquil rural area, a patchwork of small fields and farms. Then the mineral rights were leased by the owner, the Lord Skelmersdale, and coal-mining began. Within twenty years an unplanned and amorphous town had grown up around the new collieries, and the rural landscape was devastated. In 1907 the area was described as 'a particularly bare, unpleasing district, for the most part occupied by collieries, with huge banks of black refuse at intervals amongst treeless fields'.[16] The mining caused major pollution of the Tawd, although in 1902 the river got its own back by breaking through into the underground workings of the massive Tawd Vale colliery and completely drowning the workings. Nobody was killed, but over a thousand miners instantly lost their jobs and within a week 120 families had been forced to leave the town to find work elsewhere. In the 1960s, to try to resolve the problems of an acutely depressed area with a badly degraded landscape, Skelmersdale was made a new town. That the problems did not cease is well known, and now the Tawd, though far less polluted than it was a century ago, takes the run-off from a large urban area. After flowing along the edge of the great medieval deer park at Lathom, the river becomes little more than a drainage dyke as it flows across the former Hoscar Moss and joins the Douglas just above Wainblades Bridge on the road from Bispham to Ring o'Bells, below Newburgh.

The other important tributary of the Douglas is the Yarrow. After losing its headwaters in Yarrow reservoir, the new Yarrow emerges from Upper Rivington reservoir close to Cuncliffe Farm before meandering its way through Yarrow Valley Country Park, bypassing the worst of Chorley's sprawl. Some sections of the riverside here retain much of their original character, with deciduous woodland bright with bluebells in spring, and

After flowing around Chorley, the Yarrow provided water and power for a large industrial complex until the twentieth century. Industry went, but the river still flows through some of its remains.

nearby meadows which are among Lancashire sites for the autumn crocus (*Crocus nudiflorus*). The river has, in landscape terms at least, remained surprisingly unsullied by industry and urbanisation, despite the proximity of towns such as Chorley. At Eccleston it is spanned by a particularly attractive hump-backed bridge and the medieval parish church stands close to the bank, while at Croston, where the river is canalised as it passes through the little

This is now the Yarrow Valley Park, where some of the pools made by industry have developed into splendid fenland.

The Yarrow is highly canalised as it flows through Croston, though this is no hindrance to sea trout swimming upstream to spawn. Croston church is fifteenth-century, at a time when the village would still have been surrounded by unreclaimed mosslands (see page 208). The river here burst its banks in January 2008, flooding part of Croston.

As it meets the Ribble, the Douglas is renamed the Asland. Note the shipping channel training walls (see page 247).

town (mainly to avoid flooding, which in the past was a constant threat here) it provides an essential element in the attractive scene of river, church, cottages and cobbled street which makes this a favourite spot for photographers and artists. Below Croston the now embanked Douglas, joined by the Lostock, which drains the land south of Preston including the urban sprawl of Whittle-le-Woods, Bamber Bridge, Farington and Leyland, flows along the margin of Croston Finney. This was once a great tract of fen and wetland, but it was drained in the late eighteenth century to produce a pancake-flat landscape of large geometric fields and ruler-straight lanes, now crossed by the railway line from Preston to Ormskirk from which an excellent view of this man-made land may be obtained.

The urban effect on the Darwen

As soon as it flows from the moors, the River Darwen enters the town of Darwen, where it runs for almost two kilometres through an almost-continuous culvert, broken only by one short stretch of daylight in the middle. A good part of central Darwen is in fact built on top of its forgotten river. Emerging from its subterranean gloom, it continues down the valley and round the back of Blackburn Rovers football ground. Both football ground and the terraces street around are known as Ewood, a name that has been

The Darwen at Roach Bridge. From its source the water of the Darwen has been impounded, abstracted, used to provide energy, and what remains has been dammed and polluted.

traced back to early in the thirteenth century and means the 'oak wood by the stream.'[17] The Darwen then passes through the industrial outskirts of Blackburn to Feniscowles, where it is joined by the much-reduced flow of the Roddlesworth. Here, large paper-mills exploit the waters of the river, but then, suddenly and unexpectedly, it leaves town behind and, like the Douglas and its tributaries, passes into largely unspoilt countryside. From the road bridge at Feniscowles it is another five kilometres before the next road bridge, and for much of that section the river flows in a deep steep-sided valley, almost a gorge, lined with dense and inaccessible woodland: the name Wild Bottoms Wood near Samlesbury Bottoms is quite revealing! The survival of these woodlands, especially at Samlesbury Bottoms, Hoghton Bottoms and at Hoghton Tower, is remarkable, since Blackburn and Preston are so close at hand, and can be explained mainly by the topography of this section of the valley, where the steepness of the slopes has prevented access and meant that there was no agricultural potential.

The best view of the woodlands and the valley, except for those on foot who can see it from the network of local paths and tracks, is obtained from the train travelling between Blackburn and Preston, where the railway crosses the valley on a high viaduct immediately below Hoghton Tower. This splendid house is the seat of the de Hoghton family and was built in 1565 on the top of a distinct wooded knoll at 179 metres that commands a magnificent view over the surrounding country and which can be seen from as far away as the outer estuary.[18] James I visited Hoghton Tower for three days in August 1617 and the menu for the three grand dinners eaten by the king and his retinue still survives. It not only reveals the protein-rich diet on such occasions but also the extent to which wild fauna was harvested. There were boiled pullets, capons, chickens, ducks, mutton jiggits, breast of veal and sprod (sea trout). Roasted meats included shoulder of mutton, loin of veal, haunch of venison (probably red or fallow deer), wild boar, domestic pig, turkey, swan (mute), goose, quail (were these wild?), partridge, plover, capons and beef. Heron was roasted but served cold, and there were pasties of hot venison and hot mince, chicken and snipe pies, andd tongue and curlew 'pyes', also served cold.

From Samlesbury Bottoms downstream the Darwen has a more open valley and here there are several sites of industrial archaeological importance, for this was one of the first Lancashire rivers to be intensively exploited for its water power. The old mill sites at places such as Roach Bridge and Higher Walton played an important part in the county's industrial development from the 1770s onwards. The Darwen finally flows into the Ribble at Walton-le-Dale, close to the ancient bridging point over the Ribble, where Walton-le-Dale Roman supply depot once stood.

The canalised
Darwen as it flows
into the Ribble.
The City of
Preston is on the
distant bluff, while
over the flood
bank in the right
foreground was
the Roman camp at
Walton-le-dale.

The natural history of these urban tributaries

In the early 1970s I lived only a few metres from the lock through which the
Rufford branch of the Leeds and Liverpool canal opened into the mouth of
the Douglas. Then the Douglas was a stinking sewer, its stench invading our
kitchen on warm summer evenings. Usually the river ran a thick oily black,
but sometimes there was a tinge of colour: green, purple and once bright
blue. I sampled the river downstream of the Yarrow inflow: no fish or clean
water invertebrates were living there. I walked the river downstream from
Gathurst: there was no plant life at all.

From the mid-1960s I spent a considerable amount of time on Big Ribble,
downstream of Calderfoot. Salmon and sea trout ran the Ribble, mostly
swimming hard to reach the clean water above the Calder confluence for,
even when it was running 'clean', the Calder contained much pollution from
sewage outfalls and factories. Once, in July 1965, I witnessed the sort of
environmental disaster which then, occasionally, issued forth from the urban
Calder. Along about two kilometres of river I collected four dead salmon,
eleven sea trout and many dace and chub. A sudden thunderstorm had
deluged Pendle and Rossendale. So much water fell that it overwhelmed the
capability of the sewage treatment works to cope. Floodwater and raw sewage
gushed down the Calder and into the low-flowing Ribble, which had not been
hit by the storm. The pollutants absorbed all the oxygen in the clean Ribble

As water quality within the river system has gradually improved, clean-water invertebrates such as these have colonised the Yarrow.

ABOVE
Green dun; yellow may dun.

BELOW
Stonefly nymph; adult stonefly.

water and this plug of foetid, deoxygenated water swept downstream, quickly suffocating most fish life in its path.

It was not a unique event, for in his book *The Ribble Salmon Fisheries* (1952) A. T. R. Hoghton described many similar events. For instance:

18 June 1930   'Thousands of fish killed below Calder.'
12 July 1932   'ditto'
12 July 1941   'Thick black flood; many fish killed.'
4 July 1942   'Salmon and seatrout killed below Calder Foot.'
10 June 1943   'Thick black sludge; fish killed.' [19]

Beginning in the 1970s a great deal of work has been carried out in order to clean up these rivers. Millions of pounds have been invested in the modernisation of sewage works so that they are now able to cope with the regular urban waste and sudden surges of pollution and thunderstorms. Industrial sources of pollution have been identified and dealt with. There are occasional 'accidents' – the most recent on the Yarrow was on 14–15 May 2002 when the fish stocks in eight kilometres of river below Chorley were killed. Despite these, things are getting better.

My own observations have centred on the Yarrow and part of the Douglas. In 1976 there was no plant life at all in the Douglas downstream of Wigan or in the Yarrow below Chorley. By 1995, however, the rivers were clean enough to support the small pondweed (*Potamogeton berchtoldii*) and fennel pondweed (*P. pectinatus*), water crowfoot, Canadian pondweed and two water-starworts (*Callitriche stagnalis* and *C. platycarpa*).

Since 1976, collecting samples of the stoneflies and mayflies living at three sites on the Yarrow also indicates a great improvement in water quality. On the open moor above Yarrow reservoir where the water has always been very clean, the stream has nine species of stonefly and three species of mayfly. In the Yarrow Valley Park, close to Chorley, only one species of mayfly occurred

As the rivers have become cleaner, with more invertebrates, so the dipper has increased and spread.

in 1976: that was *Baetis rhodani* which can tolerate a degree of pollution. By 1995, six species of stoneflies and seven species of mayflies occurred here. Since 1995 another stonefly and three more mayfly species have been found there. Below Chorley there were no stoneflies or mayflies in the Yarrow in 1975; by 1995 there were three species of mayfly.

Cleaner water and an increasing population of aquatic invertebrates have resulted in the spread of dipper to the Yarrow and kingfishers to Yarrow and some parts of the Douglas. Supported with stocking by the Environment Agency, there are now thriving populations of coarse fish: chub, dace, roach and minnows. Most exciting has been the development of a run of sea trout in the Yarrow. These fish require clean water, not only in the higher reaches where they spawn (above Chorley), but also in the lower reaches of the Yarrow and the Douglas through which they migrate to and from the estuary. To enable them to run to above Chorley, fish-passes have been built at formerly impassable weirs.

Similar improvements and diversification of fauna have taken place on the Calder and Darwen. Clean-water weed-beds and invertebrate populations have developed. Dippers and kingfishers have spread and stocks of chub, dace and roach increased. Sea trout and salmon are now running the Calder, through Burnley town centre and into Pendle Water, and the deeper river pools now have large shoals of grayling. Calder, Darwen and Douglas may be urban tributaries of the Ribble, but they are becoming clean urban rivers.

Wildlife in the urban environment

The urban environment through which these rivers flow have their own wildlife. Foxes have invaded the towns in recent years and the American grey squirrel is now a common sight in large gardens and municipal parks. Pied wagtails nest in town centres and feed on parks, bowling greens, football pitches and supermarket car parks. Swifts (*Apus apus*) nest in church towers and mill roofs. House martins (*Delichon urbica*) nest beneath the eaves of some town centre terraces, and studies in east Lancashire have shown that they prefer houses that have either whitewashed walls or white-painted eaves.

In the sprawl of housing estates the densities of breeding blackbirds are often much higher than densities found in the countryside. As gardens mature they become colonised by woodland birds: robins (*Erithacus rubecula*), wrens (*Troglodytes troglodytes*), blue, great and coal tits (*Parus caeruleus, P. major, P. ater*), goldcrest, chaffinch (*Fringilla coelebs*), greenfinch (*Carduelis chloris*) and goldfinch (*C. carduelis*). Bird tables help maintain thriving populations of house sparrows (*Passer domesticus*), a favourite food of sparrowhawks. Even more spectacular are the peregrines which nest on church towers and

Grey wagtails are
common along all
clean Lancashire
rivers.

former mill chimneys and chase feral pigeons down the High Street. In winter
lapwings often roost by day and feed by night, and they have discovered
that the flat roofs of modern town centre factories and supermarkets are
safer roosts than farmland. Occasionally something special turns up. Black
redstarts (*Phoenicurus ochruros*) have nested in Blackburn town centre, and
parties of waxwings (*Bombycilla garrulus*) have been seen in winter, feeding
on rowanberries on roadside verges and in gardens.

Urban sprawl may be unsightly to the wildlife watcher, yet it is hardly
barren. Garden ponds attract frogs and newts as well as a wide range of

Once quite scarce, the speckled wood butterfly is now a very common species, even in gardens in the centre of towns.

BELOW LEFT
Hummingbird hawk moths (*Macroglossum stellatarum*) are migrants from southern Europe and they have begun to appear regularly in and around towns in the valley. Here one seeks nectar from a *Fuchsia* growing in a hanging basket.

BELOW RIGHT
The painted lady butterfly is a migrant that has increased greatly in towns in recent years, attracted to nectar-rich flowers such as *Buddleia*.

dewpond invertebrates such as water hog-lice, water boatmen and dragonflies. Koi carp will attract herons to the smallest garden pond. In recent years two species of butterfly have colonised towns in the region and become widespread and numerous. The speckled wood (*Parage aegeria*) lays its eggs on rank grass, and there is plenty of that in our towns, whilst the holly blue (*Celastrina argiolus*) seeks gardens with holly or ivy on which its caterpillars feed.

Houses, factories, shopping centres and roads are compatible with wildlife and their needs, provided that we make them compatible.

CHAPTER FIVE

Where the river meets the sea

I must go down to the seas again, for the call of the morning tide
Is a wild call and a clear call that may not be denied;
And all I ask is a windy day with the white clouds flying,
And the flung spray and the blown spume, and the sea-gulls crying.

John Masefield, *Sea-fever.*

The highest spring tides, backed by westerly gales, push upstream past Penwortham to Frenchwood and the A6 bridge at Walton-le-Dale. By contrast, on neap tides the flood may not reach the old tramway bridge at Preston's Avenham Park, although at least part of the oozy mud on either side of the low water channel beneath the bridge carrying the west-coast London Euston to Glasgow mainline railway into Preston station is flooded. Sea-water or full strength saltwater does not reach Preston, however. The saltwater that flows up the estuary on a flood tide is denser than the freshwater flowing downstream. So the freshwater flows over the saltwater and at the head of the estuary, around Preston, the tidal rise consists mainly of freshwater that is being pushed back or held upstream by the sea pushing up the outer estuary. Thus freshwater fish species, such as chub, dace and roach, that cannot tolerate saltwater, can live in the upper tidal reaches around Preston and have, on occasion, been caught out in the estuary at low water.[1]

Preston, then, is the head of the Ribble estuary. The outer limits of the estuary are 27 kilometres away to the west, where the low water channel of the estuary merges with the Irish Sea, four kilometres south-west of St Anne's. This is roughly a line between the shore at Starr Gate, the southernmost

The tide rushes up the Ribble estuary as a 'bore'. On a spring tide, backed by a severe gale, the bore may reach over one metre in height.

corner of Blackpool, where the tramline terminates, and Formby Point, where the shore swings south-eastwards into the Alt and Mersey estuaries.

The name of that southern tram terminus, Starr Gate, is not without interest, for it is a mix of the history and natural history that is the theme of this book. Starr-grass is the old Lancashire name for marram-grass (*Ammophila arenaria*) that grows on starr hills or sand dunes. 'Gate' is Viking in origin, meaning 'street' or 'track'. So Starr Gate was the ancient track leading into the dunes.

Today the estuary and its hinterland comprise five fairly distinct habitats. When the tide is out the only significant water is the low water channel of the Ribble, together with other smaller creeks including the river Crossens, Main Drain at Lytham, and the mouths of the rivers Douglas and Daw and Savick Brook. They flow through mudflats and sandflats that, together with the sandy beaches west of Southport and St Anne's, are flooded at high water. On spring tides, this entire 'intertidal zone' may be flooded, but on neap tides much remains exposed. Backing the mudflats from Southport and Lytham eastwards are saltmarshes. These are partly flooded on every spring tide, but are completely flooded when a high spring tide is pushed higher by westerly gales. Large areas of saltmarshes have been reclaimed and converted to rich arable land and market-gardens. Sand dunes back the sandy beaches of the outer estuary. Large areas of these have been covered with housing estates, holiday camps and other tourist 'attractions'. Inland most of the coastal hinterland is flat and covered with mossland. Little natural mossland remains, for most has been drained and is now very rich arable farmland. Except for relatively recent holiday towns, human settlements around the estuary were on raised areas, usually the low boulder clay ridges that are most apparent between Ormskirk and Burscough, at Tarleton and Hesketh Bank, and at Freckleton, Clifton-with-Newton and in the Kirkham/Wrea Green/Kellamergh area.

Around 10,000 ago, when humans began to colonise the North West as the ice retreated northwards, the coastline was much further west than it is today.

The natural evolution of the estuary

… those chaffe sands which doe in mountains rise
On shore 'tis pleasure to behould, which Hoes*
Are called in worold: windie tempest blows
Them up in heapes …

Rev. Richard James, Iter Lancastrense, 1636.

Approximately 10,000 years ago the last Ice Age released its grip on north-west Europe and the thick ice-sheets and snowfields that covered the land began to melt. Because so much water was locked away as ice and snow, at the start of the thaw sea level was about 55 metres lower than it is today and the Ribble valley then extended westwards through what is now the bed of the Irish Sea to an estuary roughly 40 kilometres west of the present estuary (see map opposite). Traces of this ancient valley can apparently still be discerned in the submarine contours at depths greater than ten fathoms; in shallower water this former valley has become buried under later sediments.[2]

As the ice melted, so sea level rose relative to the land. Until fairly recently it was thought that not only was the present Irish Sea basin flooded, but that sea level rose to inundate eastwards across what today is dry land. It was believed that the sea level was highest around 5,000 years ago, producing an ancient coastline which the geomorphologist R. Kay Gresswell termed the Hill House Coastline (see map on page 205).[3] This name comes from Hill House, an old house built on a 10-metre high ridge surrounded by

---

*   'Hoes' = Hawes, i.e. sand dunes.

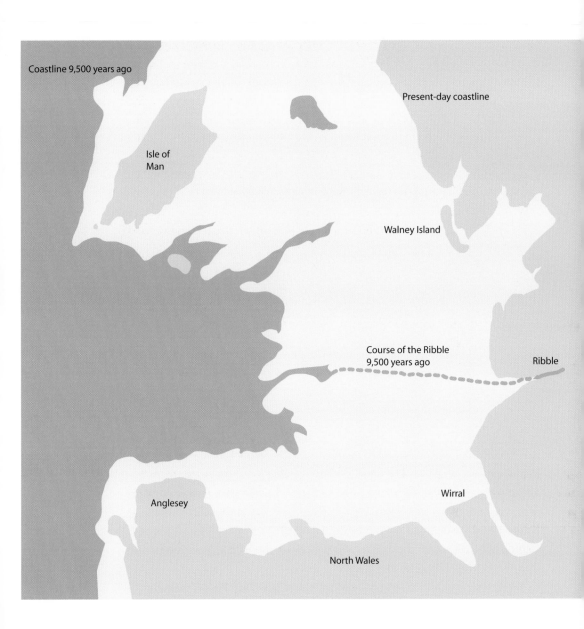

Coastline 9,500 years ago

Present-day coastline

Isle of
Man

Walney Island

Course of the Ribble
9,500 years ago

Ribble

Wirral

Anglesey

North Wales

low-lying, flat mosslands between Downholland Cross and Great Altcar, inland of Formby. Gresswell's theory was that when the coast was at its most easterly, this ridge was a promontory and the sea wuold have washed its foot to produce a low cliff that is particularly marked at Hill House. Similar low cliffs cut into boulder clay are visible on the south side of the estuary along the inland side of Shore Road between Hesketh Bank and Hundred End, south and west of the Mere Brow–Holmeswood road, and to the north of the same road near Rufford.

Clifton village on its low cliff. The fields in the foreground were tidal saltmarsh before they were reclaimed.

The south side of the estuary is mostly low and flat. In contrast the northern Fylde side rises higher with thicker sheets of boulder clay. Thus, following Gresswell's theory, when sea level peaked 5,000 years ago, there was less low-lying country for the sea to inundate. The tide then flowed between Warton and Lytham as far inland as Ballam, and east of Freckleton Naze to Newton-with-Scales, Clifton and below Lea Hall. The River Daw, that drains south from Kirkham to the estuary, flows beneath the 'Hill House' Coast cliff from Freckleton village to the Naze.

More recently, M. J. Tooley has shown that the Hill House coastline is no such thing, but is in fact the eastern shoreline of a shallow lake, lying immediately inland of the shore, which extended northwards to include Martin Mere.[4] He has also demonstrated that sea levels did not peak 5,000 years ago, but rather that 5,000 years ago the sea level was *lower* than it has ever been since. We can see that during the past 2–3,000 years, the sea has advanced eastwards to its present position, for at low water we can walk out over the shore north of Formby Point and note how, 5,000 years ago, this area was mossland where peat was being formed. Bands of peat are now being eroded by the tide as far out as the present low water mark, and in the peat we can find roots from the ancient oak forests. And not only tree roots, for at very low tide are exposed the preserved footprints of human beings and

RIBBLE: VALLEY AND RIVER

the animals that they hunted – red deer and auroch – who lived here three or more millennia ago (see page 14). Peat formation appears to have been rapid in the warm wet climate that prevailed 5,000–7,000 years ago. It has also been rapid in the last 3,000 years as a consequence of the cool wet climate and a high water table caused by high sea levels. Only drainage by humans has hindered the continued development of peat on low-lying ground around the estuary. Those areas are what we know as 'mosslands'.

The extent of the 1720 inundation and the line of the so-called Hill House coastline.

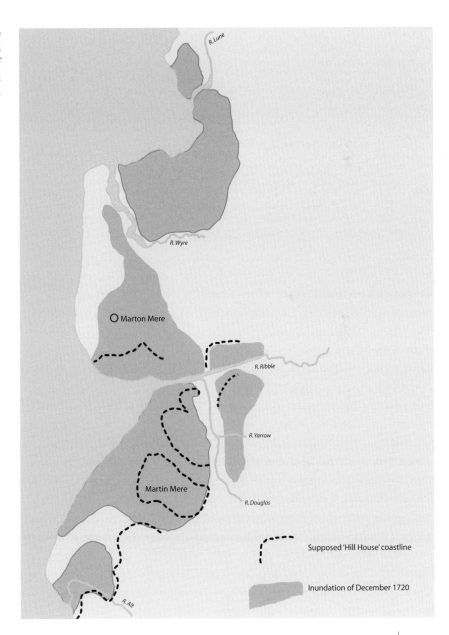

That low-lying mosslands are vulnerable to flooding by the sea is confirmed by documentary sources in recent times. For example, the diarist Nicholas Blundell, squire of Little Crosby, recorded in December 1720 that: 'Till the 10th generally Raine, then to the 16 very Faire, the four next days very wet and extreamly Windy the like scarce ever known and never so high a Tide known as these four dayes especially the 18th and 19th chiefly at the Meales, Alker, Alt-Grange and towards Lancaster, there also was very great Thunder & Litoning, toward the End of this Month generely faire but much Wind … never so much damage done by High Tides in these parts as now'.[5] The Lancashire coastal floods of December 1720 were perhaps the most serious in historical times. The sea broke through the flimsy defences on both sides of the Ribble estuary, flooding the low-lying mosslands as far inland as Rufford and Staining and destroying almost all bridges on coastal roads. Two generations later, the diarist Timothy Cragg of Ortner in Wyresdale noted, in the 1790s, instances of local flooding in the mosslands and estuaries of north Lancashire and used the measure of the 1720 floods as his yardstick, for they were 'the greatest that there was in the memory of man'.

Besides the low cliff found at places such as Hill House and between Mere Brown and Holmeswood, and the extensive peat lands, another feature to be seen widely inland around the estuary is a seam of white or very pale sand, known as Shirdley Hill Sand (from the small hamlet of the same name near Scarisbrick, where the deposits are especially thick). Gresswell thought that this sand was laid down by the sea when the sea lapped against and then retreated from the Hill House coast. However, recent research has indicated that the sand underlying the peat was blown there by cold desert winds at the end of the last Ice Age, some 10,000 years ago.[6] Some wind-blown sand reached far inland, traces having been discovered on Billinge Hill between Rainford and Wigan, and the depth of sand in some places has made it worth exploiting as a mineral resource. The so-called 'Leisure Lakes' at Mere Brow and the meres at Mere Sands Wood LWT Reserve were formed when sand was extracted there in the 1960s and 1970s. Quantities of sand have occasionally been blown inland in more recent millennia, for thin seams of wind-blown sand can be found within peat beds laid down in the last 5,000 years. Here, the historical evidence is also clear: the records of the little priory at Lytham, a daughter-house of Durham Cathedral Priory, refer many times in the fifteenth century to the loss of agricultural land which had been overwhelmed by the blowing sands, and on occasion the village of Lytham itself was partly buried. The piles of sand which often clog the gutters and roads of St Anne's to this day, and which sandblast parked cars near the shore, are the modern manifestation of a process which has been continuing for five millennia.

ABOVE LEFT
Reed fen must have been widespread on the natural mosslands.

ABOVE RIGHT
White beak sedge was once common amongst *Sphagnum* moss on the natural mosslands. It no longer occurs on mosslands around the Ribble.

White beak sedge and bog asphodel growing an a lowland raised bog.

The sand dunes of the outer estuary began to form 4,000–4,600 years ago.[7] These formed a barrier between the highest ordinary spring tides and the westernmost mosslands, though occasionally they would have been breached in storm conditions. To the east of where Crossens and Lytham are today there were no dunes. There a braided series of low water channels meandered through mudflats, backed by small area of saltmarsh. Very high tides could sweep across these mudflats and marshes on to the ancient mosslands, especially when the Ribble and Douglas were in flood after heavy rain. Even today, only drainage channels, embankments and pumps prevent large tracts of land around the Ribble being inundated by high spring tides.

The Lancashire mosslands

Men also [as well as wandering sheep and cattle] have found their last home upon this dreary place too in my memory. Nat Bell, and Radcliffe, returning home, loaded with ale, fell under the fatal burden and died before morning.

> Anon., *Manuscript on the treacherous natures of mosses*, c.1780.

One thousand years ago many small and several very large 'mosses' dominated the county's lowlands. A broad expanse of mossland extended, inland from the belt of sand dunes, northwards from Maghull, Ince Blundell and Altcar to the site of modern Southport, and then eastwards, backing the Ribble estuary saltmarshes almost to Preston. Other great mosses included the continuous belt from Simonswood and Kirkby through Bickerstaffe and Rainford, and those which formed a wide swathe of countryside from the edge of Warrington on both sides of the Mersey almost as far as Manchester. This included the celebrated Chat Moss, which was 2,600 hectares in extent in the seventeenth century before drainage began. It extended eastwards from Glaze Brook to Winton and southwards from Astley and Worsley to Irlam; across Glaze Brook, Risley Moss covered a further 1,800 hectares. North of the Ribble, mosslands backed the coast from Lytham north to the Wyre Estuary and then extended across Over Wyre from Pilling and Winmarleigh to Cockerham and on to Glasson. As one ditty put it, 'Pilling Moss, like God's Grace, is boundless!'

Of the many smaller mosses, one close to the centre of modern Manchester exists only through the name Moss Side, close to the University of Manchester. Ringway Moss has also vanished, its site is taken by Manchester International Airport. In contrast parts of Red Moss at Horwich and Risley Moss near Warrington, remain and are subject of some conservation work. My own calculations, based on old maps and fieldwork, suggest that at the end of the first millennium the total area of mossland in the Mersey Basin was approximately 18,000 hectares. Further north, there were a further 7,200 hectares south of the Ribble, 2,200 in the Fylde south of the River Wyre, and 7,400 hectares in Over Wyre and around the Lune estuary, giving, in the modern counties of Lancashire, Merseyside, north Cheshire and Greater Manchester, a total of some 34,800 hectares of mossland. Writing in 1793, when reclamation of mosslands was well under way, John Aiken (in *A Description of the County for Thirty of Forty Miles Around Manchester*) estimated the area of unreclaimed mossland then to be 26,500 acres (10,500 hectares).

Today, with the exception of the fragments of undrained virgin moss which survive, the areas of mosslands are mainly areas of flat, peaty arable farmland or market garden, drained by a network of ditches, although many small former mosses have been covered by brick and tarmac. Without continuous artificial drainage, most of the larger mosslands would rapidly revert to wild wetland, a process encouraged by wildlife organisations in some areas.

Mossland formation and plant life

Judging from radiocarbon dating of the deepest peat deposits, these mosslands began to develop around 7,500 years ago. Most of the peat was formed, however, within the last 3,000 years.[8] Extensive shallow hollows left at the end of the last Ice Age filled with water and the shallow lakes became colonised by a fenland plant community which included common reed (*Phragmites australis*), reedmace (*Typha latifolia* and *T. angustifolia*), jointed rush (*Juncus articulosus*), spike-rushes (*Eleocharis* species), sedges (*Carex* species), mare's-tail (*Hippuris vulgaris*), bogbean (*Menyanthes trifoliate*), various-leaved pondweed (*Potamogeton gramineus*), white and yellow water-lilies (*Nymphaea alba* and *Nuphar lutea*) and water plantain (*Alisma plantago-aquatica*). As the aquatic and semi-aquatic plants died, their remains partially decomposed to produce fen-peat, and as the layer of fen-peat grew thicker, so the depth of water diminished. The pollen of oak, willow, hazel, pine, lime and holly (*Ilex aquifolium*) and weed-species including stinging nettle (*Urtica dioica*), docks (*Rumex* species) and dandelion (*Taraxacum officinale*) has been found in fen-peat formed around 2,500 years ago. So too has the pollen of cereals.

This evidence allows us to reconstruct the main features of the landscape of lowland Lancashire in about 500 BC. On the better drained sloping ground, just above the level of the waterlogged ground and on the slopes which extended towards higher areas such as the Clieves Hills west of Ormskirk, or the upland of Harrock Hill on the edge of the Douglas valley, there

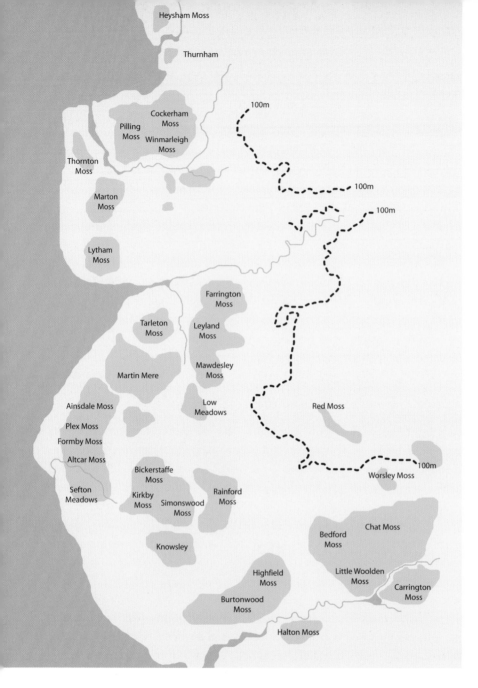

Heysham Moss

Thurnham

Cockerham Moss

Pilling Moss

Winmarleigh Moss

Thornton Moss

Marton Moss

Lytham Moss

Farrington Moss

Tarleton Moss

Leyland Moss

Mawdesley Moss

Martin Mere

Low Meadows

Red Moss

Ainsdale Moss

Plex Moss

Formby Moss

Altcar Moss

Bickerstaffe Moss

Sefton Meadows

Kirkby Moss

Simonswood Moss

Rainford Moss

Worsley Moss

Knowsley

Chat Moss

Bedford Moss

Highfield Moss

Little Woolden Moss

Carrington Moss

Burtonwood Moss

Halton Moss

100m

100m

100m

100m

A map showing the extent of wild mosslands in central and southern Lancashire around AD 1000. Subsequently the vast majority either had their peat extracted for fuel or were drained, burned and ploughed to produce rich, flat farmland. Tiny wild remnants can be seen at Red Moss (Horwich) (Natural England), Heysham and Bedford Mosses (Lancashire Wildlife Trust), Risley Moss (L.A. Reserve) and Highfield Moss (SSSI).

was extensive woodland. In places this had already been cleared to make agricultural land. The pollen of docks and dandelions indicates that farmers then, like gardeners now, had difficulty in keeping the weeds down. The flat lowlands were covered with the vast tracts of mossland or bog, with numerous areas of open water and a complex and intricate network of river channels and minor watercourses.

Cranberry creeps over *Sphagnum* moss.

A sundew plant, rooted amongst *Sphagnum* has captured a black darter, a dragonfly closely associated with natural mosslands.

Quickly the level of fen-peat would have neared the water surface and as open water disappeared, so a peat-bog plant community replaced the fenland plant community. The dominant plants on a bog are three species of bog-moss. *Sphagnum cuspidatum* dominated the wetter part of the bog, one form of this species being capable of living in shallow water. *S. papillosum* dominated the less wet areas. *S. rubellum* formed dry rusty-red mounds within the less wet *S. papillosum* areas. Also found on the bog would have been bog rosemary with its pink bell-flowers, the yellow spikes of bog asphodel, the aromatic bog myrtle (*Myrica gala*), pink-flowered cranberry, white beak sedge (*Rhynchospora alba*) and three species of insectivorous sundew (*Drosera*). Cotton-grasses (both the dominant *Eriophorum vaginatum* and, in wetter areas, *E. angustifolium*), that are really sedges, occurred the bog, single shoots emerging from the clumps of bog-moss, but where the moss cover had been broken, dense swards might be found, lighting the late spring scene with white, feathery fruit-heads. Cross-leaved heath would also have grown in the wetter areas, areas of purple moor-grass and bog-myrtle in others, and in the driest parts of the bog extensive swathes of heather would have been purple in the early autumn sun.[9]

Such bogs were not fixed; they were constantly growing upwards and outwards. From about 2,500–3,000 years ago the climate became wetter than before, and evaporation was reduced by an increased incidence of cloud-cover. Humans may have contributed to the tendency for waterlogging. Forest trees take huge volumes of water from the ground and pass it into the air from the leaves. The felling of trees in low-lying areas would have reduced this transpiration and encouraged bog formation. So as rain fell on the bog the bog-mosses absorbed the water and grew upwards, raising the level of the bog and spreading sideways onto adjacent low ground and suffocating any woodland already growing there. Thus these low-level bogs are known as 'raised bogs'.

Human communities living beside these growing bogs tried to cope with the inundation. Someone once called the Iron Age dwellers in the lowlands of north-west England 'dwellers in the country of water', and several dugout canoes as well as iron axe- and spear-heads have been found in and around

A stump of bog oak, unearthed by a plough on Martin Mere.

the mosses. In some areas of raised bog late Bronze and Iron Age people felled trees to build roadways across the bog (the most famous, Kate's Pad on Pilling Moss has been dated to 2500 BC, and traces of similar log roadways have been discovered buried in peat lands south of the Ribble); the growing bog overwhelmed these and, of course, the felling of even more trees would have exacerbated the problem. Today the stumps of oaks, which were suffocated and killed by the oxygen-starved peat, are exposed by the erosion or ploughing of peat and called 'bog oak'.

It is likely that those whose lives were being disrupted by the rapidly expanding mosslands held them in some sort of awe. Evidence for this comes from the discovery of three bodies during peat excavation on Lindow Moss, close to Wilmslow in Cheshire, during the 1980s. A severed head found on 13 May 1983 was radiocarbon dated to AD 210+/−80, a part-corpse found on 1 August 1984 was dated to between 2 BC and AD 119, and fragments of a body found on 6 February 1987 were dated at AD 25–230. Besides these, in 1824 a severed head, wrapped in a woollen cloth, was discovered in Pilling Moss, in 1942; a decapitated skull was unearthed from Red Moss (Horwich); and, on 18 August 1958, the head of a young man, severed from the body at the second cervical vertebra, with a fractured skull and with a garrotte of cord bound tightly round the throat, was found in Worsley Moss. These people had been murdered, probably as a sacrificial offering to some god, and their bodies ceremonially put in the peat beneath the bog-moss surface. Undoubtedly very many similar sacrifices have never been discovered. It is noteworthy that the stomach of the part-corpse from Lindow Moss contained the remains of a quite special meal, including seeds of mistletoe (*Viscum album*), a plant of mystical properties for ancient Britons.[10]

In the acid, oxygenless bog, these bodies did not decompose as they would have had they been laid on top of the bog or in the bog surface. Many other bodies have been recorded in the past but not scientifically examined. C. Leigh noted, in his *The Natural History of Lancashire, Cheshire and the Peak of Derbyshire* (1700), that 'sometimes in mosses are found human bodies entire and uncorrupted'.

Perhaps these early people associated peat bogs with a god, for these bogs were not predictable, inert structures. Methane, or marsh gas, was generated within the peat and, as it bubbled at the surface, it sometimes spontaneously ignited to give a weak phosphorescent flame long called 'Will-o'-the-wisp'. To simple minds a flickering flame out there on a treacherous bog in a misty winter's evening would surely seem to be an apparition from another world? The effect would be even more marked when, following the sudden ignition of a large build-up of methane the bog exploded. In either 1633 or 1663 (the two years are given by different authors) Chat Moss exploded and is said to

Lindow Moss. It was at this precise spot that Lindow Moss Man, wittily nicknamed Pete Marsh, was buried two millennia ago. Was he, and the other bog-bodies, sacrifices made to the gods of the bog?

have 'strewn the Manx, Welsh and Irish coasts with peat!' That, of course, was a gross exaggeration, yet it illustrates the awe in which these bogs were held well into the seventeenth century.

Occasionally raised bogs absorbed so much water that they simply burst open. The peat turned from a saturated and unstable solid into a viscous liquid, and began to flow – contemporary reports of such 'brasts' (to use the Lancashire dialect term) suggest that broad sheets of thick peaty water poured across adjacent farmland (for the raised bog was higher than the surrounding areas) and choked streams and rivers. While the effects were temporary, serious economic damage could ensue, though fortunately such spectacular events were very rare. In 1526, when Chat Moss burst, a contemporary anonymous report stated that the moss had grown 'as high as the top of Culcheth Mill.' John Leland, Henry VIII's antiquary, reported that, 'For Chately Mosse [Chat Moss] that with breking up of abundance of water yn hit did much hurt to landes therabout, and rivers with wandering moss and corrupte water.'[11]

When humans began to drain and reclaim the Lancashire mosslands the mossland habitat would have been a mosaic. There would have been open pools (as at Martin and Marton Meres), areas of fenland, areas dominated by bog mosses, drier areas dominated by heather and even drier areas with birch woodland.

Animals living on untamed mossland

We know relatively little of the animals that inhabited the wild mosslands, simply because they were drained before accurate recording of wildlife began. F. S. Mitchell's *Birds of Lancashire* was published in 1885 towards the end of reclamations, though there were memories provided by some of his correspondents.[12]

Several moorland birds nested on the raised bogs. Twites, also known as mountain linnets, are scarce moorland birds (page 155), but they nested commonly on the untamed mosslands. Mitchell quoted a Mr John Hardy who considered twite to be commoner than linnets (*C. cannabina*) 'near Manchester [on Chat Moss] ... during the years of the Cotton Famine [1860s], when the factory girls wandered in their neighbourhoods further than is usual with them, knitting or otherwise employing themselves to kill the time, I found some nests of the twite lined with lengths or bits of worsted, one in particular being lined with white in a neat and remarkable manner.' The last twite nests to be recorded from Lancashire mosslands were found amongst heather on Formby Moss in 1917 and on Chat Moss in June 1940.

Mitchell tells us that 'the mosses ... are the stronghold of the short-eared owl in the breeding season. Here among the heath, it nests annually.' The last mossland nests of short-eared owls were found on Cockerham Moss in about 1906, Martin Mere [the report said, 'near Southport'] in 1917, and on Carrington Moss (where the bird bred commonly up to 1893) in May 1922. Today, short-eared owls nest only on the moors and are scarce winter visitors to the mosslands.

The red grouse, Mitchell tells us, was common 'on the ling-covered mosses, both inland and adjoining the coast', and well into the nineteenth century there were several grouse-shoots on the mosses (as at Cockerham and Carrington). The 1916 Lancashire & Cheshire Fauna Committee Report stated that: 'Mr L. Greening reports that the Red Grouse is still to be found in the low-lying mosses at Holcroft and Rixton near Warrington'. It is not today, for grouse now occur only on the Pennine moors and only two have been seen on the lowland mosses in the last ninety years (singles noted in the *Lancashire Bird Reports* at Formby Moss, December 1959 and at Little Woolden Moss, 24 April 1970). Grouse still occur on mosslands close to the Solway Firth.

The nightjar (*Caprimulgus europaeus*) is a moth-eating crepuscular summer visitor. According to Mitchell it was once 'common on all South Lancashire mosses'. By the 1950s it was restricted to the small wilder remaining corners of Chat and Risley Mosses. By 2000 none remained.

That mosslands were once home to a great wetland bird community is borne out by Mitchell's description of the status of the bittern (*Botaurus stellaris*): 'It is naturally most often seen upon the low-lying peat-mosses and marsh lands, and there is no doubt that, years ago, in their unreclaimed state, these were tenanted for the purposes of breeding'. There is one dated record of bitterns breeding on the mosslands of west Lancashire: on 6 August 1708 a Mr Aldreds was found 'in ye cross-field, he had been taking young Bitterns.'[13]

But of most other water birds, such as the water rail (*Rallus aquaticus*) and the now extremely rare spotted crake (*Porzana porzana*) we have no information other than they almost certainly occurred, probably in high densities. Perhaps Leighton Moss near Silverdale in north Lancashire can give us a clue. Its 160 hectare reedbed has a wonderful assortment of fenland birds. Were even larger areas of Lancashire mosslands so rich in aquatic birds? They were probably even richer. For instance the crane (*Grus grus*) certainly bred on the wild mosslands, for its footprints have been found preserved in peat beds off Formby Point and the tenth-century Norse invaders named one of their settlements after this birds that they would have known so well from home: Tranmere, *bank of the cranes.*

However, fragmentary and casual evidence from miscellaneous documentary sources can help to give clues about wildlife. For example, *The Diaries of Nicholas Blundell* of Little Crosby cover the years 1702–28 and include many earlier notes.[14] Most of the records come from the Blundell estates in the vicinity, including not only Little Crosby but also Ince Blundell and the Altcar mosslands. For 29 April 1711 Blundell reported that 'John Bannister took a Fulmert with his hands'. The 'fulmert' is the foulmart or polecat. Polecats (*Mustela putorius*) are assumed to have been common, especially in marshy areas, but this is the only good dated record of the species from our region and it is likely that the only reason this polecat is included in the diary is because it was caught by hand and not killed in a trap or by shooting. Polecats were said to have occurred on Pilling Moss as late as 1891 (see below), while we know that in 1666 the Prestwich churchwardens gave Richard Bate a bounty of two pence 'ffor a filmard', and the bounty in 1773 at Prestbury was three shillings for a 'filmart and filchet' (both names for the polecat).[15]

On 15 December 1712 Blundell reported: 'I had a Cow cast its Calf, I Lay'd it to shoot Kits at the Long Garden Wall'; and on 21 January 1713 noted that: 'Betty Swift sent me a Mare to lay to shoot Kites'. Despite the fact that Mitchell could quote no records in 1885 of red kites (*Milvus milvus*) from the Lancashire lowlands (he gives very few from the moorlands further north), they must have been common early in the eighteenth century for Blundell to have laid out the corpses of large animals to attract them so that he could shoot them. The day after he put out Betty Swift's dead mare: 'Robert Tompson shot a Kite through the Long Garden Wall'. Other kite records include a payment of sixpence in 1664 to Thomas Hardman 'ffor 1 urchant [hedgehog] and 5 gleads [kites]' by Prestwick churchwardens, and the receipt of '3 kyte heads' by Ormskirk churchwardens in 1666.[16]

In those days all snakes were styled vipers, adders or longworms. Blundell makes several references to them, but it is clear that they were actually grass snakes, from their size and the locations in which they were often caught: Today grass snakes (*Natrix natrix*) are probably extinct on the Lancashire mosslands, yet early in the eighteenth century they appear to have been abundant. This is to be expected, for they are semi-aquatic reptiles and wet mosslands, with their large populations of amphibians and small fish, would have suited them. On 9 July 1725 Blundell noted that: 'Thomas Newton killd an Adder which was fully 3 Foot & three Inshes long.' Adders (*Vipera berus*) never grow to that length; grass snakes do. Four years earlier, he reported on 22 June 1721 that 'Some of my Servants and Thomas Syers Etc: Killed 50 Adders most of them in some old Hay as was lately put out of the Hay-Loft and lay behind the Stables, severall of them wer of the largest Size.' Grass snakes are famous for entering fermenting compost and muck heaps, seeking warm places to lay their eggs. Adders never do this, being viviparous. Blundell gave two other references to grass snakes. On 3 July 1708: 'There were 72 adders or longworms taken in ye midding on ye backside of my stable in about two hours time, 22 of which were baired and killed with lifting up only one pitchfork of dung or old straw; some were killed in other places about the house to-day or yesterday. When they were all together they were 81 in count, those of the longest size were about 3 feet and ½, the generality upwards of 2 foot 10 inch. They were in wight 45lbs.' 14 June 1712: 'Robert Tompson [he who killed the Kite?] killed about 15 Adders or Long Worms'.

Grass snakes are almost certainly extinct in the entire Ribble catchment, the last dated record coming from Samlesbury on 6 August 1922, though the *Seventeenth Report* of the Lancashire & Cheshire Fauna Committee indicated that it was still fairly common on the mosslands close to Garstang up to 1930. All subsequent reports have turned out to be of non-native subspecies of grass snakes escaped from captivity (*Lancashire & Cheshire Fauna Committee Reports*).

Today the mosslands of west Lancashire are visited in winter by thousands of pink-footed geese (*Anser brachyrhynchos*) from Iceland. They feed on

Red kites were once common on and around the mosslands, but were exterminated during the eighteenth century. Today efforts are being made to introduce kites widely across Britain.

stubbles, potato fields and meadows. On 26 September 1721, Nicholas Blundell reported, 'I saw a Large Flock of Wild Geece they are the first I have heard this Season'. But were they pink-feet? Probably not, for from the notes published in 1885 by Mitchell they were more likely to have been white-fronted geese (*Anser albifrons*), and of the Greenland race *flavirostris*: 'this species comes down to the marshes and river [Mersey] at night to feed, passing the day on the moss-lands'. But Mitchell was not absolutely right. These geese flighted to the mosslands at dawn to feed (as Greenland white-fronts still do on some unreclaimed raised-bogs and blanket-bogs in Wales, Ireland and the Inner Hebridean island of Islay) on cotton-grass rhizomes, and they flighted back to the Mersey at dusk to roost.

Pilling Moss was the last of the great Lancashire mosslands to be completely drained and turned to the plough. Cuthbert Oxendale gave a little insight into what the moss was like.[17] There, amidst 'a rough spongy piece of land' was a black-headed gull colony holding an estimated '10,000 to 12,000' birds. Oxendale described how 'I threaded my way to the breeding ground by reclaimed patches and through piles of peat drying for fuel. I had barely ascended the breast of the moss and begun to wade knee-deep through the shaggy "ling," when thousands of these startled birds rose into the air.' He also described how, 'through the droppings of the bird the heather has disappeared before so rich a manure, and rank grasses and rushes have succeeded'.

Nine years later, Thomas Newbigging described a visit to the same gallery: 'Buckbean, water-mint and cresses flourish here luxuriantly … The croaking of the innumerable frogs which haunt the marshes, to one unused to such sounds, is a rich treat.' The pools and ditches, he said, 'harbour eels in great abundance, and of large growth. Our guide, who is an adept in the art of spearing these creatures, by beating the surface of the water, immediately produced an unusual commotion underneath; bubbles of air were seen rising in half a dozen places, caused by eels boring for security into the mud at the bottom. Quick as lightning the spear was plunged into the water where a succession of air bells was rapidly rising, and on its withdrawal, an eel of large size, caught by the neck, wriggled and struggled to free itself.'[18] In double quick time they caught enough eels to provide 'a dinner that a lord might envy'. It is clear that mossland pools were great eel fisheries. But Newbigging gives a few other notes of interest. 'Large quantities of peat' were excavated annually, yet the supply 'seems almost inexhaustible.' Large tracts of the area were covered 'with a close shaven carpet of dark green moss [*Sphagnum*: see page 211] and dwarf grass, level as a bowling green.' There were hares, rabbits and weasels, and he tells us that, 'the marks of the polecat's claws may be traced on the beaten tracks'.

The *Prescot Churchwardens' Accounts 1523–1607* include bounties paid for the heads of 'vermin'.[19] Prescot is just to the south of Catchdale and Kirkby Mosses, and though this is beyond the Ribble catchment there is no reason to suppose that it was untypical of the position elsewhere in mossland Lancashire. In 1591 the churchwardens 'Payd John Olyverson for ix [nine] crowe heades and ij [two] kytes and one pye [magpie] head, vjd. [sixpence]. Payd James Taylor ix [nine] crowe heades, a pye hed and a kyte head and a hedghodg, vijd. [sevenpence].' In 1594 the record shows how hedgehogs (*Erinaceus europaeus*) were then considered vermin, with a bounty up to twice that of the red kite: 'Item, paid to Mathew Stemson for vij [seven] urchins [hedgehogs], xx [twenty] crowe heades, iij [three] mouldes [moles], iij malpes [bullfinch], ijs. jd. [two shillings and a penny]. Item, paid to Mathew Ellum for vij urchins, xiiijd [fourteen pence]. Item, paid to Peter Suttons boy for iiij mouldes and fowre crowe heades, iijd. Item, paid to Edmund Tunstall for v urchins, ixd. Item, paid to William Johnson for iij urchin heades, vd. Item, paid to Ellize Gleast for ix urchin heades, xvjd [sixteen pence] … Item, paid to George Smith for j kyte head, jd.' A penny for a kite's head!

In the 1590s red kites must have been a common sight as they sought food over the vast mosslands. In November 2002 they were so rare that crowds of birdwatchers gathered to watch two soaring over the Altcar mosses. Oh to be able to go back, with modern binoculars, to watch the wildlife of sixteenth-century mosslands!

Mossland reclamation

The process of reclamation of mossland, involving the cutting of drainage channels, the creation of fields, and eventually ploughing and top-dressing to produce farmland, was extremely protracted and undertaken largely as a result of piecemeal effort by local landowners and communities. In the Lancashire mosslands, in contrast to areas such as the Fens, the Somerset Levels and the Humber lowlands, there are very few examples of large-scale concerted projects for drainage of large areas by major engineering works. The only significant exception is the project for the draining of Martin Mere, discussed below; most other works were more local and more modest. It is possible that some drainage work predates the Norman Conquest, but there is better documentary and historical evidence to show that monastic houses were active in land drainage during the medieval period. Burscough Priory, for example, had apparently undertaken the construction of ditches and drainage channels on Burscough and Tarlscough Mosses by the end of the thirteenth century.

It is important to recognise that the mosslands, though they were invariably denounced by the agricultural improvers of the eighteenth century as being waste, useless, barren and unproductive, were in fact important and valuable elements in the local economy and served as a vital natural resource. From earliest times the peat was cut for fuel, and throughout lowland Lancashire this remained the only significant fuel for domestic use until the late eighteenth century, when coal gradually began to supersede its use. Peat-diggings, or turbaries, were an essential asset for any lowland community. They were carefully husbanded and jealously guarded, particular care being taken to prevent people from adjacent communities encroaching onto mosses belonging to others (a major consideration being that the open mossland was without visible and obvious boundaries, so that local experts maintained a store of community knowledge to ensure that the actual boundaries between townships were clearly understood). Many court cases in the sixteenth and seventeenth centuries concerned infringement of turbary rights and, indeed, a great deal of our knowledge about the mosses and how they were exploited comes from evidence given in these cases. For example, Penwortham Moss on the southern side of the head of the head of the Ribble estuary extended as far as Farington and Hutton. It had some wet areas, for reeds were cut for thatching. However, most appears to have been communal grazing and turbaries where peat, 'Twoo Yardes in depenes', was cut for fuel. On 26 February 1547, King Edward VI set up a commission to investigate the extent that the people exploited the peat and grazing there.[20] On Burscough Moss, where the people of the village had for long dug their peat fuel, the Duchy Court had to intervene following a skirmish over peat-digging rights between a band led by Sir James Stanley (who had purchased Burscough Priory and its lands after Dissolution in 1537) and the servants of Sir Hugh Huxley and William Adamson.[21]

The moss also provided other resources. Reeds and rushes were cut for thatching roofs, for strewing on the earth floors of houses, and for the pith of the *Juncus* rush which provided wicks for tallow dips and rushlights. In all mossland communities eggs of waterfowl were gathered in spring, and waterbirds themselves were killed from late summer and through the winter. We also know that areas of mossland with open water or fen were important fisheries, which represented a valuable asset for landowners and could be leased out for large sums. Of these Martin Mere was the most important. Eels would have occurred here naturally (in 1278 there was a two marks – 13s. 4d. – annual fee to fish for eels at North Meols[22]), but other species that were netted, including pike, bream and carp, were probably introduced deliberately. A 'Moat' shown on the Ordnance Survey map close to Eas Brook at Scarisbrick (SD 391128) is almost certainly the remains of a late thirteenth- or early-fourteenth century fishpond.[23] It may be that pike and cyprinids escaped or were released into the Mere from fishponds such as this.

These fish stocks were carefully and jealously preserved. In February 1354 Roger Bondesson and John Stelle of Rufford were prosecuted for taking 'bremos' (bream) belonging to Richard de Aghton from the Blowick end of Martin Mere.[24] In 1565 John Bold claimed damages for trespass against Barnaby Kytchyn, William Matthewe and Hugh Haward over the fishery at Wykes Ditch, a channel at the edge of the Mere at Blowick.[25] In a case brought to the Duchy Court it was reported that in March 1537 John Hunter and William Dobson had been going to the Mere to collect a net owned by their employer Henry Banastre when they were set upon by a band of employees of Sir Thomas Hesketh. In Court, Dobson pointed out that where they were fishing, close to Sollom and Rufford, the fishing belonged to Mr Banastre. Later Sir Thomas admitted knowing that his men were illegally fishing, but denied sending them to beat up Mr Banastre's employees.[26]

In 1620 the will of Robert Hesketh, who lived at Holmeswood Hall on the north shore of Martin Mere, included a boat propelled by three pairs of oars. At about the same time, Edward Scarisbrick, who lived close to the south-western corner of the Mere at Scarisbrick Hall, owned fourteen 'bow-nets' and several pike traps. Wicker traps made from willow were also used in weed-fringed creeks, while in deeper water long-lining with baited hooks was an important way of catching fish, especially eels. It is possible that towers at Holmeswood Hall (now demolished) and Martin Hall were used as lighthouses to guide fishermen and ferryboats in the gloom of a winter's dusk.[27]

In 1779 Parliament passed an Act 'for draining, improving and preserving the Low Lands in the Parishes of Altcar, Sefton, Halsall and Walton upon the Hill' (i.e. the mosses just inland of the coast between Southport and Liverpool). This included the drainage of three small lakes – the White and Black Otters Pools and Gettern Mere (called Barton Mere in Yates's map of 1786) – by Fine Jane's and Downholland Brooks. The names of two of these survive in White Otter Farm by Segars Lane near to Ainsdale and Gettern Farm on Plex Moss. That these lakes were once important freshwater fisheries is borne out by a report of 1662 in which Henry Blundell laid claim to wreckage on the coast at Birkdale. In his *Annals of Southport and District* (1887), E. Bland quotes this report: 'Also there was last upp a cock-boat, which was seized upon for th'use of the said Robt. Blundell, and afterwards was flitted for a ffyshing boat on the Meyre called White-oter, for the only use of the said Mr Blundell.'

Martin Mere not only covered a large area but hindered travel west of the Douglas. It was, according to Leland, the 'Greatest Meare of Lancastreshire', at its maximum extent (before the beginning of the eighteenth century) extending for nine kilometres from Rufford in the east to Blowick in the west and for about five kilometres from Scarisbrick in the south to Mere Brow in the north. The name Blowick comes from the Old Norse *bla-vik*, the black or dark bay of the mere. Its main outflow was into the River Asland (as the lower reaches of the Douglas were then known) between Rufford and Causeway Farm, but water levels were high it also flowed out to the sea along a wetland channel more or less on the line of the present outflow to Crossens. The mere was very large but very shallow – at its centre it was some four metres deep, although there were great thicknesses of mud and soft peat in the lakebed. There were several small islands in the mere, the most prominent being the Great Peel and the Little Peel, which were towards the western end of the lake in the broad bay between Tarlscough and Rufford, and the Wet Holsome which was close to the Burscough shore. Within the mere there were some deep holes in the bed, caused by springs of fresh water welling up, and here the richest fisheries were to be found. Most of the shore was not clearly defined, for open water gave way almost imperceptibly to a waterlogged alder carr, or wet scrub, which merged into thick peat bog woven

Bank Hall, by the Douglas at Bretherton, was home of Mr Fleetwood when he planned the drainage of Martin Mere. The hall was in a dilapidated state at the start of the 2000s, but work is under way to restore what was once a fine stately home.

with channels and small pools. Only on the north side, along the foot of the Holmeswood ridge, was the shore more precisely delineated.[28]

Thomas Eccleston of Scarisbrick Hall, writing in 1786, described how, in '1692 Mr Fleetwood of Bank Hall proposed to the other proprietors to drain Martin Meer on condition that a lease (for the whole) for three lives and thirty-one years should be granted him, which they agreed to do.'[29] The agreement between Fleetwood and the eight others who owned a share of the Mere was signed in 1694. In it Fleetwood would pay for all the work being carried out and compensate the others for the loss of fishing, wildfowling and reed-cutting. An Act of Parliament of 1695 approved that proposal, but ruled that the lease was for two, not three lives. The two lives were of Fleetwood himself and his daughter Henrietta, who died in 1722. The Fleetwood lease thus expired in 1753.

Fleetwood had to stop the Mere draining eastwards to the Douglas, so he dug a new outlet called the Sluice to the west so that water would drain out directly into the estuary at Crossens. This eliminated a major problem, for the natural outlet to the Douglas was too high. During summer droughts this outflow stopped and the Mere stagnated. It was hoped that the new outflow would allow continuous drainage to the sea, except at the highest spring tides. The new outflow was a canal 7.25 metres wide, with a base lower than that of the Mere, extending for two kilometres from Mere to estuary. However, the Mere was about three metres below the height reached by the maximum high water of spring tides, so Fleetwood had to solve the problem of seawater reflooding the Mere through his canal. He built a pair of sluice gates that were designed to close automatically when the tide pushed against them, but would reopen on the ebb. Unfortunately, the channel beyond the gates rapidly silted up and to prevent this Fleetwood had the gates raised by a half metre. This removed the slack flow at high water which caused the silting, but it resulted in higher water levels in the Sluice at high tide. This hindered drainage, and the lower pastures which had successfully been reclaimed soon reverted to bog. Thomas Fleetwood died in 1717, but his work was continued by his successor up to 1753 when the lease expired. In 1755 the sluice gates were washed away in a tidal surge and, though replaced, again became blocked open by silt. A large area of expensively reclaimed land reverted to swamp or, as Thomas Eccleston put it: 'The lands upon the Meer became of little value, being covered with water all winter and liable to be flooded by very trivial summer rains.'[30]

Eccleston was exaggerating a little, however, for Fleetwood was able to lease three farms on part of the land he had drained. One was to John Berry (from whom Berry House Farm at Tarlscough takes its name); one was to Henry Low (who built two houses on what is now the Leisure Lakes site); and one was taken by Eiliam Wiggins, whose name is remembered in Wiggins Lane which leads from Holmeswood towards Burscough.

In 1778 Thomas Eccleston moved into Scarisbrick Hall and in 1781 resumed the task of draining Martin Mere and its surrounding mosslands. He constructed three sets of sluice gates. Outermost was a pair of sea-gates, inside of which was a pair of flushing-gates. When the tide fell and the sea-gates opened, any silt laid down was flushed away by a sudden surge of water released by the flushing-gates. As an added precaution, close to the Mere outflow Eccleston built a pair of stop-gates which would, in the event of the other gates failing, prevent seawater flowing into the Mere. There were occasional setbacks. In April 1783 all three sets of gates failed and large areas of reclaimed land were flooded. Eccleston's sluice system had it drained off in five days. He had the Sluice re-excavated so that its bed was at sea level and its length extended to eight kilometres. As drainage proceeded he had about 175 kilometres of interlinking drainage channels cut to assist with draining and to flush away further floodwater. To help with this Eccleston purchased a special plough, invented by Cuthbert Clark, which dug ditches that led to the main drains. 'I am most gladly indebted to the inventor,' he wrote, 'for with this, in one day, I cut drains eight miles in length, thirteen inches in depth, twenty inches wide at the top, and five at the bottom.'[31]

Berry House farm gets its name from one of the first men to farm a reclaimed part of Martin Mere.

In 1784 the first of the drained areas was ploughed and produced its first crop of cereals. Within a few years, land that was formerly worth only four shillings per acre was producing a crop of barley yielding an income of £11 17s. 6d. per acre *per annum*, and land that had been worth nothing was producing an annual income of £10 17s. 6d. per acre from a crop of oats. It was reported that reclaimed areas left to grow grass produced the best pasture in Lancashire. There were still occasional setbacks. Thus, in 1789 the river Douglas burst its banks just south of Rufford (at the natural outflow of Martin Mere) and flooded the Mere. The Douglas banks were then raised to prevent this happening again. In 1813, four years after Thomas Eccleston had died and his son (also called Thomas) inherited the estate, heavy seas destroyed sea- and flushing-gates; but the stop-gates prevented massive inundation.

Thus far, drainage had depended solely on gravity, but in 1849 Sir Thomas Dalrymple Hesketh had a steam-pump installed at Crossens so that the water was pumped out. Today there is a large pumping station at Crossens, with electric pumps, and the Mere is now mostly dry farmland. However, an area south of Mere Hall is now significantly below sea level, because with continued draining and pumping the peat of the old lakebed has shrunk dramatically, lowering the land surface and requiring yet more pumping. It is now some five metres below maximum high water mark. This means that not only is Martin Mere particularly vulnerable to possible sea-level rise, but also that the cost to the public purse of maintaining the farmland in its present state is increasing inexorably.

Only one small area of Martin Mere remained boggy in summer and flooded in winter into the 1970s. This area, at Tarlscough, is now the reserve at the Wildfowl and Wetlands Trust.

Crossens pumping station. Without this Martin Mere would quickly revert to a lake surrounded by wetland. The boulder in the foreground is an 'erratic' brought here by glacier from Dumfriesshire in the last Ice Age.

The last remnant of Martin Mere that was never completely drained and that never saw the plough is now the reserve of Martin Mere Wildfowl & Wetlands Trust.

The other mossland areas have been similarly drained and converted into black, peaty, highly productive arable farmland. By the second half of the seventeenth century about 5,700 hectares between the Mersey and the Ribble had already been reclaimed to some degree. Following Acts of Parliament in 1779 and 1800 – 'for the draining, improving and preserving the Low Lands' – Banks, Tarleton, Halsall and Plex Mosses are drained to Crossens, whereas water from Downholland and Formby Mosses is pumped south to the River Alt. Further east, Mawdesley and Croston Mosses drain directly into the Douglas or via the Yarrow or Lostock, and Leyland Moss drains to the Douglas via Carr Brook; the drainage of Croston Moss resulted in the loss of Fenny Pool that covered a large area between Rufford and Croston village.

There is no heather on Heather Farm. There was when the heathery mossland was reclaimed to create Heather Farm.

Gettern Farm, in the midst of Plex Moss, grows potatoes and carrots in its peaty soil. The name comes from Gettern Mere, a large shallow lake that was drained to create the farmland.

This cottage was built in 1752, 29 years before Thomas Eccleston carried out his drainage of Martin Mere. When it was built, the Mere would have lapped close to its back door!

Further north, a main drainage channel, the Main Drain or Main Dyke was cut between the Ribble estuary at Lytham and Wyre estuary at Skipool, into which water from the southern Fylde mosslands is pumped and then carried away. This resulted in the loss of Cursed Mere, probably an area of fenland (see below), and a reduction of the area of Marton Mere, now a local nature reserve.

Not all mosslands in the Middle Ages were lakes, fens or deep bogs. For instance, large areas of the drier moss edges between Lytham and Poulton-le-Fylde provided excellent cattle grazing, but even here there were some dangerous spots. In 1527 the Duchy Court heard how the Prior of Lytham had rights on Lytham Moss beyond the Cursidmeyre [the vividly named Cursed Mere], but was told that Cursidmeyre was a mire where 'hath ben many bestes and Catelles drowned therin.' [32] Marton Mere, inland of Blackpool, is the last remnant of wet mossland in that area north of the Ribble. Until the mosslands and meres were drained, travelling through the country surrounding the Ribble estuary was notoriously difficult, and habitations were few. When Celia Fiennes made her *Northern Journey* in 1697, after fording the Mersey she headed north-east to Wigan and then continued north to Preston rather than take the more direct route on the Ormskirk/Burscough clay ridge. 'Not going by Ormskerk,' she wrote, 'I avoided going by the famous Mer call'd Martin's Mer, that as the proverb sayes has parted many a man and his mare indeed; it being evening and not getting a Guide I was a little afraid to go that way it being very hazardous for Strangers to pass by it.' [33]

Middle Meanygate is a track across Tarleton Moss. Meanygate means a gate, or track, leading to common fields (see page 76); several lanes and tracks are still called 'meanygate' in the Tarleton-Banks region.

So by the beginning of the twentieth century little natural mossland remained, apart from a few corners of Chat, Risley and Highfield Mosses in the south, part of Simonswood Moss further west, and by the end of the twentieth century no completely natural mossland remained south of the river Wyre. All the rest had been drained and turned into productive farmland, some of the best in Britain, or the rich brown peat has been excavated for the horticulture industry and so that private gardeners could grow prettier geraniums.

However, the trend to drain and reclaim is now being reversed. The remains of Red, Risley and Highfield Mosses are being preserved and returned to their natural state. Along parts of the Alt, the Environment Agency is returning areas to wetland as part of flood-prevention schemes. At Martin Mere Wildfowl and Wetlands Trust Centre, the last marshy part of Martin Mere has been saved, and a large area of drained and formerly arable mossland is being converted back into wet mossland, with open pools and reedbeds. In time, projects such as these will give us an inkling as to what Lancashire's wild mosslands were really like.

The Ribble coastline: mud and sand, saltmarsh and sand dune

We have very little contemporary information as to what the coastline from Preston westwards to Formby Point and Starr Gate was like before the late eighteenth century. Of five maps of the Ribble estuary published in the sixteenth and seventeenth centuries (Saxton 1579, William Smith 1598, Speed 1610, Johan Blaeu 1648 and Collins 1689) that of Blaeu is perhaps most useful in showing what the area was like before it was altered by man. Martin Mere and the mosslands dominate the southern side of the estuary. Water from the Mere flows east into the River Asland, into which the Rivers Douglas, Tawd and Yarrow also flow. The Asland flows into the Ribble estuary as it does today (though now called the Douglas). To the north of the estuary is Marton Mere, then a lake of considerable size. Lytham and Marton Mosses form an extensive area north of Lytham. The coastlines south of North Meols (Southport) and north of Lytham are concave in outline on this map, and not convex curves as on today's maps. In the middle of the seventeenth century the land on which Blackpool Airport and the town of St Anne's now stand was sand dune. Similarly, the land on which most of modern Birkdale, Ainsdale, Woodvale, Freshfield and the western part of Formby was then dune.

Collins's map of 1689 contrasts with the others because it lacks detail about the high water mark and instead shows the estuary channels and sand banks. The low water Ribble channel has banks on either side, but the outer estuary

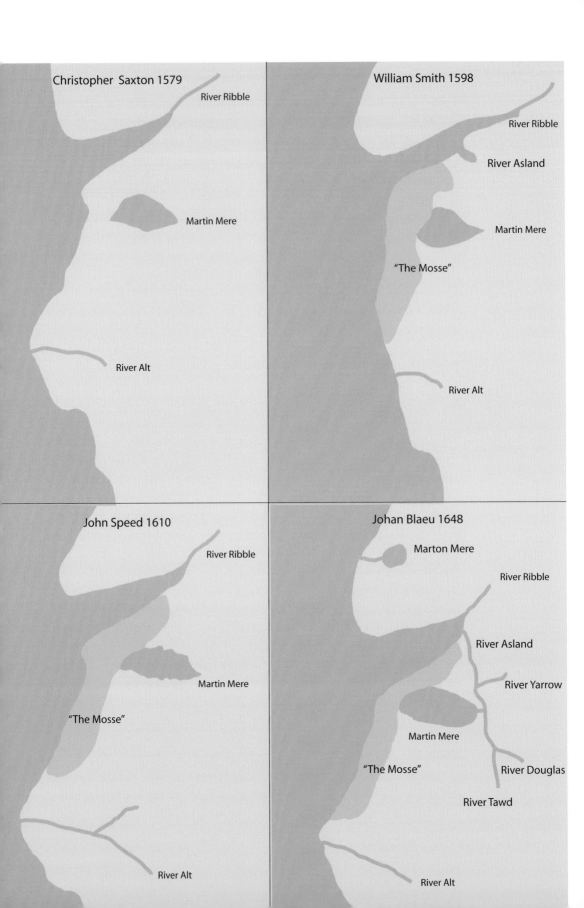

Christopher Saxton 1579

River Ribble

Martin Mere

River Alt

William Smith 1598

River Ribble

River Asland

Martin Mere

"The Mosse"

River Alt

John Speed 1610

River Ribble

Martin Mere

"The Mosse"

River Alt

Johan Blaeu 1648

Marton Mere

River Ribble

River Asland

River Yarrow

Martin Mere

"The Mosse"

River Douglas

River Tawd

River Alt

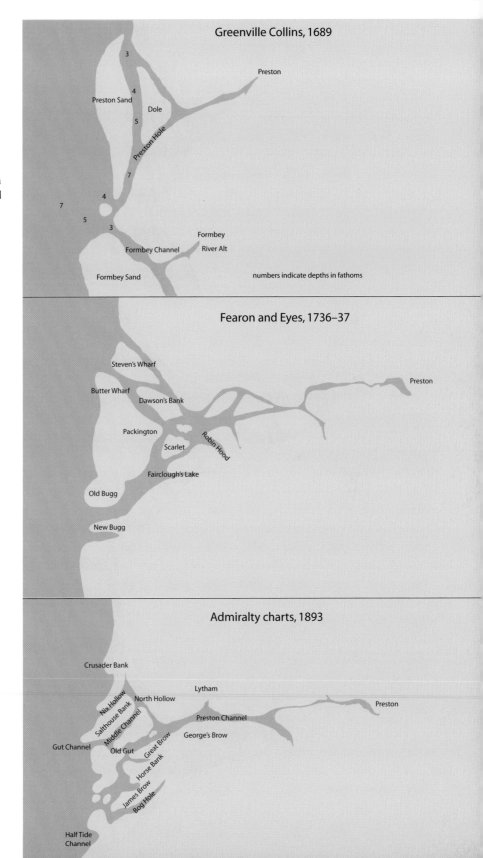

Some early maps and charts of the Ribble estuary, from the sixteenth century to the end of the nineteenth century.

Greenville Collins, 1689

3
4
Preston Sand
Dole
5
Preston Hole
7
4
7
5
3
Preston
Formbey
Formbey Channel
River Alt
Formbey Sand
numbers indicate depths in fathoms

Fearon and Eyes, 1736–37

Steven's Wharf
Butter Wharf
Dawson's Bank
Packington
Scarlet
Robin Hood
Fairclough's Lake
Old Bugg
New Bugg
Preston

Admiralty charts, 1893

Crusader Bank
Lytham
Nix Hollow
North Hollow
Salthouse Bank
Middle Channel
Preston Channel
Preston
George's Brow
Gut Channel
Old Gut
Great Brow
Horse Bank
James Brow
Bog Hole
Half Tide Channel

is protected by two long sandbars, the inner Dole and the outer Preston Sand. Boats heading to Lytham, Freckleton Naze or Preston would have had to avoid these by following the southernmost channel called Preston Hole or, if coming from the north, a channel Collins does not name.

Collin's chart is probably an over-simplification. Two more detailed ones were published before the estuary channel was trained late in the nineteenth century. Fearon and Eyes's 1736 version is perhaps most interesting, for they show a complex of banks that were exposed at low water and a network of interconnecting channels. Three inlets are shown on the north side – Lytham, the River Dow at Freckleton Naze and Savick Brook – and all three are major inlets today. The river Douglas and Crossens river are shown entering the south side of the estuary as they do today. However, between these two are other channels, at Hundred End and Old Hollow. Since the subsequent drainage of the mosslands these have become insignificant. Hundred End Creek is now a muddy ditch at Shore Road, whereas the only trace of a channel at Old Hollow is the narrow brackish pool stranded on the inside of the sea-wall close to Old Hollow Farm. That the channels and sandbanks of the estuary were subject to great change can be seen by comparing the map by Fearon and Eyes with the last chart drawn in 1893 before the Ribble shipping channel was trained. And because the low water estuary channels were so braided and occasionally altered course, we may infer that only narrow strips or patches of saltmarsh could have developed, high on the shore.

It is clear also that, in the last 700 or 800 years, sea level has risen and destroyed what were once significant areas of low-lying dry land, or, more probably perhaps, extensive coastal erosion has taken place with the same effect. The name Argarmeols (or Argarmeles) is of Old Norse origin, meaning 'Argar's (or Erengr's) sand dunes'. It is a village that appeared in Domesday (1086) and records as late as the reign of Henry VIII refer to the place, which was probably situated about two kilometres off modern Birkdale. However during the fourteenth century the sea gradually began to overwhelm Argarmeoles. A deed from Cockersand Abbey in 1346 states that it is 'now annihilated by the sea, and there is no habitation'. By 1503 the manor of Argarmeoles had completely vanished for, following a tax demand from the Duchy of Lancaster in 1583, Sir Henry Halsall objected to paying any dues because, 'the said Argarmeols and all the lands and tenements in the same area and were at the decease of Hugh Halsall, and long before within the hegh see and drowned and adnichilate with the sayd see, and out of the lawgh water mark, and also off the body of the countrye'. Halsall's protest was supported by evidence from 80-year-old John Shirlok, who pointed out that he had never seen Argarmeols but had 'hard say that such londes ther were and drowned in the see but were ne in what parte he never hard tell'.[34]

Less well documented is the lost village of Kilgrimol (or Kelgrymoles), the sand dunes that once belonged to a Viking called Kilgrim. It was situated off what is now Fairhaven and St Anne's, but was washed away sometime before 1532. The *Duchy Pleadings* for that year record a witness who stated that Kilgrimol was 'worne into the sea 2 or 3 miles', and that '2 miles of fair pasture had been worne into the sea'.[35] Walk out onto Salter Bank and you are walking over what was once Kilgrimol. The builders of St Anne's considered – with scant evidence – that Kilgrimol was buried under the sand dunes on which they built the town.

Most of the towns and villages scattered along the shores the estuary have names of Old English or Scandinavian origin, and some of these give topographical and landscape information.[36]

OLD ENGLISH

Ashton:	town with ash trees
Aughton:	town with oaks
Burscough:	fortified camp by a wood
Clifton:	settlement on a cliff
Freckleton:	settlement by dangerous pools
Greenhalgh:	a green hollow
Halsall:	low-lying land close to the hall
Hutton:	settlement on a spur of land
Kirkham:	place with a church ('kirk' is the Scandinavian form)
Lytham:	place by the slopes (probably referring to sand dunes)
Martin Mere:	place on the mere (the second Mere is tautology)
Marton Mere:	as above (Martin Mere was sometimes called Marton Mere)
Rufford:	a rough ford (across the Douglas and also across the channel draining to the Douglas from Martin Mere)
Sollom:	a wet enclosure [an Old English and Old Norse hybrid name]

OLD NORSE

Bescar:	birch carr (carr comes from *kjar* meaning a boggy willow or alder wood)
Birkdale:	birch valley
Hesketh Bank:	bank with a horse-racing track
Holmes(wood):	island in a marsh: Martin Mere
Hoscar:	the boggy area grazed by horses
North Meols:	sand dunes [north, because there was a southern Meols on Wirral]

Ormskirk:	church belonging to or founded by Orm
Ribby:	village on a ridge
Tarlscough:	(Tharald's wood)

CELTIC (ROMANO-BRITISH) VILLAGES

Haskayne:	marshy land
Penwortham:	village (Old English 'ham') with a sharp-ended hill (Celtic 'pen')

Other names from these periods are often related to people who founded or owned them, or to man-made features: For instance: Ainsdale (Einulf's dale); Becconsall (Bekan's hill); Bretherton (town owned by a younger brother); Bryning (place belonging to Bryni); Crossens (headland with a cross); Croston (town with a cross); Formby (Forni's byre); Mawdesley (Maud's land); Preston (Priests' town); Skelmersdale (Skelmer's valley); Scarisbrick (Skar's sloping land – the village is on higher ground and the land slopes down on either side); and Tarleton (Tharaldr's town).

The Norse invasion of south-west Lancashire was very significant. In 902 a large group of Irish Norsemen were expelled from Dublin, probably as a result of a small civil war, and fled eastwards across the Irish Sea to north-west England, initially, it seems, mostly to the coastal areas of Cheshire and south-west Lancashire, later further north into Morecambe Bay. Writing in 1946 of the Viking settlements in Lancashire, F. T. Wainwright noted that, 'they arrived in small separate companies seeking land to cultivate ... It is generally believed that they came as peaceful farmers not as hostile warriors ... their influence did not end with the tenth-Century: they have permanently changed the racial and social structure of the area and they have left a mark on Lancashire that persists even today. In short the Irish-Norse settlements in the North-West [of England] are no less significant that the Danish settlements in the East, and for Lancashire no other event is of greater historical importance.' Those with locally common surnames around the Ribble estuary, such as Rimmer, Bickerstaffe, Hesketh, Kirkby, Carr and Lunt may like to reflect that they have Vikings as ancestors.[37]

The development of coastal towns and villages

With the exception of Preston, Ormskirk, Lytham and Kirkham, all of which were built on high ground that could not be flooded, the major towns around the estuary are of recent origin. Though the name Blackpoole appears in

The shipyard on the River Daw, Freckleton. It is quite likely that Roman fleets anchored here, in the lee of Freckleton Naze.

1602, the growth of the town dates from the mid-eighteenth century, when it started to develop as a middle-class seaside resort. The sprawl of Lytham to Ansdell, Fairhaven and St Anne's is nineteenth-century.

Freckleton had a corn mill from at least 1199, the year that Roger de Freckleton conferred a sixth of a mill and the fishery in the Ribble to his brother Adam's son, Richard. Of a second mill, mentioned in the de Hoghton deeds for about 1290 we know nothing. The mill was powered by water in the River Daw that flows from the eastern end of the Kirkham ridge. During the twelfth and thirteenth centuries much of what is now dry land to the

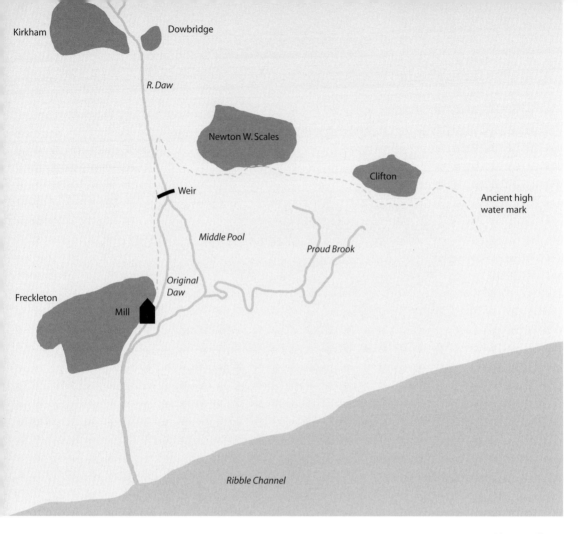

Kirkham

Dowbridge

R. Daw

Newton W. Scales

Clifton

Weir

Ancient high
water mark

Middle Pool

Proud Brook

Original
Daw

Freckleton

Mill

Ribble Channel

Freckleton Mill
and its associated
waterways.

east of Freckleton village was tidal saltmarsh and mudflat, and the mill was built at the head of the tide. As this part of the estuary silted up and the saltmarsh expanded, attempts were made to make the mill more efficient. A dam was constructed to build up a head of water, and a new channel was cut from the Daw to a stream, then called Proud Brook, that drained the land around Clifton village and flowed into the Daw downstream of the mill. The original Daw, the cut channel and the remains of Proud Brook can be seen today; the cut channel is now called Middle Pool. A weir was built where Daw and Middle Pool separated, by which flow down both streams could be regulated. But in dry summers, when the mill needed the water, Middle Pool dried up and the people of Newton were unable to graze their cattle. So in 1427 it was agreed that the manor of Newton could have the flow going down Middle Pool for three days and nights each week, and the people and mill of Freckleton could have the water flowing down the Daw the other four days and nights. Despite the problem of water supply, Freckleton Mill continued to grind corn until 1922. It was demolished in the 1960s.[38]

The Daw, sheltered from prevailing winds by the ridge on which Freckleton was built, probably also provided a sheltered anchorage probably from Roman times. The shipyard here was built in 1814 and produced many ocean-going vessels, including 18 boats especially constructed for harpooning basking sharks. However, Freckleton, along with its neighbour Warton, remained a tiny village until the warplane industry settled here in the 1940s.[39]

Lytham appears as 'Lidum' in Domesday. In 1199 Richard Fitz Roger gave land here to monks from Durham so that they could build a cell dedicated to St Mary and St Cuthbert. This was dissolved in 1537 and its site is probably beneath the present Lytham Hall. In 1606 the entire township and parish of Lytham was acquired by Sir Cuthbert Clifton of Westby, and his descendants continued as lords of the manor until the early 1960s. Up to late in the eighteenth century Lytham remained a small agricultural and fishing village, which had poor overland access because no good roads led out into the southern Fylde from Preston. There was no direct road from Lea to Warton or Freckleton, so most travellers to Lytham came round via Clifton, Kirkham, Wrea Green and Ballam.

Travel was made easier when a bridge was built over Savick Brook (close to the modern Lea Gate bridge) with a more direct route through Clifton village. The bridge and new route were funded by the Hoghton and Clifton families who owned all the land crossed by the route, with the Hoghtons responsible for the roadway east of Savick Brook and the Cliftons for the roadway to the west. Profit was their motive and those passing had to pay a toll. In 1678 John Brown and John Hornby were prosecuted at Clifton manor court for not paying the toll. In May 1781 Sir John Hoghton and Thomas Clifton constructed a new road which headed directly across Lea, Clifton and Newton Marshes to Lytham. They built a tollhouse where the Lea Gate motel now stands. The toll was removed on 28 July 1902 and, between 1904 and 1912 their bridge over the Savick was rebuilt. The direct road from Clifton via Freckleton to Lytham was opened in 1924.[40]

Lytham's growth as a resort began in the 1780s, and in 1796 the first guidebook to the infant town was published. Growth was piecemeal in the first thirty years, but in 1832 the new squire, Thomas Clifton, and his formidable land agent, James Fair, began to enforce strict controls on building quality and to lay out a new town.[41] The Green was created by the removal of the sand dunes between the village and the shore, and the long line of East Beach, Central Beach and West Beach, backed by large private houses, was laid out. In 1846 a branch of the Preston–Wyre railway reached Lytham. In 1863 a single-track line was opened that carried passengers through the

Lytham from its wooden jetty. In 1950 a sandy beach stretched to the promenade, the windmill and, to its right, the old Lytham lifeboat station. Since then Lytham has become surrounded by saltmarsh. The spiky grass making up much of the marsh is *Spartina* (see page 259).

new western end of Lytham called Ansdell (named after the artist Richard Ansdell) and on to the growing resort of Blackpool. A pier was built in 1865 at Lytham to enable promenaders to stroll out to sea and at the end of which steamers could pick up and drop off visitors. The intention of the estate, carried through with careful attention to detail, was that Lytham would be a gracious, attractive and select resort. Cheap excursions and the 'tripper' trade were rigorously excluded, and the elite tone of the town has remained

The whole of St Anne's was built on a huge tract of sand dunes, little of which remains today.

a feature of its character to the present day, in dramatic contrast with the raucous raffishness of Blackpool. Lytham in the 1860s and 1870s had a fine beach of golden sand, but the silting of the estuary and the gradual conversion of the sand to mud and saltmarsh put paid to its role as a 'proper' seaside resort, so that it became primarily a place for genteel holidays, retirement and, increasingly, commuting. As at Southport, the silting of the estuary brought an end to the steamer trade, and the pier was demolished in 1960.

To the west of Lytham and on the coast-side of the new railway was a vast expanse of deserted sand dunes. In the late 1860s James Fair, the land agent, suggested to the Clifton estate, who owned the land, that the dunes could be developed, as had already happened at Southport. In 1871 a main road, Clifton Drive, was pushed through the dunes and in October 1874, the estate granted a lease on over 600 acres of dune to a group of cotton-mill owners from Rossendale who were looking for a good investment. On 31 March 1875 the foundation stone of St Anne's-on-the-Sea was laid, the new town taking its name from its church dedicated to St Anne. St Anne's pier was opened ten years later.

The promenade at St Anne's had been built on a 'stanner' or shingle ridge on the top of the shore. Between the promenades at Lytham and St Anne's was a broad inlet called Granny's Bay that was naturally protected from heavy seas by a double stanner. Here fishing boats could safely be pulled high above the tide. In 1890 Thomas Riley took the lease of 264 acres of dune close to Granny's Bay and put in a temporary rail link from the Lytham–Blackpool line to carry machinery and materials. He excavated a lake and created landscaped gardens which were first opened to the public in August 1893. Riley named his development Fairhaven, after the Clifton estate land agent Thomas Fair, son of James.

Alas we have few records of the wildlife that inhabited what must have been a magnificent area of sand dunes before development. Lytham, Fairhaven and St Anne's have almost merged together and then continued into the sprawl that is Squire's Gate, Blackpool, Bispham, Cleveleys, Rossall and Fleetwood. Post a saucy postcard from any of these (perhaps with the exception of Lytham!) and it will simply be franked, Fylde Coast.

A continuous belt of dunes averaging about one kilometre in width lay behind the south side of the outer estuary from Crossens to Formby and beyond. Until the middle of the eighteenth century there was only one village of any size along this stretch of coastline. This was called North Meols, which had developed in the angle where estuary saltmarshes, Martin Mere and the sand dunes met. The village grew around the early medieval church of St Cuthbert, and for that reason was, as it still is, known as Churchtown. As early as 1219 the grazing at North Meols, which was primarily for sheep and exploited the potential of local saltmarshes, was owned by the de Hoghton family. In the thirteenth century Sawley Abbey owned the rights to saltpans at North Meols, where seawater was boiled in the summer months. The monks, and other landowners, protected their estates from flooding by building embankments or 'sea cops'. The line that these banks followed is approximately that taken by the lane between Churchtown and Crossens, immediately above maximum high tide levels that prevailed in the thirteenth and fourteenth centuries. Subsequently, as the accretion of mud and sand increased at the top of the shore and the high water mark retreated, the villagers of North Meols built further embankments during the sixteenth, seventeenth and eighteenth centuries. 'Inning' added more land to their properties and, besides the traditional income from fishing, agriculture grew in its economic importance.[42]

North Meols was a village when there were only sand dunes and a handful of fishermen's shacks at South Hawes (now called Southport). It is now called Churchtown, after its church dedicated to St Cuthbert.

In the 1790s the area was first affected by the growing fashion for sea-bathing. A hotel, the Black Bull, was built here and visitors bathed at Marshside. The first Sunday in August became known as Big Bathing Sunday, when people flocked to Churchtown. Two Sundays later was the turn of the tiny village of Birkdale, which hosted Little Bathing Sunday.

Unfortunately, the shore at Marshside was muddy. This presented William Sutton, proprietor of the Black Bull, with a magnificent business opportunity. Three kilometres away to the south-west and surrounded by mountainous sand dunes was South Hawes, where in 1790 a fisherman called Peter Hodges had built a crude cottage by the outflow of a narrow stream, the 'river' Nile. Instead of sending his bathers to Marshside, William Sutton took them by wagon to South Hawes, where the beach was sandy and the sea clear. In 1792 he built a special bathing-house at the top of the beach. Competition soon arrived. In 1797 Sarah Walmesley built Belle Vue Cottage close to Sutton's bathing-house, her aim being to take in paying guests, so in turn Sutton built the first hotel here. Although called the Original Hotel, it was also known as the Duke's Folly as it led to 'Duke' Sutton's bankruptcy and a spell in Lancaster gaol. Thus was the town of Southport founded, its name being selected because South Hawes did not sound attractive enough.

Quickly Southport became *the* place to be seen bathing. In 1803 William, Duke of Gloucester, bathed at Southport, and in 1815 Prince Louis Philippe stayed here to enjoy the waters. Yet it was then still a small town: in 1811 the parish of North Meols had only 2,496 people, with another 371 living in the village of Birkdale. By 1817, though, many fine houses were being built and in 1821 Christ Church was consecrated. In 1832, someone described Southport as comprising 'principally of one long straggling street, so wide that the immediate space is filled by gardens or rather small fields'.

That long street was built along a wide dune 'slack' into which spring tides flooded. As Southport was developing, the bottom of this slack became a brackish marsh. So the houses, church and other buildings were built on the higher drier dunes on either side of the slack. The houses on the south side were given long gardens that extended onto the marsh, and the marsh drained by a narrow ditch over which small wooden bridges were constructed to let the people pass. The roadway was built between the drainage ditch and the houses on the north side of the slack. Eventually the drainage ditch was culverted and the bridges removed. Thus was the famous wide and long Lord Street born; it was given its name in 1831.

At first, many visitors came to Southport by the Leeds and Liverpool canal, which deposited them at Scarisbrick whence wagons and coaches carried them the rest of the way to the sea. But then a railway link with Liverpool was completed in 1850 and with Manchester in 1855. A promenade was laid down;

later a bathing and marine boating lake constructed and in 1860 the pier, then
the longest in Britain, opened.

Eventually Southport merged with the expanding Churchtown, Marshside
and Crossens in the east, and with Birkdale in the west, obliterating vast
tracts of sand dune. In 1964 the coastal railway line to Liverpool was closed
and the track turned into a road through the dunes to Ainsdale. From the
1960s Ainsdale grew from a village into a sprawling township that included
the building of a Pontin's holiday camp on some of the most pristine wild
dunes. Freshfield merged with Formby when housing estates were built on
the dunes. Large areas of dunes were developed into golf courses, including
the championship one at Birkdale. And where the dunes are not developed,
they are now the playground of thousands of pairs of human feet.

In little over 300 years the meres and mosslands around the estuary were
drained. In little over 200 years tiny hamlets and uninhabited sand dunes
became urban sprawl. Of three wild habitats, two have been tamed. Only one
has not ... and that had a close and lucky escape!

Crossing the Ribble estuary

The Ribble estuary itself is now a barrier to overland communications. To
go from St Anne's to Southport, a ten-kilometre crow's distance, involves a

road journey of forty kilometres via the nearest road bridge at Preston. By train it is even more difficult. But in the past the estuary was far less of a barrier – here, as is also the case in the stretch of the Ribble on either side of Ribchester, communications are actually much more difficult in the motor age. Until the late nineteenth century, and the dredging of the channel to provide access to Preston dock, the river was crossed by a series of fords, usable at various stages of the tide, while the cross-river water links, by coastal shipping, fishermen's boats and small ferries, were of major importance.[43]

The two fords at the head of the estuary, one linking Preston and Penwortham and the other going from Penwortham to Tulketh across the site of what is now Preston dock and Morrisons' supermarket, have already been mentioned (page 96). Another ford, poorly documented, connected Howick with Lea. The next ford downstream was at Hutton, which was linked with Lea by a ford first recorded in the twelfth century. It was sufficiently important to have a small chapel at its southern end, for the use of travellers, and had a permanent guide who lived at Dungeon Farm and was paid an annual salary by the abbey of Cockersand (and later by the Duchy of Lancaster) for his work. A ford crossed at an angle from the shore at Longton to Clifton, and another from Longton to Freckleton Naze. Some of these crossings were very ancient indeed – the medieval references to '*strata ferrata*' ('metalled

Guide Road recalls the time when a guide would lead people across the Hesketh Bank/Warton or Freckleton ford. In those days there was little, if any, farmland here, for the braided Ribble channel meandered across its wide estuary. This farmland is reclaimed saltmarsh, and the saltmarsh grew on mudflats that emerged from the estuary as silting up occurred.

road') in connection with some of the lanes leading to the south shore imply that they may have been in use in the Roman period, and in the eighteenth and nineteenth centuries several writers refer to seeing paved stretches of causeway extending down into the waters of the estuary.

Two fords linked Hesketh Bank with Freckleton Naze and Warton. The former was, with the Hutton–Lea ford, the most important crossing below Preston. It was much used by travellers heading north along the Liverpool–Ormskirk ridge and south from Kirkham and the Fylde, for it avoided the long detour via Preston and Walton-le-Dale. A narrow clay ridge extends north from Rufford through Tarleton to Hesketh Bank. From Kirkham a similar clay ridge extends south to Freckleton Naze. Between Hesketh Bank and the Naze the Ribble was very shallow at low water. From Guide Road on the Hesketh Bank side, a guide would lead travellers on horseback across the shallow ford to either the Naze or to the Guide Inn, a short distance west of the Naze. The Guide Inn was destroyed when Warton aerodrome was built in about 1940. Although this crossing was first described in a twelfth-century manuscript, the Romans who had a fort at Kirkham may well have used it. Two events in the civil war illustrate the importance of this ford. In August 1644, Sir Marmaduke Langden, Lord Molyneux and Sir Thomas Tyldesley led a band of royalists from Kirkham to the Naze and forded the river to Hesketh Bank to escape a parliamentarian force. Normally travellers on that route would continue south to Ormskirk, but to escape from their pursuers they turned west. They 'al got over saflie and marched to Mealles' [North Meols].[44] Seven years later, in 1651, the sixth Earl of Derby landed at Rossall Point with 300 troops he had raised on the Isle of Man. He marched to Warton and then crossed to Hesketh Bank before resting at Lathom House. At Upholland the earl was wounded in a skirmish with some parliamentary troops. He escaped and later fought at the Battle of Worcester before being captured, after the royalists' defeat, at Nantwich and beheaded on 15 October at Bolton, principally for his role in the 'massacre' in that town during the war.

The importance of this crossing was borne out in 1655 (during the Commonwealth and before the return of Charles II) when a petition was presented at the court in Preston:

Petition

To the right Worshippfull the Justices of the Peace and Quorum for the Countie Pallatyne of Lancaster assembled att the Sessions of peace holden att Preston the 4th of October 1655.

The humble peticion of William Tomlinson of Warton, Guide over the Ribble to Hesketh banke.

Sheweth

That the peticioner hath served the people of the Commonwealth as guide over the same River for the space of fortie yeares and upwards and hath beene readie upon all seasonable tymes and occasions with himself and his horse to guide and preserve passengers from the danger of the water. In that tyme and service hath cost above the number of Ten horses to his greate damage and impoverishment, and being unprovided for a servicable horse such as is a requisite for that service, though willinge to serve the countrey.

His humble request is that your Worshipps would take the premises into serious consideracion and favourably to grant your Order for such an allowance towards the buying of a horse fitt for that service as in your wisedomes may seeme meete, the same being the highe road from Chester to Lancaster and into divers other parts and therefore necessarie, and the peticioner shalbee as hitherto readie to attend all passengers.

And daylie pray for your Worshipps etc.[45]

The shipping channel training walls (see also the photograph on page 191). These are breaking up in some places and eventually, unless they are repaired, the estuary may return to its ancient form with the loss of its extensive saltmarshes.

Like all the fords on the Ribble, the crossings from Hesketh Bank to Freckleton Naze and Warton had to be abandoned in the late 1880s, when the channel was deepened and dredged so that large vessels could pass upstream to the new Preston Dock (page 247). It is of interest to note, however, that in August 2000 (and again in August 2005) I was rowing a small boat in the low water channel, and between Warton and the Naze the bottom of the boat hit hard sand on several occasions. It appears, remarkably that since the Port of Preston closed the ford has slowly been re-establishing itself.

Navigating the Ribble

In the mid-1680s Preston's first historian, Richard Kuerden wrote that 'the River below [Preston] at present is much choked up with sand', and in about 1770 Murdock Mackenzie reported that the Ribble channel was 'crooked and defective'.[46] The river was shallow, with narrow and shifting channels, and its estuary was subject to constant silting. This meant that the Ribble, unlike the Lune or the Mersey, had failed to develop a significant port. A modest amount of coastal trade was carried on at Lytham (where the boats unloaded on the beach at low tide and were floated off as the tide rose), Freckleton, and the Douglas, and some small vessels did make the difficult journey up to small quay at Preston. That the upper river had been used for shipping for centuries is clear from early documentary references, but Preston, though a major centre, did not have a significant role as a port. However, as industrialisation progressed in the later eighteenth century, and as the town's merchants, like those of other centres such as Blackburn, felt increasingly aggrieved by what they saw as Liverpool's unscrupulous exploitation of its near monopoly of Lancashire's overseas trade, schemes to improve the river emerged.

In 1806 an Act of Parliament set up a company to make the Ribble estuary navigable to Preston. Some work was undertaken, with the bend at Lea Sands being improved by a new cut, but the money soon ran out and little substantial

The Albert Edward Dock in Preston is now used solely for pleasure boaters.

progress had been achieved. There were various further attempts to revive the scheme, and by 1834 boats called *Ribble* and *Enterprise* were plying trade in and out of Preston. However both had eventually to be laid up because of the shallow nature of the low-water channels and the dangers of going aground on shifting sand banks. Several surveys were made between 1834 and 1837, and in 1838 a new Ribble Navigation Company was set up with Preston Corporation taking most shares. In 1843 a new quay was built, but that did nothing to alleviate conditions out in the estuary. Nonetheless, a major aim of the strategy – the building of embankments to contain the channel, and the reclamation of the saltmarshes and other land thus protected from flooding, was pursued. A further report in 1866 by Bell & Miller, marine civil engineers from Glasgow, recommended the construction of training walls on either side of a new low-water shipping channel and the building of a dock. The estimated cost was £130,000. Little progress was made over the next 17 years, other than infighting between those for and those against the plan. But then in 1883 Preston Corporation bought out the Ribble Navigation Company for £72,862 and, with £558,000 in the coffers, began the work.

By March 1888 the new river channel between Penwortham and Preston was completed, and in 1892 the Prince of Wales (later King Edward VII) opened the Albert Edward Dock, which occupied much of the old river channel where it had formerly swung northwards towards the foot of the hillslope at Ashton. Work had also progressed with the dredging and walling of the new shipping channel (the stone coming from quarries on Parbold Hill and carried by barge down the Douglas), but this was a slow process and it was not until 1919 that it reached the sea. By the time the channel was completed in May 1926 over 13 million tonnes of sand had been excavated.

By now Preston was a busy port and through much of the twentieth century ferries from Ireland, coal-barges from Wigan, timber-carrying ships from the Baltic and Geest banana-boats from the West Indies plied their trade to Preston. Ships came and went on every tide. From the road between Lea Gate and Freckleton they seemed to be sailing through fields rather than along a channel! The port closed in 1981 and the dredging and maintenance of the shipping channel ceased.[47]

Saltmarsh development

The main effect of the trained channel on the rest of the estuary was rapidly to increase the rate of deposition of mud and silt and to encourage, especially on the south side, the spread of saltmarshes. At Churchtown the embanking of saltmarshes began in the thirteenth century, and by the middle of the nineteenth century the former shoreline was over one kilometre from the

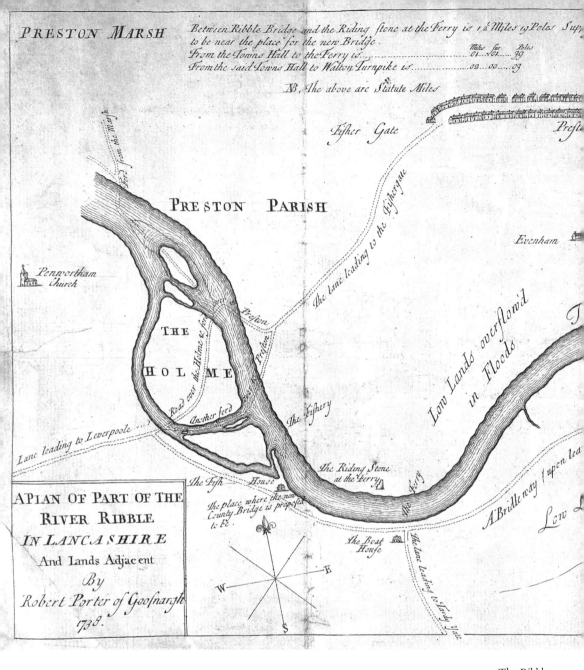

PRESTON MARSH

Between Ribble Bridge and the Riding stone at the Ferry is 1½ Miles 19 Poles Sup
to be near the place for the new Bridge.
From the Towns Hall to the Ferry is................................. 01...01.....39
From the said Towns Hall to Walton Turnpike is................ 02...00.....03

NB. The above are Statute Miles

Fisher Gate

Prest

PRESTON PARISH

The lane leading to the Fishergate

Evenham

Penwortham Church

Low Lands overflow'd in Floods

T

THE HOLME

Preston

Road over the Holme to ford

Preston

Another ford

The Fishery

Lane leading to Leverpoole

The Fish House

The Riding Stone at the Ferry

The Ferry

A Bridle way upon lea

Low

The place where the new County Bridge is proposed to be.

The Boat House

The lane leading to Lea/y gate

A PLAN OF PART OF THE RIVER RIBBLE IN LANCASHIRE And lands Adjacent By Robert Porter of Goosnargh 1738.

N

W ——— E

S

---

high-water mark. During the medieval period reclamation of saltmarsh was significant all along the southern shore of the river, from Penwortham, via Hutton, Longton, Hesketh Old and New, Inner Banks, Inner Crossens and Inner Marshside Marshes, and along the lower reaches of the Douglas. On the north side of the river the highest saltmarshes at Clifton, between Savick Brook (Lea Gate) and Newton-with-Scales, had been embanked by the 1250s, when William de Clifton permitted the people of Lea to graze their cattle on

The Ribble at Preston in 1738, prior to its taming. The two channels between Penwortham and Fishergate, separated by the low island of Penwortham Holme, made it

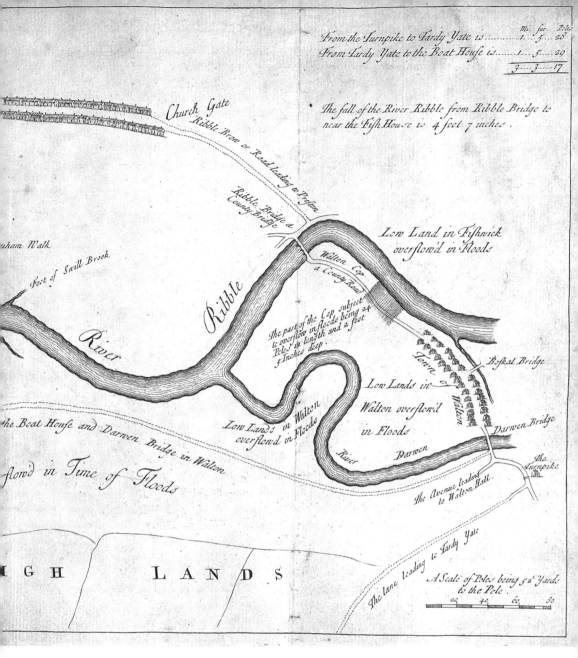

From the Turnpike to Tardy Yate is .... Mi. fur. P:le: 1 ... 5 ... 28
From Tardy Yate to the Boat House is .... 1 ... 5 ... 29
3 ... 3 ... 17

* The fall of the River Ribble from Ribble Bridge to near the Fish House is 4 feet 7 inches.

Church Gate

Ribble Brow or Road leading to Preston

Ribble Bridge a County Bridge

Low Land in Fishwick overflow'd in Floods

ham Walk

foot of Swill Brook

River Ribble

Walton Cop a County Road

The part of the Cop subject to overflow in floods being 24 Poles in length and 2 foot 5 Inches deep.

Town of Walton

Boshal Bridge

Low Lands in Walton overflow'd in Floods

Low Lands in Walton overflow'd in Floods

the Boat House and Darwen Bridge in Walton

River Darwen

Darwen Bridge

The Turnpike

flow'd in Time of Floods

The Avenue leading to Walton Hall

IGH   L A N D S

The lane leading to Tardy Yate

A Scale of Poles being 5½ Yards to the Pole
20   40   60   80

difficult to bridge. Once all the Ribble had been confined to one channel a bridge could easily be built linking Fishergate and Penwortham. (See also page 95.)

the marsh after the corn, grown on the reclaimed marsh, had been harvested. Further enclosures resulted in large tracts of Newton, Freckleton, Clifton and Lea Marshes being embanked by the end of the nineteenth century. Evidence from Hutton, which is well documented, shows that the usual method of reclamation was to drive deep piles into the marsh at low water, and then to heap earthen embankments around these, protected by hurdles of brushwood. The timber for the piles was often alder (which is particularly resistant to

From the sea wall at low water, the Ribble saltmarshes look like a large expanse of grassland, with a few flowers. Get out there, or fly over them, and you will find that an intricate network of creeks and gutters dissects them.

Longton Marsh is the most mature unreclaimed saltmarsh, first colonised by saltmarsh plants towards the end of the nineteenth century.

rot, as it grows in wet conditions) and some of this was floated down the Ribble from higher upstream. The earth embankments were consolidated over several seasons, the damage of higher tides being made good and new hurdles added as appropriate. In order to prevent flooding from inland, any tributary streams flowing down to the marsh were also embanked, and tidal sluice gates constructed to let water out at low tide but to close against the incoming tide. Usually the embankments were built in a straight line along the outer edge of the marshes; most are still visible and many shown on current Ordnance Survey maps.

By 1934 most marshes had spread only a little beyond the edge of the last embankments, the two main exceptions being at Longton and Hesketh Out Marshes, where saltmarsh had covered most of the former bare mudflats. In the following 35 years, up to 1969, a further 17 square kilometres of shore became covered with saltmarsh vegetation and in the subsequent 38 years to 2004 another 6.1 square kilometres of saltmarsh was added.[48] During this latter period two major areas of saltmarsh were embanked: most of Hesketh Out Marsh, which is now farmland, and a large section of Marshside and Crossens Marshes. The latter involved building a bank that now carries the coast road from Crossens to Southport. It was the intention of Sefton Council to drain and build houses on the reclaimed marsh, but happily they did not. This area is now a wet grassland reserve of the RSPB. There had also been plans, in the late 1970s, to embank Banks Marsh, but fortunately the Nature Conservancy (now Natural England) stepped in, and this, the largest saltmarsh in Europe, became a National Nature Reserve.

The road going from left to right is Shore Road, between Hesketh Bank and Banks. Before any reclamation was carried out, high spring tides reached this point. This is Hundred End and the lane joining Shore Road marks the boundary between the Hundreds of Leyland and West Derby. Before Tarleton Moss was drained, that lane was a track across the moss.

Because the shipping channel is close to the north bank of the estuary there has been little room there for expanding saltmarshes on that bank. The major saltmarsh formation has occurred between Warton and Lytham and mostly since about 1920. Today the saltmarsh at Lytham extends to the west of the wooden jetty and yacht clubhouse: in 1956 my mother took a photograph of me in a boat alongside the jetty with not one wisp of saltmarsh to be seen!

When Southport pier was opened in 1860, the end was in a deep-water channel called the Bog Hole. Paddle steamers plied their trade from there, taking day-trippers to other resorts such as Llandudno, the Isle of Man, Blackpool and Lytham, at any state of tide. However, following the training of the Ribble channel the Bog Hole began to silt up. By 1909, the year my own grandmother was taken by steamer from Southport pier to Blackpool for the day, the depth of water at the end of the pier was 18 metres. By 1924 the depth was only 11 metres and by the 1930s the Bog Hole dried out at low water. The last steamer sailed from Southport in 1923. However, it was not only the pleasure boats that were affected. Banks and Marshside were fishing communities up to about 1900 but, as accretion reduced water depth off both villages, it became impossible to launch every day. Banks became a farming and market gardening community while the fishermen of Marshside took to shrimping, initially with horse-drawn but today motor-driven carts which are parked at the head of the shore at Birkdale.[49]

It has been said that the tide never (or rarely) comes in at Southport. This is not true, for the fortnightly spring tides frequently make the top of the shore and, when backed by gales, cause parts of the coast road to be closed to traffic. There has been a retreat of the sea from Southport and Lytham eastwards in that the high-water mark has moved westwards as the sand banks and saltmarshes built up. In the last fifty years the low-water mark between Birkdale and Ainsdale has moved westwards by about one kilometre.

On 31 October 1981 the Port of Preston closed and the maintenance of the Ribble shipping channel – the dredging and repairs to the training walls – ceased. As already noted, at low water the shipping channel downstream of Freckleton Naze is less than a metre deep and only half that depth in a few places. Further west, breakages are appearing in the training walls and it is now possible to paddle across the channel from Salter's Bank to Foulnaze when the tide is out. (Note: this dangerous journey should not be attempted!) In the early 1970s the wide Pinfold Channel, into which the Crossens river flowed, split the vast low-water sandbanks off Southport; that channel had been greatly reduced by 1995 and the Crossens river headed north to the Ribble channel. Perhaps, in future decades, the estuary will revert to its pre-trained complexity. This may result in major problems, for if that happens large areas of saltmarsh will erode away lands which have been reclaimed from the sea become threatened. There are also suggestions that the golden sands of St Anne's beach will disappear, to be replaced by saltmarsh, while the muddy shore at Lytham will one day be a fine beach again. One thing is certain: the Ribble estuary will never remain the same.

This is the memorial, at St Anne's, to the lifeboat men who lost their lives on the night of 9–10 December 1886, trying to save the crew of the ship *Mexico*. Of the Southport lifeboat men, 14 out of 16 perished. All 13 of the St Anne's lifeboat men were drowned. The crew of the Mexico were saved, by the Lytham lifeboat. The Ribble estuary can be a very dangerous place.

The natural history of the estuary

The Ribble estuary is a mosaic of habitats. Running through it are the low-water channels, of which the former shipping channel is the largest. At low tide the water here is fresh or slightly brackish and at high tide almost full-strength seawater, so that only those fish and invertebrates which are able to tolerate a wide range of salinities can live there. The population of flounders is huge, and provides the staple diet for up to 200 cormorants. Male eels grow from the elver stage in the estuary. Female elvers head further upstream as far as Settle, where they spend several years feeding and growing in freshwater. Then, on a dark autumn night, they swim back downstream to the estuary on the first stage of their migration back to spawning grounds in the Sargasso Sea. Grey herons that feed in the estuary appear to catch more eels than flounders; 19 herons feeding one day in August 2000 at the mouth of the Douglas took 42 eels but only 11 flounders.

In summer, sea-bass (*Dicentrarchus labrax*) and thick-lipped mullet (*Chelon labrosus*) follow the tide through the estuary. Bass are predators, hunting shrimp, crabs and small fish, whereas mullet eat tiny particles of any organic matter, from algae to cattle dung washed off the saltmarshes. Salmon and sea trout pass through the estuary, as smolts heading seawards to feed and grow and as adults heading back upstream to spawn. Whilst Ribble salmon go as far as the Faeroe Banks and Greenland's Davis Straits to feed, sea trout remain within British waters, some going no further than the outer estuary.

The Ribble estuary channel has long been a salmon and sea trout whammel net-fishery, with a legal maximum of six licensed netsmen who may fish a

A bass from the estuary that had a large sprat in its throat.

There is a commercial net fishery for salmon on the estuary. The two vertical markings midway down this fish are where the net scraped away some scales.

certain number of tides per week through the season. Today there is a six and a half-inch minimum mesh size so that the majority of sea trout and smaller salmon (grilse) that hit the net manage to swim through and escape. Fishing takes place from Freckleton Naze and begins at the last of the ebb. The boat is rowed across the low-water channel as the net is played out. Then, with the boat at one end, the net drifts down the stream, its line of corks curving across the channel. When a salmon hits the net and becomes trapped by its gills, the corks in close proximity bob under. The netsman now rows along, pulls in that part of the net, extracts the salmon and kills it, and then re-sets his net. By the time the tide begins to flood and brings a stop to the fishing, net and boat will have drifted as far as Lytham. Being a netsman is hard work

LEFT
A Marshside shrimper sets off at low water.

RIGHT
Cleaning the catch.

with little reward, for many are the short summer nights when not one salmon lies in the boat as dawn breaks.

There has been a fishery for brown shrimps (*Crangon crangon*) in the outer estuary since Southport was South Hawes and St Anne's was an area of undeveloped sand dune. On the south side of the estuary shrimps are caught by towing a net through shallow water with a tractor or motorized cart, whereas on the north side, where it is easier to launch, the net is towed by a boat. A century ago there was a commercial sea-fishing industry in the outer estuary, catching mainly dabs (*Limanda limanda*), whiting (*Merlangius merlangus*), cod (*Gadus morhua*) and, in summer, mackerel (*Scomber scombrus*). Besides fishing from boats, stake nets up to 500 metres long were set at an angle on the foreshore at low water, the fish being gathered and the net reset after the following high tide. To prevent argument between netsmen and to provide revenue for the local authorities who owned the beaches, the shore was divided into 'fishing stalls' which might be short enough for one man to fish or might be fished by two men.[50] The silting up of the estuary and the over-fishing of the Irish Sea by European Union fleets have brought this local industry to an end, although some amateur fishermen continue to fish with shore lines, consisting a hundred hooks or more, set at the low-water mark.

Between high-water and low-water marks is the open shore. High up the estuary near Preston, the shore is an oozy mud, with a glutinous texture and sulphurous stench. In contrast, at Formby and St Anne's there are beaches of coarse golden sand. The majority of the open shore is a mix between the two extremes: mostly either sandy-mud or muddy-sand. Far out in the estuary, the higher banks are sandier than the hollows and, over the low-water period, wagons from the sand-winning plant at Marshside headed to the highest banks to carry away the sand. Sand-winning ceased in 2007.

At the low water the open shore may appear lifeless, save for a few gulls, piping oystercatchers and yelping redshanks. However, beneath the surface there live huge populations of invertebrates. The muddier areas have four main inhabitants. A tiny (4–5 mm), blackish snail called *Hydrobia ulvae* lives in and on the oozier mud. Where the mud is more compacted, a 1 cm long shrimp called *Corophium volutator* constructs burrows. A large (up to 5 cm) species of clam called *Scrobicularia plana*, lies buried deep in the mud but feeds at the surface when the tide is in by extending a long tube-like siphon with which it hoovers the mud surface. And preying on smaller creatures is a carnivorous rag worm, *Nereis divericolor* that creeps through the mud in search of its prey.

Where mud gives way to muddy-sand there is a completely different community of animals living within the beach. Here the fragile, pink-shelled

Baltic tellin (*Macoma balthica*) and the edible cockle (*Cerastoderma edule*) are abundant. So too are several species of worm, including the lug-worm (*Arenicola*), which make the characteristic worm casts on the beach. There are two species. The blow-lug (*A. marinus*) is reddish and lives fairly close of the surface of wet sandier banks whereas the larger black-lug (*A. defodiens*) is blackish, lives in siltier sand and burrows very deep. Both are popular sea-fishers' baits, the black-lug the favourite and sold at tackle-shops around the estuary.

Beaches and banks composed of coarse clean sand have a third community of shore invertebrates. The Baltic tellin is replaced by the common tellin (*Angulus tenuis*), which has a more orange than pink shell. Tube worms are the commonest worms of the sandy shore, including the sand-mason (*Lanice conchilega*) that has a rough rubbery tube, and *Pectinaria koreni* that makes a hard, curved, smooth tube of sand. At low water they retreat into their tubes, but when the tide covers them they filter food particles from seawater using tentacles around the mouth. Two tiny shrimps are also abundant in sandy shores. *Eurydice pulchra* lives in the surface of wet sand and emerges to feed when the tide is in, whereas *Bathyporeia pelagica* moves up and down the lower and middle parts of the shore with the tide, feeding at the water's edge.

How abundant these shore invertebrates are can be seen from the following table, that gives the maximum recorded densities (numbers per square metre of shore surface) from the Ribble estuary.[51]

MUD

Hydrobia ulvae	38,000–47,000
Scrobicularia plana	180
Corophium volutator	22,000
Nereis diversicolor	590

MUDDY-SAND

Macoma balthica	2,400
Cerastoderma edule	340
Arenicola species	132

SAND

Angulus tenuis	350
Tube-worms (all species)	1,080
Eurydice pulchra	1,400
Bathyporeia pelagica	5,900

Three of the
abundant inverte-
brates of the
estuary beaches.
Hydrobia ulvae,
Macoma balthica,
Arenicola marina.

Look closely at
the beach surface.
Lugwork casts
show that there is
life beneath. But
look more closely.
The tiny specks
are snails, *Hydrobia
ulvae*, that occur in
millions.

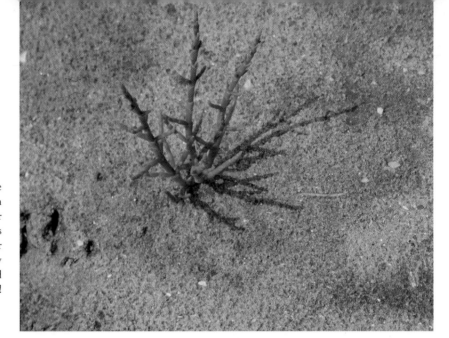

Marsh samphire growing on the beach near Southport. This is a major coloniser of bare muddy sand, and it is good to eat!

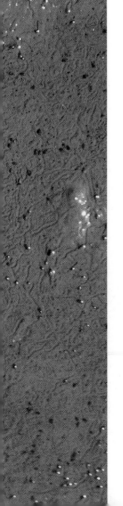

The variety and abundance of these shore invertebrates attracts many migrant and over-wintering wading birds to the Ribble (see page 276).

The open shore is bounded at and above the high water mark by either saltmarshes (where the shore is mud or muddy-sand) or sand dunes (where the shore is clean sand). The only exception to this is where man has developed the shore, as along the concrete promenades at Southport and Lytham St Anne's.

Saltmarshes develop when the height of the shore increases, through mud and silt deposition by the tide, to the level at which late spring and summer neap tides fail to cover the shore for about 28 consecutive days. This gives the seeds of plants that can colonise the mud surface time to germinate without being washed away.

There are two main plant colonisers of bare mud on the Ribble estuary. Where the mud is a drier, more compacted silty-mud, marsh samphire (*Salicornia europaea*) is the prime coloniser. This is a short, fleshy annual, is especially common between Marshside and Southport, and is popularly picked, for it makes an excellent pickle (it is sometimes called 'sea-asparagus').

The second coloniser is one of the most remarkable of plants, the common cord-grass (*Spartina anglica*). During the nineteenth century the American smooth cord-grass (*S. alterniflora*) was accidentally introduced to Britain and it hybridised with the native small cord-grass (*S. maritima*). The hybrid, which was first discovered on the south coast of England in 1878, was named Townsend's cord-grass and given the scientific name *Spartina townsendii*. Like most hybrids, such as the mule, Townsend's cord-grass was sterile. However, it was far more vigorous than either of its parent species, and a small fragment of rhizome quickly growing into a large spiky clump. In the hundred or so years following its discovery, Townsend's cord-grass was introduced to many muddy estuaries and quickly smothered the higher mudflats. It was introduced to the Ribble in 1932 with the aim that, after the cord-grass had turned tidal mudflat into saltmarsh, the saltmarsh could be embanked to yield more land. This plant has largely been responsible for the subsequent massive spread of saltmarshes. One of the most interesting and amusing cases was in the early 1970s when the plant was quickly spreading from Crossens towards Southport. To eradicate it, the local council had it bulldozed. The tide then scattered the bulldozed fragments, each of which then grew into a new plant! A remarkable change occurred in Townsend's cord-grass: the number of chromosomes in the plant's cells doubled from the usual 61 or 62 to 122, and with this change the plant became a new fertile species, the common cord-grass. Now we have a vigorous coloniser of mudflats that can produce seeds.

A third coloniser of bare substrate, in this case sand, occurs in the narrow bands of saltmarsh associated with the recent dune formation known as Birkdale Green Beach (see below). This coloniser, common saltmarsh grass (*Puccinellia maritima*) is a fleshy green grass that occurs commonly on the raised levees of the larger saltmarshes, usually associated with English scurvy-grass (*Cochlearia anglica*), which is not a grass but a member of the cabbage family.

When saltmarsh vegetation clothes a former mudflat, at high water springs, it slows down the flowing currents and, from the slack water, silt quickly settles out. Thus, once a mudflat becomes saltmarsh its level rises quickly; from that point fewer and fewer tides can reach it; its surface dries, and other plants which are less tolerant of prolonged and frequent washing by the tide can live there. The rate of accretion can be very rapid. In the years 1970–78 the mud surface of Crossens Marsh rose by an average of 1.7 cm *per annum* and on the seaward side of Banks Marsh by 1.9 cm *per annum*.[52] By 2002, one area on Crossens Marsh, which had been tidal mudflat and covered by all tides reaching 9.1 metres OD in 1970, was reached by 10.0 metre tides only when backed by a westerly gale.

Common saltmarsh grass and annual seablite (*Suaeda maritima*) colonise cord-grass and samphire marshes early, and it is quite common to find a clump of cord-grass surrounded by yet uncolonised bare mud with one of these living in the higher centre. Sea-aster (*Aster tripolium*), with its yellow-centred light purple flowers in late summer, invades areas of marsh soon after the mud has been completely overgrown. As the marsh level continues to rise, a network of gutters develops which rapidly carry away the seawater of a spring tide. Now the entire marsh might be flooded on fewer than 40 days each year, but the lapping of water on the gutter edges deposits silt and raises the edges above the level of the surrounding marsh. These raised strips by the gutters, called levees, quickly become colonised by a low, grey-green shrub called sea purslane (*Halimione portulacoides*). The levees also have large clumps of English scurvy-grass that, in spring, are a mass of white blooms. And because they are close to the gutters, lush growths of common saltmarsh grass vie for space with the sea purslane and scurvy-grass. Away from the levees and above the sea-aster zone, the Ribble saltmarshes are dominated by a second grass, red fescue (*Festuca rubra*), so called because, in late spring and summer, it gives a coppery red hue to the marsh top provided that it is not heavily grazed. Of course, the grassy saltmarshes are top-quality grazing provided the stock is taken off when the highest tides threaten. Today, beef cattle from far away are brought to Banks Marsh for the summer months, while Longton Marsh supports a large head of sheep.

Large tracts of the Ribble saltmarshes are still in the stages dominated by cord-grass, sea-aster or red fescue. However, there are corners which have progressed further. For instance, at the head of Marshside Marsh extensive stands of sea club-rush (*Bolboschoenus maritimus*) and common reed (*Phragmites australis*) now grow where, in 1965, it was open shore.

The saltmarshes provide food for internationally important flocks of winter wildfowl (page 276). They are also an important habitat for ground-nesting birds. Up to 240 pairs of redshanks together with small numbers of lapwing and up to three pairs of ruff (*Philomachus pugnax*) breed here on saltmarshes. Black-headed gulls first nested on Banks Marsh in the 1950s after disturbance drove them from the Ainsdale dunes. By 1999 over 14,000 pairs bred on Banks and Warton Marshes.[53] Lesser black-backed and herring gulls (*Largus fuscus* and *L. argantatus*) colonised Banks Marsh in the 1970s and their numbers grew rapidly to over 4,000 pairs of lesser black-backed and 850 herring gulls in 2000.

During the 1950s a ternery on the beach and dunes at Ainsdale was abandoned, the birds moving onto Banks Marsh and later spreading to Hesketh Out Marsh. By 1976 the colony had grown to 1,080 pairs of common terns (*Sterna hirundo*) and five pairs of arctic terns (*S. paradisaea*); at the time this was the third largest ternery in Britain and the largest not on a nature reserve.[54] As the black-headed gull colony grew and took over the higher levees on Banks, the ternery gradually shifted onto Hesketh Out Marsh where they had the raised levees to themselves. Because the levees were rarely flooded by the tide, the terns were very successful here, raising more than one young per pair every year. But then, in the early 1980s, most of Hesketh Out

Sea aster, one of the commonest flowers on the saltmarshes. In autumn the marsh top appears a grey mauve.

A female ruff (known as the reeve) caught on her nest on the Ribble saltmarshes She hatched her four eggs.

Lapwing commonly nest on reclaimed saltmarshes.

Avocets have recently colonised the nature reserves.

BELOW, LEFT
Shelducks are common nesters inland of the tidal marshes, most of them leading their ducklings to the tidal marshes to feed and grow.

ABOVE, RIGHT
Teal, like the wigeon and pintail, are abundant on the estuary in winter.

Golden plover are very common winter visitors to reclaimed saltmarshes.

The short-winged conehead (*Conocephalus dorsalis*) has recently colonised stands of sea club-rush on the outer estuary saltmarshes. It is thought that they arrived here as eggs, carried across Liverpool Bay from the nearest colony on Anglesey, for they cannot fly.

Marsh was embanked* and the terns forced back to Banks Marsh. But because the high levees there were now totally occupied by aggressive gulls they were forced to nest on the lower areas of marsh where flooding destroyed most nests. By 2001 only about 100 pairs of terns remained.

Of land-birds, meadow pipits and skylarks nest commonly in the red fescue sward, linnets in sea purslane and reed buntings in sea club-rush.

One feature of saltmarshes is the abundant small pools or saltpans. Some of these are semi-permanent and, on the higher areas of Longton Marsh, have growths of pondweeds. Others are temporary and dry out quickly in summer droughts. The semi-permanent saltpans attract quite an interesting fauna, including three-spined sticklebacks and the nymphs of three dragonflies: blue-tailed damselfly, brown hawker and broad-bodied chaser (*Libellula depressa*). *Hydrobia ulvae*, which occurs in high densities on mudflats (page 257), occurs in saltpans on the lower marshes whereas a close relative, *H. ventrosa*, occurs in semi-permanent pans on the upper marshes. Brown shrimps and shore crabs (*Carcinus maenas*) can be found in temporary pans on the lower marshes, whilst the prawn *Palaemonetes varians* is common in the pans of the middle and upper marshes. This prawn is a favourite food of the little egret (*Egretta garzetta*), the small, yellow-footed white heron that is becoming increasingly common on saltmarshes in north-west England. There are three species of *Gammarus* shrimps on the Ribble estuary: *G. locusta* lives among rocks in tidal areas as at Granny's Bay and on the training walls, *G. pulex* occurs in freshwater pools and ditches inland of the tide, and *G. duebeni* lives in brackish semi-permanent saltpans on the saltmarshes.

---

* Part of this embanked marsh is being opened to the sea during the development of the new RSPB reserve.

Reclaimed saltmarshes vary as a wildlife habitat depending upon how they are managed. Large areas, particularly between Banks and Hesketh Bank and between Lea and Clifton, are intensively grazed pasture or arable/market garden. Brown hares are often numerous and sometimes are pests in brassica and carrot crops. Although many nests are lost during rolling and sowing of arable fields, lapwings often nest at high densities together with a few pairs of oystercatchers in open fields, whereas grey partridges (*Perdix perdix*) raise their broods in weedy corners and by overgrown ditches. There are, however, two areas of reclaimed saltmarsh that are important wildlife sites.

Inner Marshside Marsh, which is split into two by Marshside Road, and Crossens Inner Marsh, separated from Marshside by only a barbed-wire fence, lie inland of Southport's coast road. To the seaward side of the road are unenclosed tidal marshes. They are an RSPB Reserve.[55] This is an important area for breeding shoveler (*Anas clypeata*), lapwing, redshank and skylark. Ruff lek here every spring and have been proved to breed. In recent years the reserve has also been colonised by avocets (*Recurvirostra avosetta*). Although black-tailed godwits (*Limosa limosa*) have never been proved to breed here, the numbers of birds staying on in spring and displaying suggests that they may do in the near future. Out of the breeding season these wet marshes attract thousands of godwits, lapwings and golden plovers, and a large proportion of the teal, wigeon and pink-footed geese (*Anas brachyrhynchos*) that winter on the estuary (page 276) feed here.

Newton and Freckleton marshes lie on the north side of the estuary east of the Naze and south of the A584 Lytham road.[56] Although this area has been embanked for well over a century, many of the old saltmarsh creeks are still there, now sinuous weedy pools. This is a fine area of wet grassland, with breeding shoveler, lapwing, snipe, redshank, black-tailed godwit and, occasionally, ruff. In winter it attracts large flocks of teal and golden plover.

A wide belt of sand dunes once existed from Marshside and Churchtown south and west to Liverpool between the open shore and mosslands. Urban sprawl in areas such as Birkdale and Ainsdale has reduced the area of dunes, but the large tracts that do remain are mostly protected as nature reserves, although the paths running through them are used by thousands of people on sunny days from spring to late autumn. On the north side there used to be a wide belt of dunes from Lytham to Starr Gate, but all that now remains are very narrow strips between Fairhaven and St Anne's, and between St Anne's and Starr Gate. The loss of these dunes began in the late 1830s, when the Clifton estate, which owned the entire parish of Lytham, began the deliberate levelling and removal of the southernmost section to create the superb level sward which is now Lytham Green. The aim was to landscape the area and make it more suitable for a high-status resort, while the sand

Marram-grass
covered dunes with
planted Corsican
pines struggling to
survive.

The dunes between Southport and Liverpool have a diverse and rich flora, including some quite special plants.

TOP LEFT
Grass of Parnassus.

TOP RIGHT
Wintergreen.

LEFT
Baltic rush (its most southerly site).

RIGHT
Dune helleborine.

Isle of Man cabbage.

which had been taken away was dumped on the marshes at the eastern end of the town, raising the level and providing new areas for residential and commercial development. Further losses occurred with the creation of the new town of St Anne's from the 1870s onwards, and the exclusive new suburb of Fairhaven in the 1890s.

One of the most fascinating developments on the estuary has been the growth of a new band of dunes between Birkdale and Ainsdale known as Birkdale Green Beach. Philip. H. Smith's study here has demonstrated that the first sandy ridge was formed at the top of the shore in 1986 and that by 2003 43.6 hectares of pristine new dune had formed seawards of the older dunes.[57] Growth has continued. This new area of dune has a wide range of habitats including embryo and fixed dunes, and saltmarsh on the seaward hollows and freshwater marsh in the dune slacks no longer reached by the tide. Of the 227 flowering plants that Smith had found here up to 2003, 28 were species of conservation importance in north-west England and three nationally rare.

The flora of the entire dune system is immense; P. H. Smith has recorded 880 species of plant here.[58] The outermost mobile or yellow dunes have a flora that is dominated by marram-grass and in places this has been planted to repair dunes that have been badly damaged through trampling by human feet. Inland from the mobile dunes are the fixed dunes. Here large tracts are clothed with the grey-olive of creeping willow (*Salix repens*) and the red-berried sea buckthorn (*Hippophae rhamnoides*). There are also scrubby areas with burnet rose (*Rosa pimpinellifolia*), dewberry (*Rubus caesius*), a close tart relation of the bramble (*Rubus fruticosus*), and blackthorn. Sea spurge (*Euphorbia paralias*), bird's-foot trefoil (*Lotus corniculatus*), ragwort (*Senecio jacobaea*) and sand sedge (*Carex arenaria*) are found in more open areas of dry fixed dunes. Early in the twentieth century large areas of dune between Ainsdale and Formby were planted with Corsican pine (*Pinus nigra*) and balsam poplar (*Populus candicans*). A subtly beautiful orchid can be found in semi-shade here: the widespread green-flowered helleborine.

The dune conifers are home to the declining red squirrel that is being ousted from Britain by the introduced American grey. This is an isolated red squirrel population and very popular with visitors to the Squirrel Reserve at Freshfield. It should be noted, however, that these are not true British red squirrels. They are of the continental race, with darker tails and lacking the long blonde ear tufts of the native race. They were introduced with the Corsican pines.

The damp hollows in between the belts of fixed dunes are known as 'slacks'. Many slacks used to have deeper pools, with wetland plant communities dominated by reed-mace (*Typha latiolia*), a brackish-water form of club-rush (*Schoenoplectus tebernaemontani*), yellow flag-iris (*Iris pseudacorus*), common sedge (*Carex nigra*) and brown sedge. Damp slacks have a very attractive collection of flowers including grass-of-parnassus (*Parnassia palustris*), bog pimpernel (*Anagallis tenella*), round-leaved wintergreen (*Pyrola rotundifolia*), tubular water-dropwort (*Oeanthe fistulosa*), yellow-wort (*Blackstonia perfoliata*), field gentian, autumn gentian (*G. amarella*), seaside centaury (*Centaurium littorale*), lesser centaury (*C. pulchellum*), spring beauty (*Montia perfoliata*), brookweed (*Samolus valerandi*) and several members of the orchid family: marsh helleborine (*Epipactis palustris*), twayblade (*Listera ovata*), northern marsh orchid (*Dactylorhiza purpurella*), spotted orchid, late marsh orchid (*D. incarnata*) and bee orchid (*Ophrys apifera*). Rare plants found in dune slacks here include sharp club-rush (*Schoenoplectus pungens*) that is found only on the island of Jersey away from the south Lancashire dunes, the Baltic rush (*Juncus balticus*), which is at its most southerly here, and the very rare dune helleborine (*Epipactis leptchila dunensis*). The lowering of the water table in the late 1960s and early 1970s to reduce the risk of flooding in nearby new building developments resulted in the loss of many pools, though in recent years conservation groups have excavated pools to compensate for the losses.

The natterjack (*Bufo calamita*), a small olive-green toad with a diagnostic yellow stripe down its back, was once abundant in dune slack pools. From late March to late May the din of thousands of male natterjacks 'singing' on a warm still afternoon and evening was almost deafening. The lowering of the water table in the 1960s resulted in the near collapse of the natterjack population, and, until the development of Birkdale Green Beach, its survival was largely down to conservationists excavating ponds for them or deepening dried-out slacks. Crested newts (*Triturus cristatus*) are often found in the deeper pools and, because they are considered to be endangered, provide a conundrum for conservationists, for they are very fond of eating natterjack tadpoles.

In the nineteenth century common terns and black-headed gulls nested in large numbers on the dunes around Ainsdale, and little terns (*Sterna albifrons*) had a colony near Lytham. Oystercatchers and ringed plovers (*Charadrius hiaticula*) nested in scrapes in the sand on both beaches and in dunes. In late spring evenings, nightjars (*Caprimulgus europaeus*) churred in the dune scrub. By the middle of the twentieth century these were nearly all gone because of the tremendous increase of disturbance. The last tern nest at Freshfield was at the top of the beach. A family of day-trippers had unknowingly parked their car over the nest and were throwing the crusts from their picnic sandwiches to the parent terns that were frantically calling overhead!

The sand lizard (*Lacerta agilis*) has one of the most remarkable distributions of any land animal in Britain, being found on the heaths of Kent,

Some very special animals live in the dunes.

TOP
Natterjack toad (note the characteristic yellow line running down its back).

LEFT
Sand lizard.

Surrey, West Sussex, Hampshire, Dorset, the Isle of Wight ... and the dunes between Southport and Formby. It is probable that the sand lizard population spread northwards between 2,500 and 5,000 years ago, when the climate was much drier and warmer than it is today, and that when the climate cooled and became wetter those living between the south Ribble dunes and southern heaths died out. The male is a most beautiful lizard, the sides and back having a bright lime-green or yellow-green hue. The sand lizard has declined since the 1950s. Then they were so common that pet-shops in Preston and Liverpool

Among many species of butterfly, the dark green fritillary is a very special dune species.

The dune tiger beetle.

Ruddy darter dragonly. The dune slacks are home to many dragonflies, including the recently arrived ruddy darter and emperor.

had them for sale. Housing estates and the holiday camp at Ainsdale removed much prime sand lizard habitat. Where Pontins holiday camp is today, I caught eight in one warm July afternoon in 1960.

The dunes are also home to a wide range of invertebrates. Twenty-three species of butterflies have been recorded, at least 17 of which breed here, six are regular visitors and one very rare vagrant: wall (*Lassiommata megera*), grayling (*Hipparchia semele*), gatekeeper (*Pyronia tithonus*), meadow brown (*Maniola jurtina*), small heath (*Coenonympha tullia*), small skipper, large skipper (*Ochlodes venata*), brimstone (*Gonepteryx rhamni*), large white (*Pieris brassicae*), small white (*P. rapae*), green-viened white (*P. napi*), orange-tip, small copper (*Lycaena phlaeas*), common blue (*Polyommatus icarus*), holly blue, small tortoiseshell (*Aglais urticae*), peacock (*Inachis io*), comma (*Polygonia c-album*), dark-green fritillary (*Argynnis aglaja*), speckled wood, clouded yellow (*Colias croceus*), red admiral (*Vanessa atalanta*) and painted lady (*Cynthia cardui*), and the vagrant pale clouded yellow (*Colias hyale*).

The dune slacks have at least 11 species of dragonflies proved breeding, plus about five others recorded but not proved breeding. They include the southern hawker (*Aeshna cyanea*), the emperor (*Anax imperator*) and two very recent arrivals, the yellow-winged darter (*Sympetrum flaveolum*) and ruddy darter (*S. sanguineum*).

Mosslands lie between the saltmarshes and dunes at Lytham and from Leyland and Croston south and west to Liverpool. They have all been drained and are now mostly arable farmland, market garden or pasture. None is lacking in wildlife interest, for the mosslands have among the highest densities of breeding barn owls, grey partridge and corn buntings (*Miliaria calandra*) in Britain, while in winter thousands of pink-footed geese feed there.

There are two major wildlife reserves on the mosslands. The Wildfowl and Wetlands Trust refuge at Martin Mere includes the last area of the ancient

Martin Mere WWT Reserve attracts well over 1,000 Icelandic whooper swans through the winter months.

Martin Mere never completely to have dried out and one of the few parts never to have seen the plough. Before the WWT purchased the land in 1973 it was rough wet pasture, with extensive stands of soft rush and reed-fringed channels. Then there were large populations of nesting lapwing, snipe, mallard, moorhen, sedge warbler and reed bunting, with fewer teal, shoveler and redshank. Black-tailed godwit nested here in 1971, and since the WWT took over the site ruff has nested. Today, looking from the Miller's Bridge hide out across the mere, two large excavated pools attract winter waterfowl, details of which are given in the next section. In 2002 the Trust purchased a further 65 hectares of drained Martin Mere which, for over a century, was arable farmland. The plan here is to convert it back into the original wetland, with reed-fen and marsh, a scheme that is a very exciting prospect!

Mere Sands Wood, a reserve of the Lancashire Trust for Nature Conservation, lies a couple of kilometres north-east of Martin Mere. It is an area of mixed woodland with large shallow weedy pools. The pools are the result of sand extraction before the area was handed over to LTNC as a reserve. The management strategy for Mere Sands Wood aims to enhance the great diversity of habitats here. The woodland is being managed to encourage the growth of native trees. The pools hold a wealth of caddisflies and dragonflies, ten species of fish, and breeding great crested grebes, little grebes (*Tachybaptus ruficollis*) and eight species of duck. One pool is slowly being turned into a reed-fen so that it may attract species such as the bittern (*Botaurus stellaris*), water rail (*Rallus aquaticus*), bearded tit (*Panurus biarmicus*) and other fen birds which are in need of special conservation in Britain.

The natural woodland of the mosses is birch woodland. Blocks have been allowed to regenerate or have been planted to provide cover for pheasant shooting. Sparrowhawks and long-eared owls (*Asio otus*) are by-products of pheasant shooting for they nest in the pheasant woods. Recently buzzards have colonised the mosslands and they too nest in the pheasant woods. Here too can be found the very scarce willow tit (*Parus montanus*) that excavates its own nest hole in the soft wood of a dying birch.

As one looks across the vast flat mosslands of south-west Lancashire, one's eye is drawn to the great gasometer of Southport. It is a landmark, used by sailors out in the Irish Sea and by landlubbers from as far away as the tops of the Bowland and West Pennine moors. In 1975 not one pair of raven or peregrine nested anywhere in Lancashire. Today they do, and that they do is a testament to the conservation drives made in the second half of the twentieth century. And among the many places that you can watch nesting peregrines and ravens without disturbing them is at the gasometer. After all, to them it is just a cliff!

The estuary is used by large numbers of pink-footed geese, that winter here and breed in Iceland and Greenland (in October 2007 a record 46,000 were counted in Lancashire). In the day they feed on mossland fields and the saltmarshes and at dusk they fly to the tidal mudflats to roost.

Winter wildfowl and waders

The Ribble estuary is one of the world's major areas for wintering and migrating wildfowl and waders that breed in the arctic and subarctic lands of north-eastern Canada, Greenland, Fenno-Scandinavia, and both European and Asiatic Siberia.[59] For seven species of wildfowl and eleven species of wader the Ribble is of paramount international importance. If the Ribble mudflats and saltmarshes and the WWT refuge at Martin Mere were destroyed, all these now fairly abundant species would immediately be internationally endangered. The wildfowl are the Bewick's swan (*Cygnus columbianus*), whooper swan (*C. cygnus*), pink-footed goose, shelduck (*Tadorna tadorna*), wigeon, teal and pintail. The waders include oystercatcher, ringed plover, grey plover (*Pluvialis squatarola*), lapwing, knot (*Calidris canutus*), sanderling (*C. alba*), dunlin, black-tailed godwit (Icelandic race), bar-tailed godwit (*Limosa lapponica*), whimbrel (*Numenius phaeopus*) and redshank.

Bewick's swans first wintered on the Ribble saltmarshes in 1970–71 and since then the population has grown, but not to the extent many expected with the establishment of the Martin Mere refuge in 1973–74. The reason seems to be that the larger Icelandic whooper swans have adopted the refuge in large numbers and ousted their smaller Russian relations. Both swans feed either on saltmarsh grasses, on mossland stubbles, winter wheat or potato fields, and on

food put out for them at the refuge. On a winter's evening, watching all the swans gather on the Mere is one of the great wildlife spectacles.

So too is the sight of the great flocks of pink-footed geese that visit the estuary from September to April or early May. Many flocks feed on mossland farmland or the saltmarshes by day and at dusk flight onto the estuary or Martin Mere to roost. On moonlit nights they will flight out to their feeding grounds until moonset. Over 30,000 pink-feet – over a quarter of the world population – have been recorded feeding on and around the estuary.

Shelducks are the typical estuary duck. They breed in holes in banks around the estuary and most pairs lead their broods to the tidal marshes after they have hatched. However, many nest at Martin Mere and raise their young there. After breeding the adults depart on moult-migration to the Mersey, Bridgwater Bay or the Heligoland Bight, returning in pristine plumage in autumn. One of the favourite foods of the shelduck on the open shore is the tiny snail *Hydrobia* which they filter with their sieve-like bills from oozy mudflats.

The winter wigeon population has increased dramatically in recent years, the flock now being the largest anywhere in the world. In the winter of 1998–99 the numbers on Banks Marsh reached a staggering 97,000, and in most years far exceeds 50,000. Wigeon are grazers of grass, and their population seems to have responded to the great increase in area of grassy saltmarsh since the 1960s.

Teal have increased at Martin Mere, aided by the excavation of the two shallow pools on the refuge and also on the estuary through the increase of seeds produced by saltmarsh vegetation. Pintail have increased for the same reasons, though their populations fluctuate widely, with small numbers one year being followed by internationally important numbers the next.

Average peak populations of more important wildfowl at the WWT Martin Mere refuge

	1974–76	1983–86	1995–2005	Origin
Bewick's swan	2	290	93	S
Whooper swan	4	160	1,300	I
Pink-footed goose	–	11,100	17,100	I and G
Shelduck	18	80	930	NWE
Wigeon	600	3,100	1,900	EE and S
Teal	640	4,100	3,900	EE and S
Pintail	1,700	1,900	320	EE and S
Pochard	2	98	800	EE and S

Average peak populations of more important wildfowl and waders on the Ribble estuary shore and saltmarshes

	1970–75	1983–86	1995–2005	Origin
Bewick's swan	86	360	240	S
Whooper swan	6	81	210	I
Pink-footed goose	12,500	10,500	16,000	I and G
Shelduck	1,600	2,600	3,800	NWE
Wigeon	4,400	13,100	71,000	EE and S
Teal	1,400	4,400	5,500	EE and S
Pintail	2,300	560	2,600	EE and S
Oystercatcher	4,600	8,300	17,000	NWE (F)
Lapwing	7,000	9,300	16,500	NWE
Ringed plover	1,600	2,600	3,500	NWE, I, G, S
Grey plover	1,300	3,500	6,500	S
Golden plover	3,500	4,000	4,100	NWE, I, S
Whimbrel	60 – [580]*			NWE and I

	1970–75	1983–86	1995–2005	Origin
Curlew	900	1,500	1,700	NWE
Black-tailed godwit	1,100	2,400	3,600	I
Bar-tailed godwit	8,700	13,800	5,100	S
Redshank	6,100	1,500	3,100	NWE and I
Knot	81,200	40,700	22,000	G and NEC(?)
Dunlin	70, 700	18,800	44,000	G and NEC, NWE, S
Sanderling	7,600	5,400	6,200	G and NEC

NWE: = North-west Europe, including the British Isles and (F) Faeroes
EEE = Eastern Europe; S = Siberia; I = Iceland; G = Greenland;
NEC = North-eastern Canada

*Most of these are recorded in spring roosting on Longton Marsh.
The wader populations on the estuary have been well studied since the late 1960s.

Oystercatchers have increased in past decades as the densities of cockles have recovered following the near extermination of this favourite food in the severe 1962–63 winter. Lapwing and golden plovers are mainly feeders on insect larvae and worms on saltmarsh and reclaimed saltmarsh. In contrast grey plover feed on the open shore, preferring sandier areas, on sand-dwelling shrimps and worms.

Knot feed almost exclusively on *Hydrobia* at the top of the shore and, when the tide is fully out, on Baltic tellins in the outer estuary. Dunlin feed on *Hydrobia*, *Corophium* and the small ragworm *Nereis diversicolor* in the muddy parts of the estuary, whereas the closely related sanderling prefers sandier areas where it feeds on *Bathyporiea* and *Eurydice* at the water's edge. The two godwits are equally separated, for the black-tailed godwit concentrates on worms in mudflats and insect larvae on reclaimed saltmarshes, and the bar-tailed godwit feeds on worms in sand or muddy-sand. Most redshanks feed at the top of muddy shores on *Hydrobia* and *Corophium*. Both wintering curlew and migrating whimbrel feed by probing wet fields and saltmarshes for worms and insect larvae; they also take seeds and will glean stubbles. The latter food may seem unusual for waders, but the small wintering population of ruff at Martin Mere, that numbers up to about 150, feed on grain put out every afternoon for the wintering wildfowl.

The BBC Natural History Unit sends crews out seemingly every year to bring the Serengeti spectacular to our television screens. Goodness only knows why! The Ribble saltmarshes, as a spring tide floods them and the evening flights of wildfowl, are no less of a wildlife spectacle, with peregrines, merlins and short-eared owls playing the role of lion and cheetah and the waders and wildfowl the parts of wildebeest and zebra!

Conservation and the future of the estuary

Even if any potential human influence is ignored, the Ribble estuary will never remain the same. Through the twentieth century the area of saltmarsh increased greatly as a consequence of silting up resulting from the training of the shipping channel. This led to an increase of Bewick's and whooper swans, wigeon, teal and pintail that feed on saltmarsh vegetation. Similarly there was a great increase in the numbers of birds breeding on the saltmarshes, such as the gulls and redshank. If tidal currents change in the estuary, as they seem bound to do now that the low water shipping channel is no longer being maintained, it is likely that there will be at least some erosion of saltmarshes and a reduction in these bird populations.

Alongside the development of the huge saltmarshes, the twentieth century also saw large areas of sandy beach being turned into a sand-mud beach or mudflats. This was a consequence of a slowing down of tidal currents over the higher sandbanks following the construction of the shipping channel. Where there was sand between Lytham and St Anne's, now there are mudflats. Where there was pure sand at Southport, there is now sandy-mud. Mud and sandy-mud is much more stable than pure sand, and a consequence of this is that invertebrate population densities are much higher in mud and sandy-mud than in sand (see page 257). Should current changes in the estuary result in an increase of pure sand and a reduction in the area of mud and sandy-mud, there will thus be a reduction in the populations of waders and shelducks that feed over these more stable, productive beaches.

However the greatest threats to the wildlife of the estuary is *Homo* sometimes-not-all-that *sapiens*. The first of these comes from the fact that the estuary is a major obstacle for transport between the towns of the Fylde coast and the Merseyside conurbation. A black-headed gull has to fly only 12 kilometres to get from St Anne's to Southport, but a bread van must drive 45 kilometres, facing in its journey the traffic queues of Preston.

Several schemes have been proposed to put an embankment across the estuary to make transport easier. One, proposed in 2007, was to build a barrage across the estuary below Preston dock. There would be other spin-offs: a marina where folks could go sailing, with bars and restaurants where the weary day-tripper might take refreshment. The plan was abandoned by the City Council in December 2007 following overwhelming opposition.

The second threat comes from developers who see vast areas of mudflat and saltmarsh as 'waste' that generates little wealth. Tidal saltmarshes are useful for nothing other than grazing sheep and cattle. Sand was until recently taken from the sandbanks off Southport for profit, but other than that they constitute an unproductive flat desert that the tide floods twice a day.

It was this attitude that led to the embankment of most of Clifton and Hesketh Out Marshes in the early 1980s and that almost led to the embankment of Banks Marsh. It was this attitude that resulted in large tracts of sand dune in the outer estuary being flattened and developed for housing and a holiday camp in the late 1960s and 1970s. It was this attitude that resulted in much of Crossens and Marshside Marshes being embanked in the 1970s. The road on that embankment relieved traffic congestion in Southport town centre; happily plans were shelved to drain and build houses on the reclaimed area that today is an RSPB reserve. It was this attitude that saw the destruction in the early 1970s of the second largest reedbed and fenland in north-west England after Leighton Moss (near Silverdale) to produce 'Leisure Lakes' at Mere Brow.

It is this attitude that has led the government to encourage developers, with nice 'grants', to build those eyesores of white wind farms that generate relatively so little electricity. There is, off Blackpool and just outside the estuary, an area of very shallow water called Shell Flat. In recent years it has been discovered that Shell Flat is the winter feeding ground of a large proportion of Europe's common scoter (*Melanitta nigra*) population. This large black duck feeds by diving for molluscs and crustaceans, of which there are immense quantities on Shell Flat. In February 2003 an aerial survey revealed 42,000 scoters there, together with a further 3,500 about four kilometres off the mouth of the estuary and 2,200 off Formby Point. At the time of writing there are proposals to cover the 'waste' of Shell Flat with wind generators, and this will oust the scoters.

It was this attitude that, in years long gone, resulted in the destruction of so much of the countryside in north-west England and, when the destruction was at its height in the Victorian era, naturalists accepted the destruction as inevitable. Leo Grindon was a Manchester botanist who produced a *Manchester Flora* in 1859. There he described the wonderful species that flowered on the wild mosslands around the city. The snake's-head lily (*Fritillaria meleagris*) was 'plentiful every spring', the bog rosemary 'upon all the moors and mosses of the district', and the marsh gentian (*Gentiana pneumonanthe*) had formerly been abundant on marshy ground close to the Mersey. Grindon had witnessed the draining and ploughing up of this marshy ground, but his reaction had been so different to that of the modern naturalist: 'Nothing can be lamentable which is productive of benefit to a whole community. The right onward furrow of a generous utility is more to be admired than the bloom of a thousand gentians.'[60]

But would Grindon have been happy to see the complete annihilation of the countryside? I hope not.

Happily much of what remains of the dunes and saltmarshes around the Ribble estuary is nature reserve, while a large area of the open shore is a statutory sanctuary for wildfowl. Nevertheless, planners still tend to see the empty vastness of the estuary as a waste that ought to be developed. Let us hope that this never happens. For in this part of north-west England the Ribble marshes and beaches are an oasis in the desert of human sprawl and clutter and the infernal internal combustion engine.

You do not believe me? Then walk, on a winter's evening, along the track across the shore at Marshside, as the tide ebbs. Out there will be silence, broken only by the hissing of sand creatures as they retreat into their burrows as the tide leaves them, the peeping and piping of waders, the whistles of wigeon, the croaking cries of shelduck, and the murmuring of geese as they try to settle for a good night's rest. If the lights of the towns and villages around the estuary were all switched off, the experience would have been as it was in the days before humans began, thousands of years ago, to drain, develop and build. Long may this last bit of wilderness remain.

Notes and references

Notes to Chapter 1: The source of the River Ribble

1. Jessica Lofthouse, *Lancashire's Fair Face* (Robert Hale, 1952), pp. 21–2.
2. William Dobson, *Rambles by the Ribble* (W. Dobson, 1877), p. 13.
3. The Lancashire section of Drayton's *Polyolbion* was published in *The Palatine Note-book* (May 1884), pp. 64–8.
4. F. Riley, *The Ribble from its Source to the Sea* (J. W. Lambert, 1914), p. 1.
5. Many statistics included here are from G. Manley, *Climate and the British Scene* (Collins, 1952), p. 231; Arthur Raistrick, *The Pennine Dales* (Eyre Methuen, 1968), pp. 21–50 includes the climate of Ribblehead and the moorland tops.
6. W. T. Palmer, *Wanderings in Ribblesdale* (Skeffington, 1951), with W. Dobson and F. Riley, op. cit., give much information on the history of the valley.
7. C. B. Andrews (ed.), *The Torrington Diaries, vol. III* (Eyre & Spotiswood, 1936), pp. 88–9.
8. F. W. Houghton and W. H. Forton, *The Story of the Settle–Carlisle Railway* (Norman Arch, 1948).
9. A. Raistrick, *Prehistoric Yorkshire* (Dalesman, 1965) gives a concise account.
10. W. Pennington, *The History of British Vegetation* (Hodder & Stoughton, 1974) gives a good overall view, while W. H. Pearsall, *Mountains and Moorlands* (Collins, 1950) describes Pennine habitats.
11. M. A. Girling, 'The bark beetle *Scolytus scolytus* (Fabricius) and the possible role of elm disease in the early Neolithic,' in M. Jones (ed.), *Archaeology and the Flora of the British Isles* (Oxford University Committee for Archaeology, Monograph XIV, 1988), pp. 34–8.
12. J. Hutton, *A Tour to the Caves* (London, c.1790), pp. 42–3. M. Hartley and J. Ingliby, *The Yorkshire Dales* (J. M. Dent, 1956), p. 102 gives a history of the exploration of this cave system.
13. A. Raistrick, *Green Tracks on the Pennines* (Dalesman, 1962) describes these ancient routes.
14. A. Raistrick, op. cit., 1965 and 1968 (chapter 3) describes the exploration of these caves, while D. Yalden, *The History of British Mammals* (Poyser, 1999), pp. 29–129, gives a full account of mammals in prehistory. J. W. Jackson, 'Lynx remains from Yorkshire caves', *Naturalist*, dcccxci (1931), pp. 115–16 lists species found in Moughton Fell Cave.

15. W. Pennington, op. cit., and H. Godwin, *The History of the British Flora* (Cambridge UP, 1956) provided the foundation for this section.

16. M. Bennett, *Campaigns of the Norman Conquest* (Osprey Publishing, 2001), pp. 52–3.

17. F. Musgrove, *The North of England: A history from Norman Times to the Present* (Basil Blackwell, 1990).

18. Wool Education Soc., *Proceedings* (1953), p. 54.

19. A. Raistrick, *Malham and Malham Moor* (Dalesman, 1976), pp. 100–20.

20. J. Turner, in D. Walker and R. G. West (eds), *Studies in the Vegetational History of the British Isles* (Cambridge UP, 1970), p. 105.

21. A. Raistrick, *The Pennine Walls* (Dalesman, 1981).

22. M. E. Greenhalgh, 'The mayflies of Lancashire, Cheshire, Merseyside and Greater Manchester,' (Lancashire & Cheshire Fauna Soc. Report, 2008) includes all upwinged flies in the Ribble system.

Notes to Chapter 2: Little Ribble, Big Ribble
1. Quoted by F. Riley, *The Ribble from its Source to the Sea* (Lambert, 1914), p. 49.

2. M. Drayton, *Polyolbion* (in *The Palatine Note-book*, May 1884), pp. 65–6.

3. Quoted in W. T. Palmer, *Wanderings in Ribblesdale* (Skeffington, 1951), p. 57.

4. B. Shorrock (ed.), *Settle Bird Report 1984*, p. 8.

5. Personal observations, 1978–2005.

6. D. Mills, *The Place-names of Lancashire* (Batsford, 1976).

7. F. Riley, op. cit., p. 72.

8. T. B. Whitaker, *An History of the Original Parish of Whalley and Honor of Clitheroe* (3rd edn, Thomas Edwards, 1818). See also J. McNulty, 'Clitheroe Castle and its chapel: their origins', *Trans. Hist. Soc. Lancs. & Cheshire*, xciii (1941), pp. 45–53.

9. M. Slack, *The Bridges of Lancashire and Yorkshire* (Robert Hale, 1986), p. 75.

10. Quoted in F. Riley, op. cit., p. 109.

11. Notes in the *Lancashire & Cheshire Naturalist* (May and July 1924) state that the Osbaldeston ferry dated back to *c*.1300, that the ferry closed in 1907 when the boat was swept away in a flood, and that a new ferry would start running in the summer of 1924 with a new boat called *Mawdsley*.

12. J. H. Lumby, *A Calendar of the Deeds and Papers in the possession of Sir James de Hoghton, Bart., of Hoghton Tower, Lancashire*, Record Society of Lancashire & Cheshire, lxxxviii (1936), p. 70.

13. A. Lumby, op. cit., p. 76.

14. A. Lumby, op. cit., pp. 93–4.

15. A. Lumby, op. cit., p. 143.

16. A. Lumby, op. cit., p. 143.

17. A. Lumby, op. cit., p. 144.

18. A. Lumby, op. cit., p. 120.

19. A. Lumby, op. cit., p. 159.

20. Note text missing.

21. R. Cunliffe Shaw, 'The Townfields of Lancashire', *Trans. Hist. Soc. Lancs. & Cheshire*, cxiv (1962), p. 28. See also R. Cunliffe Shaw, *Kirkham in Amounderness* (R. Seed, 1949), especially pp. 224–36 and two other papers: G. Youd, 'The common fields of Lancashire', *Trans. Hist. Soc. Lancs. & Cheshire*, cxiii (1961), pp. 1–41 and F. J. Singleton, 'The influence of geographical factors on the

development of the common fields of Lancashire', *Trans. Hist. Soc. Lancs. & Cheshire*, cxv (1963), pp. 31–40.

22. John Leland, *The Laboryouse Journey and Serche of J. Leylande for Englandes Antiquites, Given of Hym as a Newe Yeares Gyfte to Kinge Henry the VIII* (1549), MS. Bodleian Library, Oxford.
23. C. Morris, *The Journals of Celia Fiennes* (Penguin, 1949).
24. F. J. Singleton, op. cit.
25. W. T. Palmer, op. cit., pp. 141–8, 157–65; J. Lofthouse, *Lancashire's Fair Face* (Robert Hale, 1952), pp. 13–78 describe the halls along Big Ribble.
26. D. Shotter, *Romans and Britons in North-West England* (3rd edn, Centre for North-west Regional Studies, 2004), especially pp. 26–48, 69–72.
27. B. J. N. Edwards, *The Romans at Ribchester* (Centre for North-west Regional Studies, 2000) is essential reading to accompany a visit to the Roman Museum at Ribchester.
28. See D. Hunt, *A History of Preston* (Carnegie Publishing, 1992; second, revised edition, 2009).
29. See Alan Crosby, *Penwortham in the Past* (Carnegie Press, 1988).
30. Arthur Young, *A Six Months Tour through the North of England* (Strahan, Nicholl, Collins & Balfour, 1770), iii, pp. 78–9.
31. M. E. Greenhalgh and D. W. Ovenden, *Collins Pocket Guide to the Freshwater Life of Britain and Northern Europe* (HarperCollins, 2006) illustrates all aquatic plants and animals found here.
32. M. E. Greenhalgh, 'The freshwater fishes of Lancashire, Merseyside and Cheshire', *Lancashire & Cheshire Fauna Soc. General Report*, cv (2004), pp. 23–33.
33. R. Sutterby and M. E. Greenhalgh, *The Atlantic Salmon* (Merlin Unwin, 2005), p. 23.

Notes to Chapter 3: The Hodder

1. J. K. Stanford, *Grouse Shooting* (Percival Marshall, 1963).
2. J. Bannon in R. Pyefinch and P. Golborn (organisers), *Atlas of the Breeding Birds of Lancashire and North Merseyside 1997–2000* (Hobby Publications, 2001), p. 79.
3. Personal observations.
4. M. Greenwood and C. Bolton, *Bolland Forest and the Hodder Valley* (privately published 1955, facsimile by Landy Publishing, 2000), pp. 30–2.
5. P. Marsh in R. Pyefinch and P. Golborn, op. cit., pp. 94–5.
6. D. Yalden, *The History of British Mammals* (Poyser, 1999), pp. 196–8.
7. M. Greenwood and C. Bolton, op. cit., pp. 8, 29.
8. D. Mills, *The Place-names of Lancashire* (Batsford, 1976), pp. 65–6.
9. D. Brazendale, *Lancashire's Historic Halls* (Carnegie Publishing, 2004), pp. 6–24 is the latest summary of the Forest's history. J. Porter, 'A forest in transition: Bowland 1500–1650', *Trans. Hist. Soc. Lancs, & Cheshire*, cxxv (1974), pp. 40–60, provides much other detail. Useful information can also be found in C. Ironfield, 'The parish of Chipping during the seventeenth century', *Trans. Hist. Soc. Lanc. & Cheshire*, cxxvii (1978), pp. 25–46.
10. H. Fishwick (ed.), *Pleadings and Depositions in the Duchy Court of Lancaster: Time of Edward VI and Philip and Mary*, Record Soc., xv (1898), pp. 215–17.
11. H. Fishwick, op. cit., pp. 82–3.

12. J. Porter, 'Waste reclamation in the sixteenth and seventeenth centuries: the case of south-eastern Bowland, 1550–1603,' *Trans. Hist. Soc Lancs. & Cheshire*, cxxvii (1978), pp. 1–23. J. Porter, *The Making of the Central Pennines* (Moorland Publishing, 1980).

13. H. Fishwick, op. cit., p. 217.

14. F. A. Lees, *The Flora of West Yorkshire* (London, 1888).

15. Personal observations.

16. Miss D. Worsley-Taylor, personal communication, June 2002.

17. H. B. Rogers, 'The Lancashire cotton industry of 1840', *Trans. Inst. Brit. Geographers*, xxviii (1960), p. 136.

Notes to Chapter 4: Calder, Darwen and Douglas

1. Thomas Hurtley, quoted in F. Riley, *The Ribble from its Source to the Sea* (Frederick Riley, 1914), p. 95.

2. G. Brigg, 'The forest of Pendle in the seventeenth century', *Trans. Hist. Soc. Lancs. & Cheshire*, cxiii (1961), pp. 65–90.

3. Lancashire Record Office, DDB/62/1.

4. W. Farrer *et al.* (eds), *The Victoria History of the County of Lancaster* (Constable, 1907), vol. ii, p. 461.

5. M. Brigg, op. cit., 72.

6. G. B. Leach, 'Flint implements from the Worsthorne Moors, Lancashire', *Trans. Hist. Soc. Lancs. & Cheshire*, ciii (1951), pp. 1–20.

7. W. Southern, 'Roads about Burnley', *Trans. Burnley Lit. & Scientific Club*, ix (1891), pp. 24–5.

8. D. G, Coombs, 'Excavations at the hillfort of Castercliff, Nelson, Lancashire, 1970–71', *Trans. Lancs. & Cheshire Antiquarian Soc.*, lxxxi (1982), pp. 111–30. J. Forde-Johnston, 'The Iron Age hillforts of Lancashire and Cheshire', *Trans. Lancs. & Cheshire Antiq. Soc.*, lxxii (1962), pp. 9–46. I. H. Longworth, 'A Bronze Age hoard from Portfield Farm, Whalley, Lancashire', *Brit. Museum Quarterly*, xxxii (1967), pp. 1–2, 8–14.

9. D. Beattie, *Blackburn: the Development of a Lancashire Cotton Town* (Ryburn Publishing, 1992), pp. 15–17. See also D. Beattie, Blackburn: A History (Carnegie Publishing, 2007), Chapters 1–2.

10. T. D. Whitaker, *An History of the Original Parish of Whalley and Honor of Clitheroe, in the Counties of Lancaster and York* (Thomas Edwards, 3rd edn, 1818).

11. P. Hesketh, *Rivington* (Peter Davis, 1972) gives a thorough history of the Rivington area, while M. D. Smith has produced two well-illustrated accounts: *Leverhulme's Rivington* (Wyre Publishing, 1998) and *Old Rivington and District* (Wyre Publishing, n.d. [*c.*1995]).

12. D. Kenyon, *The Origins of Lancashire* (Manchester UP), p. 27; this also gives information of most prehistoric sites in the Ribble catchment.

13. D. Mills, *The Place-names of Lancashire*, pp. 55–6.

14. D. Mills, op. cit., pp. 79, 97.

15. M. Clarke, *The Leeds and Liverpool Canal* (Carnegie Press, 1990), pp. 43–53.

16. W. Farrer *et al.* (eds), *The Victoria History of the County of Lancaster* (Constable, 1907), vol. iii, pp. 282–3.

17. D. Mills, op. cit., 78.

18. G. C. Miller, *Hoghton Tower* (Preston Guardian, 1948) is the standard work

on the Hoghton estate, but the section on natural history is suspect in places (K. G. Spencer and the author).

19. A. T. R. Houghton, *The Ribble Salmon Fisheries* (John Sherratt, 1952), pp. 82–3.

Notes to Chapter 5: Where the river meets the sea

1. Jack Wilkinson, in a discussion with R. Ball and the author on 17 September 2005, told of a three kilo carp and four kilo chub that he caught in his salmon net between Freckleton Naze and Lytham in 2004. R. Ball, with the author caught a 5kg carp of Lytham on 19 July 2006.

2. R. K. Gresswell, *Sandy Shores in South Lancashire* (Liverpool UP, 1953), pp. 16–17. See also G. F. Mitchell, 'The Pleistocene history of the Irish Sea', *Presidential address Brit. Ass. Adv. Sc.*, 1960.

3. R. K. Gresswell, op. cit., pp. 17–22.

4. M. J. Tooley, *Sea level changes in north west England during the Flandrian stage* (Oxford Research Studies in Geography, Clarenden Press, 1978).

5. J. J. Bagley (ed.), *The Great Diurnal of Nicholas Blundell, Volume 3: 1720–1728* (The Record Society of Lancashire & Cheshire, 1972), pp. 28–30. See also Joan Beck, 'The church brief for the inundation of the Lancashire coast in 1720', *Trans. Hist. Soc. Lancs & Cheshire*, cv (1953), pp. 91–105, and Alison Maddock, 'Watercourse management and flood prevention in the Alt Level Lancashire', *Trans. Hist. Soc. Lancs & Cheshire*, cxlviii (1999), pp. 59–94.

6. D. Atkinson and J. Houston, *The Sand Dunes of the Sefton Coast* (National Museums and Galleries on Merseyside, 1993), pp. 3–4.

7. P. H. Smith, *The Sands of Time* (National Museums and Galleries on Merseyside, 1999), pp. 18–19.

8. W. Pennington, *The History of British Vegetation* (Hodder & Stoughton, 1974), pp. 51–54, 59, 79–88.

9. Personal observations, and W. G. Travis, 'The plant-associations of some south Lancashire peat-mosses', *Lancashire & Cheshire Naturalist*, viii (1914), pp. 171–6.

10. R. C. Turner and R. G. Scaife (eds), *Bog Bodies* (British Museum Press, 1995), especially pp. 208–10.

11. T. Edmondson, 'Some aspects of the natural history of western Chat Moss', *N.W. Naturalist*, n.s. i (1953), pp. 401–2.

12. F. S. Mitchell, *Birds of Lancashire* (van Voorst, 1885), pp. 67–68, 89, 102–3, 127, 163–5.

13. A. W. Boyd, 'Early natural history records in Cheshire and South Lancashire', *N.W. Naturalist*, xxi (1946), p. 231.

14. J. J. Bagley, op. cit., also *Volume 1: 1702–1711* and *Volume 2: 1712–1719*. M. E. Greenhalgh, 'Early records of polecat, red kites and grass snakes from North Merseyside', *Lancashire & Cheshire Fauna Soc. General Report*, cv (2004), pp. 14–16.

15. A. W. Boyd, op. cit., p. 54.

16. A. W. Boyd, op. cit., p. 231.

17. 'A Lancashire gullery', *The Field Naturalist* (1882), pp. 145–6.

18. 'The gull moss' in *Lancashire Characters and Places* (Manchester, 1891), pp. 42–8.

19. F. A. Bailey (ed.), *The Churchwardens' Accounts of Prescot, Lancashire, 1523–1607*, Record Society of Lancashire & Cheshire, civ (1953).

20. H. Fishwick (ed.), *Pleadings and Depositions in the Duchy Court of Lancaster: Time of Edwards VI and Philip and Mary*, Record Society of Lancashire & Cheshire, xl (1898), pp. 11–16.

21. H. Fishwick (ed.), *Pleadings and Depositions in the Duchy Court of Lancaster: Time of Henry VIII*, Record Society of Lancashire & Cheshire, xxxv (1897a), pp. 184–8.

22. 'Stray notes' in *Trans. Hist. Soc Lancs. & Cheshire*, lxix (1927), p. 145.

23. J. M. Steane, 'Excavations at a moated site near Scarisbrick', *Trans. Hist. Soc. Lancs. & Cheshire*, cxii (1960), pp. 147–53.

24. W. Farrer, *A History of North Meols* (Henry Young, 1903), p. 116.

25. H. Fishwick, op. cit. (1898), p. 202.

26. H. Fishwick, op. cit. (1898), pp. 241–2. A Lancashire Chancery Deposition (*P. L. Chan. Deps. Bundle 144*) of 1717 included the argument that most of Martin Mere had 'been common to any one to fish in'; this was when the Mere was being drained and the boundaries for land-ownership being mapped.

27. D. Brazendale, *Lancashire's Historic Halls* (Carnegie Publishing, 2004), pp. 241–2.

28. Personal observations; A. Coney, 'Fish, fowl and fen landscape and economy on seventeenth-century Martin Mere', *Landscape History*, xiv (1992), pp. 51–64 and W. G. Hale and A. Coney, *Martin Mere: Lancashire's Lost Lake* (Liverpool UP, 2005). The latter gives a thorough account of Martin Mere from the last Ice Age to the present.

29. John Virgoe, 'Thomas Fleetwood and the draining of Martin Mere', *Trans. Hist. Soc. Lancs. & Cheshire*, clii (2003), pp. 27–47.

30. Lancs Record Office, DDSc 78/3 (7).

31. Lancs Record Office, op. cit.

32. H. Fishwick, op. cit. (1897), pp. 14, 206–8.

33. *The Journals of Celia Fiennes* quoted in P. Aughton, *North Meols and Southport* (Carnegie Publishing, 1988), p. 73.

34. H. Fishwick (ed.), *Pleadings and Depositions in the Duchy Court of Lancaster: Time of Henry VII and Henry VIII*, Record Society of Lancashire & Cheshire Vol. xxxiii (1896), pp. 20–1. H. Fishwick, 'Place names in Lancashire destroyed by the sea', *Trans. Hist. Soc. Lancs. & Cheshire*, il (1897b), pp. 87–96.

35. H. Fishwick, op. cit. (1897b), p. 95.

36. E. Ekwall, *The Place-names of Lancashire* (Chetham Soc., 1922), D. Mills, *The Place-names of Lancashire* (Batsford, 1976).

37. F. T. Wainwright, 'The Scandinavians in Lancashire', *Trans. Lancs. & Cheshire Antiq. Soc.*, lviii (1945–46), pp. 71–116.

38. R. Walker, 'Freckleton water mill', *Trans. Hist. Soc. Lancs. & Cheshire*, xciv (1942), pp. 94–110.

39. P. Shakeshaft, *The History of Freckleton* (Carnegie Publishing, 2001).

40. R. S. France, 'The highway from Preston into the Fylde', *Trans. Hist. Soc. Lancs. & Cheshire*, xcvii (1945), pp. 27–58. P. Shakeshaft, op. cit., 143–51, gives some information.

41. G. Harrison, *A Rage of Sand* (Ernest Benn, 1971) is a full account of the development of Lytham/Fairhaven/St Anne's. H. C. Collins, *Lancashire Plain and Seaboard* (Dent, 1953), pp. 86–104, gives a summary.

42. T. K. Glazebrook, *A Guide to Southport North Meoles in the County of Lancaster* (J.

Haddock, 1819) gives the first of several histories of the town, with P. Aughton, *North Meols and Southport* (Carnegie, 1988) the most recent. H. C. Collins, op. cit., pp. 33–54, gives a concise account, while F. H. Chetham, 'Notes on North Meols', *Trans. Hist. Soc. Lancs & Cheshire*, lxxvi (1924), pp. 71–90 provides early records.

43. A. Crosby, *Penwortham in the Past* (Carnegie, 1988), pp. 41–7, and personal communication.

44. H. C. Collins, op. cit., pp. 74–5.

45. H. C. Collins, op. cit., pp. 72–4.

46. Richard Kuerden, MS (1688), Chetham's Library.

47. D. Hunt, *A History of Preston* (Carnegie, 1991), pp. 218–21.

48. Personal observations.

49. Harry Foster, *Don e want ony Shrimps* (Birkdale & Ainsdale Historical Research Soc., n.d., *c*.1990,, gives an excellent account of the effect of silting up on the fishing community at Banks/Marshside/Southport.

50. S. A Harrop, 'Fishing stalls on the south-west Lancashire coast', *Trans. Hist. Soc. Lancs. & Cheshire*, cxxxi (1982), pp. 161–4.

51. Personal observations.

52. Personal observations.

53. M. E. Greenhalgh, 'Aspects of the ecology of an increasing black-headed gull colony', *Naturalist*, cmxxxiii (1975), pp. 43–51 and Lancashire Bird Reports (annual).

54. M. E. Greenhalgh, 'Population growth and breeding success in a saltmarsh common tern colony', *Naturalist*, cmxxxi (1974), pp. 121–7, and further personal observations.

55. B. McCarthy, *Birds of Marshside* (Hobby Publications, 2001).

56. M. E. Greenhalgh, 'The breeding bird communities of Lancashire saltmarshes', *Bird Study*, xvii (1971), pp. 199–212, and 'The breeding birds of the Ribble estuary saltmarshes', *Nature in Lancashire*, v (1975), pp. 11–19.

57. P. H. Smith, personal communication, November 2004.

58. P. H. Smith, op. cit., 1999.

59. M. E. Greenhalgh, *Wildfowl of the Ribble Estuary* (WAGBI, 1975). P. H. Smith and M. E. Greenhalgh, 'A four-year census of wading birds on the Ribble estuary, Lancashire/Merseyside', *Bird Study*, xxiv (1977), pp. 243–58. Annual Lancashire Bird Reports (Lancashire & Cheshire Fauna Society).

60. Quoted by K. J. Dormer and J. H. Tallis, 'Interesting features of the local vegetation and flora', in *Manchester and its Region* (British Ass. for the Advancement of Science, Manchester UP, 1962), pp. 74–5.

Appendices

Dragonflies and damselflies to be found in selected areas within the Ribble system

	Headwaters: Hodder, Whitendale, Brennand/Dunsop, Croasdale	Little Ribble: Settle–Clitheroe	Mere Sands Wood and Nucks Wood	Brockholes Quarry	Sefton Dunes
Banded Demoiselle *Calopteryx splendens*	–	Breeds (arrived 1990s)	Recorded	Breeds	Visitor
Emerald Damselfly *Lestes sponsa*	Breeds: bog pools	–	Breeds	Breeds	Breeds
Azure Damselfly *Coenagrion puella*	Adults observed	–	Breeds	Probably breeds	Breeds
Common Blue Damselfly *Enallagma cythigerum*	Breeds	Breeds	Breeds	Breeds	Breeds
Blue-tailed Damselfly *Ischnura elegans*	Adults observed	Breeds	Breeds	Breeds	Breeds
Large Red Damselfly *Pyrrhosoma nymphula*	Breeds: bog pools	–	Recorded, may breed	Recorded	Vagrant
Southern Hawker *Aeshna cyanea*	Adults observed	Occasional adults observed	Breeds	May Breed	Visitor
Brown Hawker *Aeshna grandis*	Adults observed	Breeds at a minimum of 2 sites	Breeds	Breeds	Breeds
Common Hawker *Aeshna juncea*	Breeds: bog pools	–	May breed	May breed	Scarce breeder
Migrant Hawker *Aeshna mixta*	Adults observed	Breeds at a minimum of 4 sites	Breeds (arrived 1996)	Breeds	Breeds (arrived 2000)

	Headwaters: Hodder, Whitendale, Brennand/Dunsop, Croasdale	Little Ribble: Settle–Clitheroe	Mere Sands Wood and Nucks Wood	Brockholes Quarry	Sefton Dunes
Emperor *Anax imperator*	Adults occasionally observed	One sighting (2006)	Breeds	Breeds	Breeds (arrived 1976)
Lesser Emperor *Anax parthenope*	–	One sighting (2004)	–	Recorded	Vagrant (arrived 2006)
Gold-ringed Dragonfly *Cordulegaster boltonii*	Breeds in streams at a minimum of 3 sites	–	–	–	–
Broad-bodied Chaser *Libellula depressa*	–	–	Probably breeds	May breed	Breeds (arrived 1988)
Four-spotted Chaser *Libellula quadrimaculata*	Adults observed	–	Breeds	Breeds	Breeds
Black-tailed Skimmer *Orthetrum cancellatum*	–	–	Breeds (arrived 1997)	Breeds	Breeds (arrived 2003)
Black Darter *Sympetrum danae*	Breeds at a minimum of one site (bog pool)	–	Recorded (may have bred)	Visitor	Rare visitor
Yellow-winged Darter *Sympetrum flaveolum*	–	–	–	–	Has bred (arrived 1995; 1999; 2006)
Red-veined Darter *Sympetrum fonscolumbii*	–	–	Vagrant	Bred 2006	Vagrant (arrived 2006
Ruddy Darter *Sympetrum sanguineum*	–	–	Recorded (arrived 1995)	Recorded	Breeds (arrived 1989)
Common Darter *Sympetrum striolatum*	Adults observed	Adults observed	Breeds	Breeds	Breeds

Sources: P. H. Smith (1999), 'Dragonflies of Lancashire' in *Lancashire Bird Report 1998* (Lancashire and Cheshire Fauna Society) pp. 74–7; P. H. Smith (2005), *The ecological interest of Nucks Wood, West Lancashire* (privately circulated); P. H. Smith (in press), *Odonata of the Sefton coast sand-dune system*; S. White (2007), 'Dragonflies in Lancashire in 2006' in *Lancashire Bird Report 2006* (Lancashire and Cheshire Fauna Society), pp. 175–6; Author's records. Several species from Southern Europe have colonised the region in recent years (see years of arrival in the table) and one other – the Small Red Damselfly (*Ceriagrion tenellum*) – is expected to colonise peaty moorland and mossland pools here within the next few years. This movement northwards of formerly very southern species is one consequence of global warming.

	Headwaters: Hodder. Moorland/ Bowland	Hodder Valley	Big Ribble Valley	S.W. Mosslands: Martin Mere, Nuck's Wood, Mere Sands Wood	Sefton Dunes
Small Skipper *Thymelicus sylvestris*	Very scarce breeder (arrived *c.* 2000)	Recorded	Recorded	Breeds	Breeds (arrived 1994)
Large Skipper *Ochlodes venata*	–	–	Recorded	Breeds in small numbers	Breeds in small numbers
Clouded Yellow *Colias croceus*	–	–	Vagrant	Vagrant	Visitor
Pale Clouded Yellow *Colias hyale*	–	–	–	–	Vagrant
Brimstone *Gonepteryx rhamni*	–	–	Visitor	Visitor	Vagrant
Large White *Pieris brassicae*	Common breeder around farmsteads and hamlets	Common breeder	Common breeder	Common breeder	Occurs (breeds off dunes)
Small White *Pieris rapae*	Common breeder around farmsteads and hamlets	Common breeder	Common breeder	Common breeder	Common breeder
Green-veined White *Pieris napi*	Common breeder	Common breeder	Common breeder	Common breeder	Common breeder
Orange Tip *Anthocharis cardamines*	Common breeder in meadows and hedgerows	Common breeder (arrived *c.* 1980)	Common breeder (arrived *c.* 1975)	Breeds in small numbers	Breeds in small numbers (arrived 1984)
Green Hairstreak *Callophrys rubi*	Common breeder on bilberry moor	–	–	[Once common on mosslands]	–
Purple Hairstreak *Neozephyrus quercus*	–	Scarce breeder in oak woods	–	–	–
White-letter Hairstreak *Satyrium w-album*	–	Recorded at Whitewell	Scarce breeder (needs Elm)	Recorded at Martin Mere (2006)	–
Small Copper *Lycaena phlaeas*	–	Very scarce breeder	Scarce breeder	Breeds in small numbers	Common breeder

	Headwaters: Hodder. Moorland/ Bowland	Hodder Valley	Big Ribble Valley	S.W. Mosslands: Martin Mere, Nuck's Wood, Mere Sands Wood	Sefton Dunes
Common Blue *Polyommatus icarus*	—	Common breeder	Common breeder	Common breeder	Common and abundant breeder
Holly Blue *Celestrina argiolus*	—	Fairly common breeder	Fairly common breede	Scarce breeder	Visitor (breeds off dunes)
Red Admiral *Vanessa atalanta*	Visitor to heath moors	Common breeder	Common breeder	Common breeder	Breeds
Painted Lady *Vanessa cardui*	Visitor to heather moors	Visitor (small numbers)	Visitor (small numbers)	Visitor (small numbers)	Visitor (some breed)
Small Tortoiseshell *Aglais urticae*	Breeds in nettlebeds in lee of stone walls	Common breeder	Common breeder	Common breeder	Common breeder
Peacock *Inachis io*	Visitor (may breed nettlebeds in lee of stone walls)	Common breeder	Common breeder	Common breeder	Common breeder
Comma *Polygonia c-album*	Very rare visitor to heather moor	Very scarce breeder	Scarce breeder	Scarce breeder	Scarce (may breed)
Small Pearl-bordered Fritillary *Boloria selene*	One colony on moorland edge	—	—	—	—
Dark Green Fritillary *Argynnis aglaja*	—	—	—	—	Fairly common breeder
Speckled Wood *Pararge aegeria*	Common around wooded streams	Common breeder	Common breeder	Common breeder	Common breeder (arrived 1982)
Wall Brown *Lasiommata megera*	—	—	Very scarce (may breed)	Very scarce breeder	Common breeder
Grayling *Hypparchia semele*	—	—	—	—	Common breeder
Gatekeeper *Pyronia tithonus*	—	—	Scarce (probably breeds)	Common breeder	Abundant
Meadow Brown *Maniola jurtina*	Recorded on heather moor	Fairly common breeder	Fairly common breeder	Common breeder	Abundant

	Headwaters: Hodder. Moorland/ Bowland	Hodder Valley	Big Ribble Valley	S.W. Mosslands: Martin Mere, Nuck's Wood, Mere Sands Wood	Sefton Dunes
Small Heath *Coenonympha pamphilus*	Fairly scarce breeder	Recorded	–	Scarce breeder	Very common
Large Heath *Coenympha tullia*	Occurs at one site	–	–	–	–

Sources: S. J. Hayhow (2000), 'The butterflies of Lancashire and North Merseyside' *Lancashire Bird Report 1999*, (Lancashire and Cheshire Fauna Society), pp. 103–108; P. H. Smith (1999), *The Sands of Time* (National Museums & Galleries on Merseyside); Author's records.

The occurrence of mayfly (Ephemeroptera) and stonefly (Plecoptera) species through the Ribble system

Mayflies	Parsonage Reservoir	Brockholes Quarry	Ings Beck (Downham)	River Ribble tributaries above Settle
Ephemera danica			+	
Ephemera vulgata		+		
Leptophlebia marginata	+			
Paraleptophlebia cincta			+	+
Paraleptophlebia submarginata			+	+
Habrophlebia fusca			+	+
Serratella ignita			+	+
Caenis horaria	+	+		
Caenis rivulorum			+	+
Caenis robusta				+
Caenis luctuosa				
Baetis vernus			+	+
Baetis fuscatus				
Baetis scambus			+	+
Baetis rhodani			+	+
Nigrobaetis niger			+	+
Alainetes (Nigrobaetis) musicus			+	+
Centroptilum luteolum				+
Centroptilum pennulatum			+	+
Cloeon dipterum		+		
Cloeon simile	+	+		
Procloeon bifidum				
Siphlonurus lacustris				+
Ameletus inopinatus				+
Rhithrogena semicolorata				+
Kageronia (Heptagenia) fuscogrisea				+ (1 specimen)
Heptagenia lateralis				+
Heptagenia sulphurea				+
Ecdyonurus dispar				+
Ecdyonurus insignis				+
Ecdyonurus torrentis			+	+
Ecdyonurus venosus			+	+

Little Ribble: Paythorne–Nappa	River Hodder: Whitewell–Hodderfoot	Pendle Water	Tosside Beck	Duddel Brook (Ribchester)	River Yarrow	Big Ribble: Calderfoot–Ribchester
+	+					
						+
			+			
+		+				
+	+	+	+	+		
+	+	+	+	+	+	+
+						+
+	+	+	+	+	+	+
+	+					
+						
+	+	+	+	+	+	
+ 1 specimen						
+	+	+	+			
+	+	+	+	+	+	+
+	+					
+	+	+	+			
+	+	+	+			
+	+					
+	+					
		+				
+	+	+	+			
	+	+	+			
+	+	+	+	+	+	+
	+					+ (1 specimen)
+	+					
+	+	+	+		+	
+	+	+	+		+	

Stoneflies	Ings Beck (Downham)	River Ribble tributaries above Settle	Little Ribble: Paythorne–Nappa
Taeniopteryx nebulosa		+	
Brachyptera risi	+	+	+
Protonemura meyeri	+	+	+
Protonemura montana		+ 1 specimen	
Protonemura praecox	+	+	+
Amphinemura standfussi			
Amphinemura sulcicollis	+	+	+
Nemurella picteti	+	+	+
Nemura avicularis			
Nemura cambrica		+	
Nemura cinerea			+
Nemura dubitans			
Nemura erratica	+	+	
Leuctra fusca		+	
Leuctra geniculata	+	+	+
Leuctra hippopus	+	+	+
Leuctra inermis	+	+	
Leuctra moselyi			
Leuctra nigra	+	+	
Capnia bifrons		+	
Capnia vidua		+	
Perlodes microcephala	+	+	
Diura bicordata		+	
Isoperla grammatica	+	+	+
Dinocras cephalotes	+	+	+
Perla bipunctata		+	
Chloroperla torrentium	+	+	+
Chloroperla tripunctata		+	

Sources: The Alan Brindle Collection (Entomology, Manchester Museum; author's records.

River Hodder: Whitewell –Hodderfoot	Pendle Water	Tosside Beck	Duddel Brook (Ribchester)	River Yarrow	Big Ribble: Calderfoot– Ribchester
+					
+	+	+	+	+	+
+	+	+	+	+	
+	+	+		+	
				3 specimens	
+	+	+	+	+	+
+	+	+	+	+	
		+			
+	+			+	
+	+	+	+		
+					
+	+	+	+	+	
+	+		+		
+	+	+		+	+
+	+	+	+	+	+
+	+	+	+	+	
+	+		+		
	+	+	+	+	
+	+				
		+			
+	+	+			
+					
+	+	+	+	+	+
+	+	+			
+	+				
+	+	+	+	+	
+	+	+	+		

Index

Most individual animals and plant species are indexed under their group, for example birds, butterflies, fish, flowering herbs, grasses, mammals, etc.